The attraction of the contrary

Hubert Robert, "L'exposition des cendres de J.-J. Rousseau aux Tuileries la nuit du
10–11 Octobre 1794"

The attraction of the contrary
Essays on the literature of
the French Enlightenment

WALTER E. REX
University of California, Berkeley

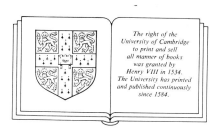

The right of the
University of Cambridge
to print and sell
all manner of books
was granted by
Henry VIII in 1534.
The University has printed
and published continuously
since 1584.

CAMBRIDGE UNIVERSITY PRESS

Cambridge
New York   New Rochelle   Melbourne   Sydney

Published by the Press Syndicate of the University of Cambridge
The Pitt Building, Trumpington Street, Cambridge CB2 1RP
32 East 57th Street, New York, NY 10022, USA
10 Stamford Road, Oakleigh, Melbourne 3166, Australia

First published 1987

Printed in Great Britain at
the University Press, Cambridge

British Library cataloguing in publication data
Rex, Walter E.
The attraction of the contrary: essays on
the literature of the French Enlightenment.
1. French literature – 18th century –
History and criticism
I. Title
840.9'005   PQ261

Library of Congress cataloguing in publication data
Rex, Walter E.
The attraction of the contrary.
Bibliography.
Includes index.
1. French literature – 18th century – History
and criticism.   2. Enlightenment.   3. France –
Intellectual life – 18th century.   I. Title.
PQ263.R48   1987   840'.9'005   86–34322

ISBN 0 521 33386 5

FP

For
DANIEL HEARTZ

In Memory of
MICHAEL MANN

Contents

Illustrations

List of illustrations

Acknowledgements

This project has been many years in the making and was carried forward thanks to generous grants from the Committee on Research of the University of California at Berkeley. The staffs of several libraries have given me assistance, notably those of the Arsénal, the B.N. and the Bibliothèque de l'Opéra in Paris, the Houghton Library at Harvard, and the Doe Library of the University of California at Berkeley. A rather large group of scholars have, at various times, made comments on all or parts of the manuscript: Leo Bersani, Malcolm Bowie, Joseph Fontenrose, Lionel Gossman, Judd Hubert, Marie-Hélène Huet, Dorothy Johnson, Leonard W. Johnson, Jean Le Corbeiller, Robert Niklaus and Jack Undank. I have been grateful for their criticisms and encouragement. My analysis of libertinage owes much to discussions, long ago, with Mr Paul Sabbah and also to Robert Ellrich who put me on the track of *Le Portier des Chartreux*. Special thanks are due to my friend Jonas Barish who generously saw the book through, from almost the beginning to the very end.

The English translations of the French passages in chapter 2 are by Lee Hildreth; those in the Introduction and chapters 3, 6, 10 and 11 are mainly by Robert Hurley, who has also been helpful, throughout, on matters of style. Early versions of some of the chapters have already appeared in print: chapter 6 was published in *Studies in Eighteenth-Century Culture*, 9 (1979); chapter 7 in the *Acts* of the *Twelfth Congress of the International Musicological Society* (New Haven, Conn.: American Musicological Society, 1980); chapter 8 in *The Eighteenth Century: Theory and Interpretation*, 24:3 (1983); chapter 9 in *Eighteenth-Century Studies*, 16 (1983); part 1 of chapter 10 in J. Undank and H. Josephs, eds., *Diderot: Digression and Dispersion* (Lexington, Ky.: French Forum, 1984); part 1 of chapter 12 in *PMLA*, 89 (1974).

My patient typist was Nancy Laleau.

Photo credits: Photo Service, University of California, Berkeley: 1, 7–12, 14, 16–24; Réunion des Musées Nationaux: 2, 4, 5; Giraudon: 3, 25, 28, 30; Bibliothèque Nationale, Paris: 13, 15, 29. Number 6 is taken from *French Drawings from the 11th Century Through Géricault* and appears with permission of Shorewood Fine Art Reproductions, Inc., publishers. Number 26 is

Acknowledgements

taken from Ph. Huisman and M. Jallut, *Marie Antoinette* (Lausanne: Edita, 1971) and appears with permission of the publishers.

Note to the reader: English translations of the French quotations have been provided in the notes at the end of the volume whenever possible. Spelling and punctuation of the French texts generally follow the original.

Introduction

Long ago, Paul Hazard, in *La Crise de la conscience européenne*[1] studied a series of traits which he had seen coming into prominence, particularly in French literature of the 1680s; he maintained that their emergence signaled the birth of a new era, the Enlightenment. Many of the traits – rationalism in philosophy, historiography, and Biblical exegesis, for example, or the new search for scientific explanation and the attack on miracles – have long since become an accepted part of the way scholars define this period. Hazard was not always original, or even correct in matters of detail, and his researches have been superseded in some areas; yet the work still makes splendid reading, not only for the marvels to be found in individual chapters (he was among the first to understand Bayle in the modern sense; he may have misspelled the name, but he was surely right about Pajon's place in intellectual history), but because with his vast erudition, the excitement of his ideas, and his astonishing insight, his synthesis remains convincing. One gets the sensation, reading Hazard, that the whole philosophical era is falling into perspective.

It is hard to imagine anyone today undertaking so gigantic a task, if only because scholarly material on authors of the seventeenth and eighteenth centuries has swollen to mountainous proportions. Naturally, as our familiarity with the period has grown deeper and more detailed, we find it increasingly difficult to generalize about it. One is also aware, in this connection, that scholars of the French Enlightenment are less convinced now of the simple valences Hazard sometimes attributed to the terms he employed. "Rationalism," for example, which he valorized so positively as the spearhead for the Enlightenment's attack on established institutions ("Ecrasez l'infâme!") has come to look so riddled with questions and problems that what impresses us today is the singular precariousness of its eighteenth-century accomplishments in France.[2] No doubt the smaller-minded *minores* – d'Holbach, Helvétius, Jaucourt, etc. – remain in our eyes roughly as before. But modern views of "rationalism" in the major figures have undergone radical transformation. Who would have believed twenty years ago that researches would uncover a clear current of "illuminism" in

Introduction

Diderot?[3] Or that some of the dominant thought processes of this editor of the *Encyclopédie* would turn out to be essentially non-Aristotelian and even non-logical?[4] No doubt the author of the *Social Contract* has always resisted easy classification, but in our time Rousseau has become more difficult than ever to define as scholars have recognized a fascinating web of contradictions that inform not only certain of his fictions, but parts of the "philosophical" writings as well.[5] For both these great figures of the Age of Reason the term "rationalist" probably obscures more than it reveals. Even in the case of the most impressive accomplishment of the French Enlightenment, the *Encyclopédie*, which purported to order and arrange all the branches of human knowledge according to rational criteria, we are becoming aware that in certain instances the two main editors could not concur on what the order and arrangement should be. Reason apparently couldn't settle the issue. D'Alembert did his best, in the Preliminary Discourse, to hide his impatience with Diderot's Chart of Human Knowledge, but the rift between them distinctly shows through, and it not only points to the fragility of their rational classifications, it foreshadows also the grand-scale breakdown in the usefulness of the System which developed, when the editors tried to categorize each and every article according to the Chart.[6] As Diderot had surely known all along, strictly and "objectively" speaking, human knowledge had no rational order.

One of the most curious changes in perspective has occurred in respect to the *philosophe* we think of as wearing the original "smile of Reason," Voltaire. Whereas earlier generations had sometimes stereotyped him as a reassuring symbol of the triumph of rationality in the Age of Philosophy, today scholars are more inclined to stress the tensions and hesitancies in the rationalism of the author of *Candide*. Though he used a methodology one might term "rationalist" until the end of his life, the Reason to which he clung lost much of the trenchancy of the early years, and as time went on, became noticeably less broad in its effective application. Eventually Voltaire found himself operating on a diminished terrain, bounded by irrational superstition and fanaticism on one side, by insoluble dilemmas such as the problem of evil on another, and on a third, by the menace of atheism – another form of rationalism, and which threatened insidiously from within.[7] Voltaire's last great metaphysical work, the *Dialogues d'Evhémère* of 1777, is a courageous attempt to reaffirm the essentials of a "rationalist" point of view, which in Voltaire's case included deism, and belief in progress as well. Yet there is a slightly hollow ring to his ironic thrusts against Plato, Aristotle, Leibniz, and the rest, as the Patriarch lords it over them for their foolish ideas and inconsequential logic. The jibes do not prevent one from noticing just how precarious Voltaire's deism has become, nor do they brighten the somber tone of his pessimism concerning the follies of mankind.

Introduction

Another issue which was considerably less aggravating for earlier generations than for us concerns the relationship of the intellectual life of the Enlightenment to history. To be sure, in one sense nothing could be simpler: what we call the Enlightenment *was* history, Voltaire and Rousseau (if only *malgré lui*) being its beacons. It has been obvious for a long time that literature in that age embodied social and political conflicts in a manner far more immediate than the preceding century had done. Such events as the condemnation of the thesis of the Abbé de Prades, the expulsion of the Jesuits, the earthquake in Lisbon and the alleged injustices of Maupeou's Parlement all found direct expression in the important literature of the period. The final words Voltaire wrote, almost literally his dying gasp, concerned the rehabilitation of a man who had been unjustly sentenced by the judicial authorities – an ultimate gesture by the Patriarch which generously symbolized the Enlightenment's vital engagement in the affairs of its time.

Yet even here our viewpoint is starting to shift. For, as some scholars have pointed out, the most consequential political event of the century, prior to the Revolution itself, namely, the Seven Years War, made scarcely any impact on the significant literature of the age. Though it is evident that the war had the most serious sort of political and economic consequences, aside from the battle scene in *Candide*, virtually nothing in the literature reflected this importance. The same can be said of the great famines of the century in France: literature is virtually silent about them. In other words, the Enlightenment was distinctly selective in its reactions to the events of history, even to those involving "humanitarian" concerns. In the last analysis, the *philosophes* only reacted strongly when, one way or another, the survival of their ideas was threatened, or, contrariwise, when their own programs were being furthered. One might hazard a number of explanations of this logically unexpected phenomenon. My own view is that it suggests how much the movement we call the French Enlightenment was defined in relation to the past, particularly the reign of Louis XIV. Then was the moment – even more than the reign of Louis XV – when the great potential enemies of the Enlightenment – tyranny, religious superstition, intolerance, persecution, legal injustice, class privilege, and so on – crystalized into their purest state. To the *philosophes*, the abuses of their own time were intolerable not merely in themselves, but because they emanated from a social, religious, and political past which all of them – even Voltaire when he was not being mesmerized by it – judged unpardonable. This was why the Seven Years War never provoked the ferocious reaction one observes in the fiftieth chapter of Diderot's *Bijoux indiscrets* where the author suddenly condenses into the most grotesque sort of puppet imagery the rage and indignation he felt about the atrocities of the reign of Louis XIV and his hated mistress–wife – including the Revocation of the Edict of Nantes. No doubt Diderot exaggerated the role of Mme de Maintenon; the point is that his deepest feelings against monarchy were rooted not only in the present, but in the past. Hazard was even wiser than he himself knew.

But if the history of ideas is being obstructed by concepts that refuse to retain their traditional status, if the relationship of eighteenth-century literature to history is beclouded and confused by blanks or emanations from the past, and if large syntheses such as Hazard produced are now out of reach simply because today's scholars know so much, then are those whose concern is literature left, perforce, with the deconstructionist and semiotic aftermaths of *nouvelle critique* as a last resort? I do not think so. In fact, not at all.

If vast syntheses no longer appear possible, there is nothing wrong with fragmentary, rather than synthetic, approaches. Fragments make for diversity: the eighteenth century itself thrived on them. The *Encyclopédie*, except for the unworkable Chart, is essentially bits and pieces arranged in alphabetical order. Certain chapters in Montesquieu, and all the chapters of *Candide*, have the appearance (at least) of fragments. Facts and experiments are, first of all, bits. No doubt all these fragments were thought of by the *philosophes* as belonging to larger wholes, as d'Alembert rather ponderously insisted in his Preliminary Discourse, but this does not damage their usefulness as points of departure. Indeed the element of synecdoche suggests the direction the explorations may take.

Likewise, although terms like "rationalism" and "superstition" are indeed turning out to be clumsily ambiguous, perhaps one may control them somewhat better if one stops looking at them directly for their content and attempts to view them contrapuntally, as working against other terms. Even trained musicians may have difficulty hearing certain pitches if they are given in isolation. Musical sounds achieve their full identity by being heard amid contrasting tones, in other words, against what they are not. (Obviously a similar observation might be made of colors.) Presently I shall suggest one way in which this concept might usefully be applied to the Enlightenment.

Finally, the selectivity which governed the response of the *philosophes* to historical events may also be placed in a more useful perspective: if it indicates, as I believe it does, that their responses were tied in some respects to the past, it also signifies, paradoxically, that they were participating in a movement that was heading towards the Revolution. This is the other side of the same coin: the issues they selected (some of which I have just mentioned) were, incipiently, the revolutionary ones, although these would only achieve gradually the kind of virulence that makes citizens risk their lives to topple governments.

In this connection, scholars are only beginning to appreciate the importance in the eighteenth century of the phenomenon rhetoricians and certain

Introduction

historians of art and iconography refer to as "prolepsis": the French Enlightenment's way of foretelling the future and writing its own destiny on the wall.[8] We are just now realizing how often and in how many different ways the fantasies produced by artists and writers of that era – even when their creations were allegedly set in antiquity – represented an effort to imagine a way out of a present that was perceived as intolerable. Furthermore, these imaginings occasionally came true: the fantasies were sometimes acted out in historical reality, as if they embodied in some mysterious way not only the discontent of the present, but the will of the future. One of the most revealing instances of this unconsciously (?) prophetic side of the era is afforded by the career of the painter, Hubert Robert (1733–1808). Admittedly it is not easy to deal with this figure briefly, as must be done here. His artistic personality was deeply complex – quite contrary to his social personality which, according to contemporary accounts, was all smiles and winning affability. He and his pleasure-loving wife were constantly seen in society, indeed, according to the fashionable Mme Vigée-Lebrun, they seldom dined at home. Though not himself of noble lineage, he was closely acquainted with members of the highest aristocracy, and even, because of commissions for the gardens at Versailles, came to know the Queen, Marie Antoinette. According to reliable reports, these persons of quality enjoyed his engaging personality and treated him as an equal. Yet none of these mundane activities prevented him from exploring in his art dimensions that had nothing to do with the glamorous world in which he chose to spend his leisure hours, dimensions in fact that were profoundly subversive to it.

The significant part of his professional life started in 1754 when he went to Rome,[9] a city not only full of ruins (fortunately for his temperament), but one which also had a strong academic tradition of ruin painting. (Piranesi, Servandoni and above all Panini were to have the most lasting influence upon him.) Robert linked up with this tradition, became a professional ruin painter himself and, in an entirely free and imaginative way, used what he saw, real or painted, for inspiration. To be sure, back in Paris, where he journeyed in 1765, ruin painting was not quite so firmly established as a tradition, nor were so many actual ruins available as subjects; indeed France's greatness did not reside in a past so distant as that of Rome. But significantly, even though there was far less material at hand, Robert kept on the same path, reworking what he had recorded in his Roman sketchbooks, inventing his own ruined landscapes, and seizing upon the meagerest occasions to exploit whatever "ruins" he could discover: the dead and fallen trees in the Parc of Versailles, for example, or the Paris Opéra as it was burning down – in the very process of becoming a ruin – or the aged Mme Geoffrin, another ruin in the making, sitting alone at her meal and being read to by a domestic standing behind her chair. One wonders what was

going on in the mind of this gifted artist as he painted so many broken arches
and fallen columns of buildings that had once been the palaces of kings, as
he depicted scenes that might so easily imply the destruction of the kind of
monarchy under which he himself lived. How much was he aware, as the
Revolution approached, of the latent message of his art, his art as presage,
even as secret desire?

Perhaps such a politicizing of the painter's motives will appear tenden-
tious or exaggerated. Yet, in the eighteenth century Diderot at least might
have agreed with it – at one point in his life. For, even though Diderot did
not later follow through with his idea, one of the reasons behind his original
enthusiasm for Robert's ruins when he encountered them at the Salon of
1767 had been political. Indeed their purely antiquarian interest paled
when he perceived in one of them an almost Ozymandian warning for
despots [N.B. English versions of French passages appear in the notes]:

Grande fabrique occupant la droite, la gauche et le fond de l'esquisse. C'est un
palais ou plutôt c'en fut un. La dégradation est si avancée qu'on discerne à peine la
demeure d'un de ces maîtres du monde, d'une de ces bêtes farouches, qui dévoraient
les rois qui dévorent les hommes. Sous ces arcades qu'ils ont élevées et où un Verrès
déposait des dépouilles des nations, habitent à présent des marchands d'herbes, des
chevaux, des boeufs, des animaux, et dans ces lieux dont les hommes se sont
éloignés, ce sont des tigres, des serpens, d'autres voleurs. Contre cette façade, ici
c'est un hangar dont le toit s'avance en pente sur le devant, c'est une fabrique
pareille à ces sales remises appuyées aux superbes murs du Louvre. [. . .][10]

The Louvre? What an intriguing, arresting choice of a palace to mention,
however briefly, in the middle of this hostile meditation on the destruction,
the just deserts, of tyrants:

Eh, bien ces puissans de la terre qui croyaient bâtir pour l'éternité, qui se sont fait de
si superbes demeures et qui les destinaient dans leurs folles pensées à une suite
ininterrompue de descendans héritiers de leurs noms, de leurs titres et de leur
opulence, il ne reste de leurs travaux, de leurs énormes dépenses, de leurs grandes
vues que des débris qui servent d'asyle à la partie la plus indigente, la plus
malheureuse de l'espèce humaine, plus utiles en ruines qu'ils ne le furent dans leur
première splendeur.   (Ed. Seznec, p. 246)[11]

Obviously ruins meant many contradictory things to Diderot; and if, as
here, they could set off ruminations on the vulnerability of despots to the
retribution of history, they could also symbolize the awesome endurance of
bygone power (as they did also for Robert). And of course for Diderot ruins
could evoke reflections on the precariousness of the present. It is in this vein
that Professor Mortier, in his classic study,[12] finds Diderot's most strikingly
original contribution to the literature of ruins. For Diderot realized that
ruins were not merely emanations from the past: they could also suggest
anticipations or prophecies of the future. This is the movement I term
"prolepsis":

Introduction

Nous attachons no regards sur les débris d'un arc de triomphe, d'un portique, d'une pyramide, d'un temple, d'un palais, et nous revenons sur nous-mêmes. Nous anticipons sur les ravages du temps, et notre imagination disperse sur la terre les édifices mêmes que nous habitons.   (Ed. Seznec, III, p. 227)[13]

These reflections bring one back to the problem of foreshadowing in Robert. For we would very much like to know at what stage, and to what degree, he comprehended the politics of his own motives as the depiction which apparently started in 1759 as a Roman scene showing a great ruined gallery with the statue of Marcus Aurelius, gradually branched into new forms, developing into a vast series of ruined gallery depictions, endlessly varied and lasting for almost forty years, until finally in 1796 the gallery which had haunted – obsessed – him for so long turned into the gallery of the kings of France, the Louvre – seen as an imaginary ruin.[14]

The best answer we have, that is to say, the closest we can come to specifying the moment of his *engagement*, is to be found in a large painting in the Musée Carnavalet, which depicts the prison of the Bastille, towering massively, with red-hued walls (the color of blood, of tyranny).[15] The building is being shown at the very instant, in July 1789, when the patriots had started to tear it down – another ruin in the making, of course. But now

1. Hubert Robert, *Galerie romaine* (1759)

7

2. Hubert Robert, *Vue imaginaire de la Grande Galerie du Louvre en ruines* (1796)

3. Hubert Robert, *La Bastille dans les premiers jours de sa démolition* (20 Juillet 1789)

the creation of a ruin is openly identified in the Revolutionary sense with the destruction of tyranny, so that the picture also memorializes the precise moment when Robert's art crossed the line and became an overt social and political statement, when his secret message was rendered visible and proclaimed in deed, and perhaps even when his own artistic personality fully revealed itself as a practicing member of the new social order. Catherine the Great was rather perspicacious in 1791 when Robert refused her invitation to abandon Revolutionary France and go to Russia: she remarked sarcastically that no doubt he was loath to leave France because he enjoyed painting ruins so much, and France was now the "country of ruins."[16] Though he would have valorized the remark quite differently, Robert would have agreed with the main point: the Revolution did indeed make ruins, and in his painting of the destruction of the Bastille he took the stand his life as an artist had prepared him to take, and publicly bid them welcome.[17]

It is my conviction that, broadly speaking, the literature of the French Enlightenment underwent a similar transformation from latency to manifestation, and from symbol to reality, as it flowed with the grand current of history towards the cataclysm at the end. The following chapters will explore the terrain in order to suggest a few of the ways in which this occurred. But before setting out on that path, a major point in the logic of my argument needs to be addressed.

II

In Hazard's great work on the intellectual crisis at the end of the reign of Louis XIV all the main authors he treated were characterized by a vigorous turning away from the traditions that had nurtured them, and this gesture of denial was destined in the Enlightenment to become a wholesale rejection of one of the most sacred values of the age of Classicism: the ideal of *emulation*.[18] The reasons for this shift are too numerous even to be listed here; it was, as Hazard saw, a question of a vast movement from one age to another. One must be content with the mere stipulation that towards the end of the seventeenth century, the basic principle of Classical education, the belief that perfection in any area of learning was attained through the positive assimilation of models and the attempt to outdo one's predecessors by following their principles, began in significant ways to be questioned and lose ground – even as the Ancients were losing out to the Moderns and the doctrine of imitation was being brought into question. When one moves into the eighteenth century, rejection, either implied or explicit, of the ideal of emulation is endemic, at least among artists and writers of the time who dared to express a new vision of things. One has only to think of the extraordinary lengths Rousseau went to, in *Emile*, to have his pupil tricked into believing he was not being schooled by an all-knowing sage; or, in religion, of the campaign by deists such as Voltaire to shrink God the Father into an invisible, abstract principle of goodness, ultimately the emanation of convictions that individuals found graven in their own hearts: or even, in painting, of the telling absence of the portrait of the King from Chardin's various "Attributs des arts." Perhaps this is the larger sense, too, of Diderot's marvelous anecdote, recounted at the opening of his essay on Terence, about the Roman slave who was offered up for auction, billed as a "ruler of men." There were no buyers, of course, and Diderot wittily proposed a moral by innuendo: no one wanted a master.[19]

Though proposed in humorous terms, the lesson of Diderot's anecdote had implications that were potentially revolutionary and that were in fact translated into action, so to speak, when the great Revolution occurred. We find a curiously literal enactment of just the sort of political message Diderot had implied in an account of one of the Revolutionary demonstrations, a procession that went from the Bastille to the Champs-de-Mars in April 1792. The purpose of the event was to commemorate an uprising of galley prisoners ("La Fête de Châteauvieux") and it is clear from the newspaper account that every aspect of the demonstration, down to the least detail, had been devised to exhibit symbolic import:

Le cortège se mit en marche fort tard, vers midi; ce n'est pas que le peuple se fit attendre, à l'exemple de despotes aux fêtes de cour. Il s'était rendu dès le matin et en grand nombre à la Barrière du Trône; mais la fête n'attendit pas qu'on prit route pour commencer. Du moment qu'on se trouva rassemblé, on goûta le plaisir d'être ensemble; il fallut pourtant partir. [. . .]

On fit sur le terrain de la Bastille une espèce d'inauguration de la statue de la liberté. Nous omettons les détails pour mieux saisir l'ensemble de cette fête populaire, la première de ce genre et qui, nous l'espérons, pourra se répéter. Le temps qui s'écoula pendant les premières stations donna le loisir aux citoyens mal disposés et crédules de se rassurer un peu, et de venir sur le passage de cette marche triomphale, favorisée d'ailleurs de toute la sérénité d'un jour de printemps.

La pompe n'était pas riche; l'or n'y éblouissait point les yeux, et n'insultait pas à la douce médiocrité ou à l'indigence honorable des citoyens. Une soldatesque chargée de galons ne jetait pas en passant, de droite et de gauche, des regards méprisants sur la foule des assistants mal vêtus. Ici les acteurs et les témoins, souvent confondus, formaient tour à tour le cortège: il y eut peu d'ordre, mais beaucoup d'accord; on ne sacrifia point à la vanité d'offrir un coup d'oeil superbe; on ne chercha point à se donner en spectacle; l'ennui, fils de l'uniformité, ne se glissa point dans les différens groupes; à chaque pas la scène changeait; la chaine du cortège se rompit bien des fois, mais les regardans en remplissaient les lacunes: tout le monde voulait être de la fête de la liberté. . . .

Le cortège parcourut la moitié du circuit de Paris, et se fit jour à travers une foule immense et continue, sans rencontrer d'obstacles. La gendarmerie à pied et à cheval n'eut pas besoin de lui tracer sa route; deux haies de baïonnettes ne furent point nécessaires pour lui ouvrir un passage; le ministre de l'intérieur ne se mêla en rien de

Introduction

la haute police; le département recommanda le bon ordre à la municipalité, et il fut pris la veille un arrêté relativement au port d'armes et aux voitures mais ce fut le peuple qui se chargea de le mettre lui-même à exécution, et sa conduite fut une leçon pour les magistrats, et un exemple pour la garde nationale. Quatre cent mille citoyens furent hors de chez eux pendant toute une demi-journée, et se portèrent tous sur le même point, sans qu'il en soit résulté le moindre accident. Des paroles de paix continrent tout ce monde; il se rangea, il s'aligna à la vue d'un épi de blé qui lui fut présenté en guise de baïonnettes, depuis la Bastille jusqu'au Champ-de-Mars.[20]

The most salient feature of the procession is that it is not, ostensibly, being led by anyone: no one in particular is at its head or is even central to it. The "galériens" it commemorates are simply identified, rather than dramatized as heroes.[21] Not so much as a drum-beat forced the participants to march in step. And since no visible authorities presided over this festivity, the leisurely procession moved of its own accord, when and where it desired. It was a living demonstration of the pleasures of existence when no one is giving, or taking, orders. As though following Diderot's suggestion, this procession celebrated a society without masters.

But if, theoretically at least, there was no authority telling the paraders where and when to move, how to behave, and what to wear, how then could the citizens know the right way to conduct themselves and make their procession a suitable expression of patriotism? The answer suggested in this account is that the demonstration was organized (or disorganized) according to negative principles: everything was performed precisely in the way traditional processions of the *ancien régime* were not. As the account informs the reader, traditional processions were exclusive affairs, pompous spectacles set apart from the populace. They reproduced all the hateful class barriers of the old régime. This told the paraders that, contrariwise, theirs must be an *inclusive* procession: simple, rather than pompous, in which the onlookers would be hardly distinguishable from the participants. In this Revolutionary procession, class barriers should totally disappear. The newspaper states that traditional processions featured brilliant uniforms, proud, in fact arrogant deportment, and rich and fancy clothes. This meant that the Revolutionaries should *not* be uniform, but variegated, and that their attire, as well as their behavior, should be unassuming: the honest poor were welcome among them. As the account states, traditional processions used military men to charge their way through the crowds and ensure that strict order was maintained. This told the Revolutionaries that their demonstration should not use force of any kind, that strict discipline should not prevail, but instead, that the procession should calmly wend its way to its destination, in its own good time. This was not a princely, but a popular affair: not anyone in particular, but the people in general were to decide what to do.

"La Fête de Châteauvieux" was devised as a civic lesson in the meaning of the words "liberty" and "equality." But, in the account, the virtues the procession embodied and preached were not being presented as values desirable in themselves (indeed, one might question whether the deliberate inefficiency and the helter-skelter quality of the occasion were virtues at all), but rather as liberations from those *ancien régime* vices which were contrary to them. The procession was an anti-body, which is to say, a liberation, through the principle of contrariety and opposition, from an undesirable state which it cancelled out. Finally, the account leads one to infer that this amiably milling cortege, with its worthy poor and modest demeanor, stopping and starting according to whim, generously picking up all who wished to join in on its peaceful stroll through Paris, was deliberately contrived as an inversion, a mirror image, of the social values that had prevailed in times past. This celebration of liberty represented all the unwanted stratifications, disciplines and prohibitions of the *ancien régime* negated by being turned topsy-turvy.[22]

There is something rather bland in the account of the festivity: like the spring weather, the procession was all friendliness and peaceful welcome (Diderot would have loved it.)[23] And yet there was nothing inherently bland or peaceful about the negative principle, the inversion of values, which structured the ceremony. On the contrary, the inversion had often been associated with violence and disruption. One can be rather categoric about the matter, for this kind of inversion had a long history in France, and, during the eighteenth century, an especially interesting one in literature.

Let us return to the notion of emulation which, as previously noted, was starting to lose ground at the end of the reign of Louis XIV, as more and more authors rejected it. The most revealing of these rejections were the radical ones which, not unlike the Revolutionary procession, created anti-bodies based on principles of total opposition. Like the Parisian demonstrators, these literary radicals felt the urge to stand accepted norms on their heads. This sort of negative inversion turned into an enormous source of literary creativity for the authors of the pre-Revolutionary Enlightenment. One finds the principle at work in virtually every kind of intellectual activity: in philosophy, in the novel, in the theatre, in painting, even in music. Perhaps the reason for its efficacy was the perfect ambiguity it implied: just as in Revolutionary Paris, the practice of negative inversion created release from the past, new and untried paths to explore, with all the excitement such liberation might entail. Yet at the same time (predictably enough), the fact that the creations of these authors were dictated by tradition – albeit negatively – implies that they were still very much tied to the values they were rejecting.[24] Revolt against accepted norms meant dependence on them, if only for the negative charge, and much more than a mere negative explosion is involved in the birth of these curious literary inventions which spring into life structured throughout as inverted images of the traditions they reject. This phenomenon is rather familiar to psychologists, of course, and to parents in general, who readily interpret the nay-saying stages of their offspring as a form of recognition of authority, if not exactly obedience to it. Even worldly-wise churches, like the Catholic or the Anglican have known for ages that real blasphemy, the kind one finds in Rimbaud and the early T. S. Eliot, may actually be a promising sign of incipient spiritual conformity. This suggestion of a sort of identity between a positive tradition and the negative mirror image of it accords quite well with the first two steps of the dialectic we attribute to Hegel, though the crucial third step, the synthesis, remains in suspense.

In short, this many-faceted phenomenon – which has an established tradition in folklore, psychology, and religion, as well as in literary theory, and which has a number of technical names including "symbolic inversion" and "symbolic negativity"[25] – could function either radically or conservatively, or both at the same time, which may explain its extraordinary success in a period we usually think of more simply as an age of reform.

Some authors were entirely conscious of the element of radical rejection involved in their creative impulses (many of the authors of the *théâtres de la foire* were; so was the author[s] of *Le Portier des Chartreux*). Sometimes the negative inversion operated on an unconscious level (as it so often did for Diderot). But some of the most interesting authors come in the twilight area between the conscious and the unconscious. Abbé Prévost is a fascinating case in point: he was sufficiently aware of the negative forces at work in the inspiration for *Manon*'s underworld to be quite uneasy about the reader's reaction. Yet, despite his apprehensiveness, he probably never saw their whole extent or grasped their import in his own creative process.

Nothing could be more natural than this kind of blindness: in literature, just as in life, negative inspiration often proceeds from hostility, discontent, desire for revenge – a whole range of urges that may not be pleasant to confront in broad daylight, and of course, given the repressive reality of pre-Revolutionary French régimes, it might have been dangerous to do so. Finally, since the forces at work here include the desire to flaunt and undo the values held most sacred by society, they regularly turned up as pornography and/or eroticism and sometimes they combined with unorthodox philosophy to form a mixture known as "libertinage." This is one of the most characteristic manifestations of "symbolic negativity" and the following pages will attempt to pay fitting attention to it.

Logically the hero of this study should have been Diderot, for no one else demonstrates so many aspects of "symbolic negativity" in so fascinating a way. H. Dieckmann first suggested how Diderot's mind operated in this regard, observing that Diderot's literary or philosophical inspiration is often antithetical, taking off in contradiction to a previously affirmed idea.

Scholars have since realized that Diderot's thought usually doesn't move forward in linear fashion at all: most often it proceeds via contradictions, opposites, reversals, and paradoxical inversions – as when, in *Jacques le fataliste*, le frère Jean is replaced by le père Ange, mainly because their names (Jean, Ange) phonetically reverse each other.[26] This example is but the tip of the iceberg, of course, for Diderot's thought continually liberates itself from itself, through contradictions – usually unseen by the author. This is one reason why it took so long for Diderot's genius to be fully recognized. His ideas cannot be summed up in the normal way, nor can his "doctrines" be set down in formulations without destroying their reason for being in the first place, along with the impulses that gave them life.

Though of course he is endlessly challenging when taken as an object of study in himself, Diderot is just as provocative when viewed as a symptom, or as part of a movement that reaches outside of himself. Diderot's followers have just as much to tell us about the possibilities of negative anti-bodies as he does. One has only to consider, for example, what happened to Diderot's anti-Classicism, surely one of the most rewarding aspects of his art to study, and one of the most complex, since his rejection of Classical notions seldom if ever exists in the pure state, and he so often builds upon the very principles he undermines. On the other hand, once his ideas have been filtered, ordered, and radicalized in the far less intelligent, imaginative, and creative mind of L.-S. Mercier, the inversion of Classical values assumes a dynamism, a virulence, that opens a new social dimension in literary theory. In Mercier one hears the kind of electrifying message that, earlier in the century, only Rousseau had been capable of producing, a tremor that reverberated throughout society.

Another Diderot disciple was Beaumarchais, who was not only a master of the dramatization of revolutionary antithesis, but a creative artist whose inner contradictions are only just now being recognized and explored. In Beaumarchais the inversions sometimes occur within single elements of the work itself, the contraries functioning in some strange way as an energizing principle that sustains the action. We will study the phenomenon in more detail in his mentor, Diderot, but even in *Le Mariage de Figaro*, we note how often the characters actually speak like someone else, or contain within themselves two irreconcilably contradictory traits. Who would expect that the Count, the very personification of injustice and evil laws that must be abolished, would turn over the coin and declare for judicial integrity, advocating just the sort of legal reform that Beaumarchais himself desired, for reasons of personal experience (III, 15)? How can Figaro, who holds our sympathy as a victim of the evil designs of the lecherous, unprincipled Count to steal his bride, himself brashly, callously boast of stealing another man's wife and producing an illegitimate offspring by her (III, 13)? How can Marceline be, on the one hand, a ridiculous, lusting old prude, the exact stereotype so risibly familiar through Régnier's Macette and Molière's Arsinoë, and at the same time claim our sympathy and affection as a spokesperson for women's rights, denouncing their enslavement in a world dominated by the mighty male (III, 16)? At the end of the play, these contradictions reach truly amazing proportions. In the final vaudeville, almost no one sings verses appropriate for him/herself: Bazile's verse should have belonged to Figaro; Suzanne sounds just like Marceline; the Moral of Figaro's lines would better suit the Count, who sings words that are surprisingly unsuitable for his situation – already the cast is tending to forget the lessons of the plot they have just completed. In short, the characters have become unstuck, wandering loose from their "true" identities (one is reminded, rather, of the parodies of the *théâtres de la foire*, or of the end of Le Sage's *Crispin*). But then, this was a giddy age. One cartoonist of Beaumarchais' time drew a shop (1784) where people could go to buy new heads for themselves. The heads came complete with wig and *chapeau*, so that to become someone else, one had only to step up to the counter and take one's pick. Beaumarchais' play gives something of the same feeling, and ironically, it seems not at all inappropriate that the Age of Enlightenment, of Philosophy, of Revolution, would end thus, in a blur of contradictions.

In our own generation in French Studies we have witnessed the temporary partial eclipse of traditional literary history, which became for a time a semi-casualty of the movements we labeled structuralism, semiotics, and deconstructionism. Likewise, aesthetics, or the work of art considered as experience – created out of life, heard, understood, felt here and now – fell very much by the wayside. And yet, as everyone in music, painting, and the theatre at least knows full well, the experience of art, or art as experience has always stood, and will always stand, waiting to be discovered – the merest strain from a concerto by Mozart, the merest cadence from a Bach fugue, the merest kitchen pot by Chardin, the merest indecency by Rameau's nephew instantly proving the point beyond controversy. It is true that literary history (at least as it was practiced by traditionalists) may have found itself for a while in an impasse. But perhaps the problem here has been that literary historians have generally assumed that the dynamic elements of the aesthetic object work in straight lines, and that the tensions in the structure of a piece of literature should be seen as resolving positively to form a coherent unity. Fortunately there are indications from many quarters (and symbolic negativity is one of them) that it is time not just to bring these assumptions into question, but to put them out of commission (at least for the present). If we can manage to take a fresh look, the possibilities are simply boundless; in fact the study of literary history is not at all at an end, it is just beginning. Perhaps a consideration of some of the literature of eighteenth-century France can reinforce this suggestion. In any event, it is a starting point.

I

Manon's hidden motives

Wherever one looks one feels the crushing weight of institutions, the inhuman steepness of the social hierarchy, the denial of instinctual life.

[Emrys Jones on *The Duchess of Malfi*]

Few lovers of opera are able to resist entirely the insinuating charm of Massenet's *Manon*. One could never claim that the libretto by Meilhac and Gille makes great poetry, but at least it hews fairly closely to Abbé Prévost's immortal story, capitalizing on some of the finer dramatic moments. The famous aria, "Ah! fuyez, douce image,"[1] may be slightly facile as a melodic statement, yet it has a way of clinging on in the mind; the tune is likely to haunt one whenever one recalls the Chevalier des Grieux's lovelorn distress. The magic spell of the piece is cast near the middle of act I, during the famous encounter at the inn. This is usually staged as a busy and colorful scene, with the arrival and departure of coaches, travelers collecting their baggage or trying to get fed – but punctuated by a somber note too as Manon's cousin (at this point, a pure invention of the librettists) warns her to mind her behavior. The cousin leaves and the Chevalier makes his appearance. Catching sight of Manon, he finds himself strangely, irresistibly drawn to her. They exchange a few words, but rather shyly, with touching hesitation. (Here for the moment they speak rather than sing.) As he asks her name, he realizes he is losing control of his feelings, but no longer cares. There is a crescendo in the music, and suddenly the moment the audience has been waiting for:

> Enchanteresse au charme vainqueur!
> Manon, vous êtes la maîtresse de mon coeur![2]

sings the tenor, his high notes already proving that his heart belongs to her alone, the horns, woodwinds, and strings all joining together to confirm it. In the intensity of the moment one realizes that his course is now set, his destiny fixed forever.

This moment is the enactment of a kind of Romantic love which the French call *amour coup de foudre*. Its excitement comes precisely from the impulsiveness, the gratuitousness, the daring disregard for practicalities, the promise to create a whole world in which to lose oneself, in which absolutely nothing matters except passion – not even death. Though Rousseau and his followers had pointed the way, it was of course Romanticism proper that developed this kind of sentiment to the fullness one finds in Massenet. In fact, the composer's task was simplified considerably because he had a "prepared" audience who knew what they wanted: to leave their reason behind in just the crescendo of Romantic emotion Massenet would provide for them.

How different these emotions are from those generated by the original story from which the opera came. Of course, Prévost's *Manon Lescaut* was not Romantic at all; it was early, pre-Rousseau eighteenth century, an era that felt quite differently about loss of self-control and sentimental oblivion. No doubt it is true, as scholars maintain, that the original *Manon* reflects the easy morality, the debauchery of the period we call *la Régence*, but even at the time there were critics who remained rather cool to the heroine's charms and the novel's decadent love theme: the great Montesquieu saw Manon first of all as a whore.[3]

Naturally, to approach the novel one must try to forget all the colorful sights and sounds of the opera. By comparison, Prévost's text looks rather stark on the page. The words have a lean, uncolored, carefully picked, very eighteenth-century feel – they give us anything but an emotional blur. We are at an inn which the author doesn't bother to describe (one has seen such inns before; the only appearance that counts is that of Manon. Before she arrives, we are waiting among life's banalities). A coach, which the Chevalier and his friend, Tiberge, have been following out of indolent curiosity, draws up in the courtyard, an event so ordinary we scarcely notice it. But suddenly, there she is, lingering behind the other women passengers while an elderly gentleman takes care of the baggage. The narrator does not describe her beyond that single, arresting word, "charmante":

Elle me parut si charmante que . . . je me trouvai enflammé tout d'un coup jusqu'au transport (p. 1229).[4]

For the Chevalier this is literally love at first sight; he had never so much as looked, sexually, at a woman before, and this erotic vacuum has allegedly created in the Chevalier the astonishing readiness for passion we witness, the irresistible surge of emotion which instantly establishes Manon as sovereign of his heart. Emboldened by these feelings, he approaches, makes polite conversation, and ascertains that her present situation is not unlike his own: they are both in their last moments of relative liberty before a life of confined regularity. He manages to convey his (passionate) sentiments, to which she eagerly responds, and, one thing leading to another, they agree on stratagems to give their gullible guardians the slip, and run off together towards Paris. Thanks to the speed of events as they occur, and the author's remarkable economy of style, all this takes just five pages!

One point is made crystal clear by the author, speaking both as the fictional narrator of the story, and also as the protagonist: the Chevalier's impulsive conduct has no rational explanation whatsoever. One may call it destiny (which has put the hero in the wrong place at the wrong time) (p. 1230; p. 1260), or fate (which has made Manon's charms so irresistible (p. 1340); or a lack of grace, which makes it theologically impossible for the hero to fight against the false attractions of things terrestrial (p. 1247); or one may call it a thunderbolt of love (p. 1248), but the author and his characters unite in their resolve to keep us from imagining for a second that there is anything voluntary, willful (in the ordinary sense) in this behavior, or that the Chevalier would truly want to act that way. Even before the start of the novel proper, the author has his narrator, in an *Avis* (pp. 1219–21), give a lecture, apparently in the Bayle manner, explaining – quite awkwardly, and with noticeable gaps in his logic – that there are occasions when people actually want to do the right thing, but are prevented from doing so by very compelling immediate circumstances, by distractions, confusions that obscure the right path, so that their conduct turns out to be just the opposite of what they originally intended. Indeed, his novel may serve the useful purpose of alerting everyone to these perils.

Perhaps it may seem to some that the novel does bear out the Abbé's slightly incoherent theories. Certainly Manon is depicted as the most compelling sort of distraction for the Chevalier, addling his brain so that he can think of nothing else. Whenever she is not in his thoughts, he is shown as embodying everything the eighteenth century thought virtuous: he is a gentleman, an aristocrat who takes the aristocratic code of honor very seriously (at the Académie, where the Chevalier was heading at the opening of the novel, young men were trained not only to bridle a horse, but to bridle their passions as well). He was supposed to be on the way to becoming a sort of churchman, that is, either a priest or a Chevalier de Malte at the beginning, a candidate in theology later on. These vocations implied celibacy, at least for purposes of fiction, and presumably they come under the "discipline de l'Eglise." And there is more: the reader is to imagine he was, *en principe*, an obedient, devoted son, everything a proud father could wish for, an honor to the family, a faithful friend to Tiberge. Since Abbé Prévost was so partial to theological arguments, one might also concede some measure of virtue in the Chevalier's conduct even when he is under Manon's spell, however tarnished and perverted it may have become (p. 1234). For, undeniably, his devotion to Manon may be unwise and regrettable, but it appears nonetheless utterly selfless, and self-sacrificing. To Manon at least he is loyalty and generosity itself, and these might actually have counted as virtues, if only (as the narrator, the Chevalier, and Tiberge never tire of exclaiming), cruel fate (that is to say, the author's well-founded psychological intuition) had not taken him down the wrong path.

Unfortunately, after a rather promising start, the theory comes up against a blank wall, as empty as the courtyard at the inn, as bare as Manon's indeterminate charms, as unyielding as words on a page sometimes are. Eventually I will suggest that the reader has been, not enlightened by all the official explanations, but anesthetized. For we must assume that there was something extremely important behind the Chevalier's sudden rush of energy and determination if we are to believe that this loyal friend, this dutiful son and pride of the family, this would-be churchman at the beginning of an exemplary career, would so suddenly falter and crash into a life of lying, cheating, stealing, blaspheming; that he would use his noble appearance and fine manners to play confidence games (p. 1262), live almost as a pimp by preying on his mistress's rich lovers (p. 1271; pp. 1314ff.), land himself in jail (pp. 1275–88), and even commit murder (p. 1288); that he would destroy almost systematically all the values he and his class supposedly esteemed the most.

According to the narrator and all the characters, the sole explanation for this moral collapse is the Chevalier's libido and Manon's charms – twin powers, it's true, that one would be foolish to underestimate. For (to go along with the narrator's presentation for a moment) it is quite plausible to read *Manon* as a tale of a nice young gentleman gone astray, lured – partly by his own gratuitous desires, and partly by the seductions of a siren – into a kind of hell that, while providing abundant sensual enjoyment, also corrodes his self-esteem and progressively destroys his will. It is very much a tale of a man's degradation through the agency of, and for, a woman. Perhaps for some readers it will be reminiscent of the classic German film with Marlene Dietrich and Emil Jannings, the *Blue Angel*; for certain of Prévost's scenes combine the most intense poignance with a tawdriness that very much suggests the psychology of the great German film. One thinks, in particular, of the supremely artful moment, so terrible for the Chevalier as he struggles to avoid contemplating the wreckage of himself, when Manon, having stood him up at a rendezvous, sends him a whore to occupy him for the night, while she sleeps with someone else (there are carriages here, too) (p. 1317). Just as in the *Blue Angel*, the hero is destroying everything he had for a woman who has no sense of the values he is giving up. Yet Prévost's tale, if only because of its origins in a society of early Enlightenment – not to mention the Christian values it claims to embody – cannot founder and sink in its degradation, as the German story does. On the contrary, the hero will start building a new life and restoring his self-esteem in the New World – at Manon's expense, this time, rather than at his own (he has no real understanding of her sacrifice, either). So that, after the Chevalier has been her inadvertent victim for so long, she finally becomes his. And then there is the final irony: Manon dies in a desert landscape uncannily like the bleak one the Chevalier had for a brief moment imagined himself in, at that most critical juncture in the novel (p. 1249), just before he slid back into Manon's fatal power.

Perhaps this is something of what the author of the story wanted the reader to understand, and of course it has an admirable sort of integrity, with just the consistency and the feeling of truth associated with the greatest works of art. Certainly, due homage should be paid to Manon's formidable charms, which the author claims precipitated his unfortunate hero on his course. However, it is time to add that his conduct itself proves that these are of themselves insufficient to make the plot credible.

If family, religion, and moral convictions really were props that fortified virtue, the hero could never have fallen so fast, so easily, so totally. This is, I believe, the secret that the Abbé would have us enjoy in his story, but never be quite cognizant of: all the alleged barriers against vice, adduced as such at every turn by the narrator, the Chevalier himself, and by Tiberge, actually afford no protection at all. Far from it. Psychologically they incite and abet the guilty pleasures they are supposed to repel.

Let us return once more to the courtyard of the inn where the hero, out of idle curiosity about its occupants, has followed the arrival of the Arras coach. Until that moment (asserts the author's hero), the Chevalier's conduct has been nothing but "sage et réglée." But that is precisely the point: since the beginning of the world (one doesn't have to be a psychologist to know this; just being a parent will do), the imposition of rules has, ipso facto, created the desire to break them. *Conduite réglée* bears within it and, under the right circumstances will actually engender, *dérèglement*, as if all the unruliness it excluded were still alive, waiting to fight back and take revenge. A confining wall, by the very fact that it restricts, can create the irresistible urge to break out.[5]

Something much more serious than a love affair with the wrong woman is taking place in *Manon Lescaut*, nor is it just a story of personal degradation. For Manon is not merely a siren luring the reader and the hero into her thrall, she is a catalyst, an agent, that unleashes both in the hero and in the reader's imagination the uncontrollable desire (unconscious, to be sure) to hurl oneself free of all life's confinements: family duties, rigors of social caste, religion, moral prescriptions, disciplines of all kinds. The courtyard that seemed so bare of motives was actually teeming with them; the Chevalier's perpetual virginity was one. His approaching vow of celibacy either as a priest, or as a Chevalier de Malte (later as a candidate in theology) called for something special – like *dépucelage* out of wedlock with a whore. The point is that a deflowering so spectacular took place not *despite* the hero's preceding chastity and the continence into which he was about to be locked, but *because* of them, *règlement* bringing on *dérèglement*.

21

One finds the same pattern in the famous friendship between the Chevalier and Tiberge,[6] who is described as being so loyal, trusting, and honest that any dishonesty, disloyalty, or distrust was simply out of the question if one frequented him. And that is just the point: the constricting demands of the situation, on an unconscious level, called for release. And so, in the name of Manon, one observes the hero cheating, betraying, even robbing the gullible Tiberge (p. 233; p. 1300; p. 1344), whose virtues only served to make him easier to deceive, as the Chevalier himself noted. Certainly, if one wishes, one can explain this by observing that Tiberge is supposed to have gotten in the way of the Chevalier's passion – as indeed he tried to do. But the total pattern of the Chevalier's behavior suggests that Manon functions not only as an object of his (and the reader's) desires, but as a pretext. This is the hidden danger and excitement of Abbé Prévost's novel, one of the reasons it has always cast such a spell, even as it awakens a certain uneasiness in the reader.

Following this same line of thought, one may wish to reconsider the hero's behavior towards his father: ostensibly the Chevalier truly wants to be a dutiful, worthy son, upholding the family honor and his own rank in society. But when it turns out that the Chevalier dishonors the family name through his unworthy conduct, betrays his father's kindness (p. 1339; p. 1347), and eventually through his disgraces even manages to contribute to his father's death (p. 1371), the reader's willingness to accept such conduct cannot be explained exclusively in terms of Manon's charms.[7] On the contrary, the charms are in part a decoy, conveniently fixing the attention, even blinding one with a thunderbolt of passion, so that no one will notice, except subliminally, that through Manon the Chevalier (the reader too, by sympathetic vibration) is able to rid himself of the whole formidable burden of the family and the onerous responsibilities it entailed in the *ancien régime*.

Similarly, the aristocratic code of honor turns out to be another weighty millstone the Chevalier throws off thanks to Manon – all the while protesting that it is against his will. But the Chevalier's masterstroke was in getting rid of everyone's most burdensome *entrave* in the eighteenth century, the yoke whose rigid strictures made themselves painfully felt in everyone's daily life, from cradle to grave; namely, the Church, and behind that, religion, and behind that, simply belief in a God who punishes or rewards according to obedience to His will. The situation, if only because of its awesome, eternal demands, called for especially inventive subversion, and the Chevalier meets the challenge (pp. 1283–5) with a series of arguments spoken with eloquence and conviction. But if one gives full play to his starting device (remembering, too, what he says elsewhere about the *délectation victorieuse*, p. 1250), one discovers he has, with the utmost contentment to himself (and presumably to the reader as well, though unconsciously), substituted his mistress (who is a whore after all) for the divinity, and has explained why, in the circumstances, he was quite right to love her instead. It is a stunning performance; even the author sensed he had gone rather far; perhaps that is why he made straitlaced Tiberge (standing in for the well-meaning reader) look so appalled that the Chevalier quickly applies some casuistry to take the sting out of his own words.

Neither the narrator, nor the Chevalier, nor the reader would tolerate such behavior, were it not for repeated assurances that everyone disapproves of it, that it was wrong, and that the author (speaking through his narrator), who dreamed the whole plot up, was deeply sorry it happened.[8] As for the Chevalier, it was not any wicked *penchants* that led him astray, but the blindest of passions. Particularly serviceable in this regard are Tiberge's sermons in favor of virtue – for several reasons. First, they relieve the reader's mind (one can enjoy this as a *moral* work, after all). Second, by outlining right conduct so emphatically, they set off and dramatize by contrast the Chevalier's wrong-doings. Lastly, if my theory is correct, they paradoxically recreate and reinstill in the Chevalier (and the reader), on an unconscious level, the desire to do all the things they condemn. They are fuel to the flame; insurance that the Chevalier's wayward course, and even the course of the novel, will continue, as will our participation in it. Tiberge's sermons are indeed creative acts, but in more ways than we are prone to acknowledge.

The point is that the enormous energy – destructive energy – set loose in *Manon Lescaut* derives from the unconscious desire to get free of the institutions and conventions that composed the whole fabric of eighteenth-century society, that made disciplined and civilized society in France possible. The energy released is specifically subversive; it comes from the secret urge to undo, prey upon, and break down everything society has constructed. As with the ring in *Les Bijoux indiscrets*, these forces could only be released under special, almost magical circumstances (for the Chevalier, the sudden appearance of the siren; for the reader, the occasion of this strange imaginary voyage, the book itself). Ordinarily such destructive motives are neither so visible, nor so active, because they have been systematically blocked, channeled, sublimated, or otherwise rendered innocuous by institutions – all the things the Chevalier wars against as the author has him wander further and further into the labyrinth of conscious desires for Manon, and unconscious, unexpressed, in fact, denied urges to be rid of society's shackles. Thus it is entirely plausible that the Chevalier, following these blind impulses, would find himself almost of necessity in an inverted mirror-world, literally an "underworld," striking against the values he, in "real" life, is supposed to esteem most highly. But real society in the early eighteenth century was as hostile to natural impulses as it was to nature itself, when untamed. Inevitably when the hero follows his natural instincts, he becomes an outcast, living beyond the pale of decency, a criminal, a marauder. Nor will the author allow him to be integrated into society again until he has tamed, killed off, and put behind him, the instrument and symbol of these instincts, Manon herself, the magic ring.

Our point of departure was the observation that *règlement* sometimes actually produces *dérèglement*. In *Manon Lescaut* this meant libertinage, sexual, religious, even social. Yet, given the Abbé's world view, there were safeguards, guarantees that the energy released would run its course, that – as was just mentioned – reintegration would inevitably take place. Like the monster in *Phèdre*, Manon and the instincts she awakened have to be ultimately expelled. This reverse process is inherent even in the terms of the situation. For, if *règlement* engenders *dérèglement*, by the same token, unruly behavior depends by definition on the continued existence of rules, if only rules to be broken. Society with all its confining traditions and institutions will have to prevail; the protest against it affirms its importance; guilty pleasure cannot survive without sources of guilt.

Forewarnings of an eventual return to the fold are everywhere in *Manon Lescaut*, the strongest indication being the Chevalier's efforts to turn his mistress – the very embodiment of wanton, untamed desire, the agent of his own social marauding – into something fixed, stable, and even respectable at the end, by taking her hand in marriage (p. 1360). His efforts eventually kill her, of course – though, once again, neither he nor the narrator sees it that way, and it is true that the final scenes have a rich complexity of symbolism that it would be unwise to simplify. Again the text astonishes by its bareness, its total lack of descriptive, or even psychological detail. There they are, hero and heroine, fleeing across the blank desert (an utter figment of Abbé Prévost's imagination) (p. 1366). Manon is dying from unspecified causes, the main one probably being simple exposure to the elements (she had always been a fragile creature of art and artifice; it is no wonder exposure to pure sunlight and fresh air was fatal to her). Nor does this eventuality come without precedent, since nature – through the Chevalier's uncontrolled impulses – had been claiming its victims all along, from the start. It had always been clear that nature was dangerous. The reader also sensed all along that the Chevalier's total enslavement to Manon demanded a release that was likewise total, that only Manon's death could set him free – the passions, the bliss, the ecstasies, the miseries, the crimes fading into memories, fading into text, *écriture*, while civilized society reasserted its dominance –

Ah! fuyez, douce image.

The tunes of the opera preserve, even enlarge, the whole sentimental side of the story. Naturally, they eliminate completely the philosophic and social import of the original – which is what most concerns us here. Somehow, as dramatically as a burst of the full orchestra, Abbé Prévost's bare words on the two-dimensional page have suddenly turned into a Pandora's box, sending out in a great rush not only illicit passion of astonishing force, but subversive impulses as well. And even though we know from the beginning that ultimately these figures of crime and passion will be reabsorbed and disappear, the contemplation of their energy and destructive potential in the novel is an awesome, disturbing experience.

It is the urge one finds in *Manon Lescaut*, the urge to undo, subvert, *to free oneself by becoming totally other in respect to established values*, that I call "attraction of the contrary." Although it did not always function so dramatically as in *Manon Lescaut*, and though not much critical attention has been paid to it, it was one of the most dynamic forces at work in eighteenth-century literature. This is a phenomenon that is worth examining, for as one tracks it past the mid-point of the century, one notices rather significant patterns starting to emerge: perhaps in a sense Abbé Prévost was lucky that everything would still go back into his box, and that he had a decoy in Manon to mask the secret motives. For the time would come when the will to subvert would be so explicitly political, the sexuality so blatant, that no cover-up was possible; a time when all these dangerous passions, these natural impulses, were constructed, not to return home to law and order, but to stay loose and free in society. To study them is to observe a social crisis in the making.

2

Three literary approaches to the art of love

Traditional wisdom has sometimes implied that literary eroticism and literary pornography are two closely related versions of the same phenomenon: eroticism is supposed to stop shorter and be more reticent, while pornography goes further and says more, but essentially, we are told, these are two forms of the same creative impulse and they belong in the same literary bracket.

It is true, to be sure, that one can find cases that apparently bear out the theory: cases in which the erotic and the pornographic loosely combine with one another to make a shapeless mixture that breaks down distinctions. Nevertheless (and this is what the present chapter will attempt to prove), the possibility has always existed that if one could somehow isolate these two forms and examine them separately in their original state, one might discover their relationship to be quite different from the one traditionally assumed. Fortunately, it has been possible to locate two perfect, laboratory-pure, specimens of eroticism and pornography for the study, and, naturally enough, they both come from eighteenth-century France, a country and a century that proudly excelled in niceties of distinction, whose Cartesian ambiance fostered clear thinking, and whose social stratifications made class differences particularly apparent. The first example is *Le Sopha* (1740), by Crébillon, *fils*, a veritable archetype of an erotic novel in the gallant style; the second is *L'Histoire de Dom B[ougre], Portier des Chartreux* (1741), attributed to Gervaise de Latouche, a quintessentially pure example of pornography, pornography uncontaminated by either gallantry or Sadism. An impartial investigation of these two archetypes will show that, far from being restfully compatible members of the same family, eroticism and pornography are separate species whose natural condition is to be at war with one another.

I

Unfortunately for pleasure-seeking readers of today, the first author, Crébillon, *fils*, had a style of writing which strikes one as coyly mannered and *précieux*: his fancy sort of art simply does not appeal much to this generation.

Three literary approaches to the art of love

Thus it may come as a surprise to observe that one of Crébillon's main stylistic devices also occurred in the far more down-to-earth novel we have just been considering, *Manon Lescaut*. Scholars have long been aware that the author of *Manon* never described his famous heroine for the reader.[1] We never learn whether Manon is tall or short, blonde or brunette, whether her proportions are generous, or petites; we know nothing of the sound of her voice (her intonation and pitch, her accent). The narrator depicts her as very *distinguée* when he first catches sight of her, but the description is not very specific. In short, Manon is a blank, a constant invitation to the reader to write his own ticket, create his own idol, project his own image. The advantage is that, since she has no being except that which the reader himself chooses to endow her with, no one can find anything objectionable in her, or even anything not quite perfect. It is no wonder that she is everyone's favorite heroine.

This technique of the blank is pushed to the extreme in Crébillon, *fils*, whose entire fictional world sometimes turns into a void, calling for the reader to fill it in. In his erotic novel, *Le Sopha*,[2] the only terms used to describe the many female sex objects that people its pages are all vague, hollow, without substance: *ses charmes, ses beautés, ses attraits, sa délicatesse, sa pudeur, sa bouche, ses yeux* – none of it exists unless we create it subjectively in the terms of our own private imagination, becoming in the process as much the authors of the novel as Crébillon himself. It leads to narcissism, since our own images are constantly before us. It also involves seduction, the reader being constantly teased into participation in the creative act, which is then reproduced in the seduction scenes of the story itself.

Un instant après que je m'y fus placé, je vis entrer la divinité à qui j'allais appartenir. C'était la fille de l'omrah chez qui j'étais. La jeunesse, les grâces, la beauté, ce je ne sais quoi qui seul les fait valoir, et qui, plus puissant, plus marqué qu'elles-mêmes, ne peut cependant jamais être défini, tout ce qu'il y a de charmes et d'agréments, composait sa figure. Mon âme ne put la voir sans émotion, elle éprouva à son aspect mille sensations délicieuses que je ne croyais pas à son usage . . .
(pp. 274–5)[3]

This style with its relentless abstractions and generalized terms, utterly devoid of color, form, or any sort of concreteness, derives directly from the high style of seventeenth-century Classicism. It fits perfectly with the aristocratic settings of *Le Sopha*, although the thinness of Crébillon's psychology, the continual boudoir ambiance and the endless gallantries, cheapen the effect.

But the plot situation of the novel is undeniably clever: an Indian Brahman, whose soul has transmigrated into many kinds of persons and objects in previous incarnations,[4] now finds he remembers perfectly the former incarnation when he spent an entire existence as a sofa (presumably Brahma's punishment for his over-active sex life, although such a vulgar word as "sex" in the usual sense could never appear in a high-style novel such as this). The rest of the book recounts, in the vaguest possible terms, the amorous exploits the soul-in-the-sofa had been forced to witness, but could never participate in, a punishment lasting until two utterly chaste lovers made love for the first time upon him, at which point the soul would be released. Virgins of either sex being extremely rare – virtually non-existent – in the eighteenth century, the book becomes quite long before two of the right kind are found. Occasionally the soul is given permission to change sofas, and it can move anywhere it pleases in the particular sofa where it finds itself, in order to have the best vantage points for close-ups on the girl's "beautés," whose location is practically never specified.

Je choisis avec soin l'endroit d'où je pouvais le mieux observer les charmes de Zéïnis, et je me mis à les contempler avec l'ardeur de l'amant le plus tendre, et l'admiration que l'homme le plus indifférent n'aurait pu leur refuser. Ciel! que de beautés s'offrirent à mes regards! . . .   (p. 276)[5]

The quote is from the penultimate sequence of the story, just one step away from the soul's final release. Immediately after this passage, the soul-in-the-sofa tries to start a romance with Zéïnis, the lovely virgin who is sleeping upon him, and actually comes to believe he has succeeded in making her aware of his amorous efforts. She really seems to be responding, as if someone had been kissing her, just as he was trying to do . . .

Alas for him, it was only her dreams of someone else, of the chaste young man who then appears in person, and the final lovemaking begins. The description, or rather the non-description, of their activities takes some fifteen – admittedly rather small – pages: the girl is clad in a veil that at once hides and at the same time suggestively hints at the incredible attractions of her unspecified charms. The same enticing-while-forbidding strategy dominates all the action throughout the scene, and what generates the hero's passion are the obstacles she places in the path of her irresistible charms: for fifteen pages she is saying "No!": trying to push him away and escape from his embraces, entreating him to stop, bursting into tears, she employs every conceivable stratagem to protect/lose her virtue. At last he breaks through her defenses and she lets out what is called "un cri plus perçant" (p. 295), the double-entendre suggesting for the first and only time something concretely sexual. And at that very moment the tale is over, the lights go out, the paragraph goes blank, it is the end.

In other words, the story depends entirely upon obstacles and resistance. It cannot exist otherwise; it will vanish. The obstacles in question are first of all the resistance of the girl, the central matter, of course; but also the resistance of the words on the page that, by their lofty indefiniteness, refuse to specify what we want to see; the resistance of the sofa that keeps the soul within range, but unable to take action; the resistance of the book itself, that suggests the enticing pleasure of penetrating nature, while confining the reader to empty art, and disappearing into thin air the moment anything tangible starts to emerge.

This is not only a witty but a brilliantly unified conception – one of the most perfect structures for an erotic novel in the whole eighteenth century. Yet since its initial period of popularity, the work has never been widely read; today it is not even so well known as Crébillon's *Egarements du coeur et de l'esprit*. Nor is this merely because the work grows far too long in the middle. There's a strange coldness about *Le Sopha* that puts one off, and after a number of readings one even begins to find something vaguely distasteful about it. Perhaps this is due partly to the vast discrepancy between the high level of the style – always so elegant and illusively discreet – and the sexy subject matter: combining the two yields an annoying coyness and artificiality, typical of the *style galant*, that quickly palls. One notes too that as the style constantly strives to embellish, using innumerable times the same contrived and empty words – *charmes*, *beautés*, *attraits*, and so on – one begins to suspect that if the author so constantly felt the need to prettify something with compliments so vague, it may be because he didn't find that something – sex in its physical reality – so pretty at all. And the least one can infer is that the pleasure the hero works towards so energetically is extremely brief; it hardly has time to exist before the story ends.

One might suggest an intriguing parallel here between the effort to mask all the natural realities of lovemaking, and certain specimens of rococo furniture that seem determined to hide the fact that this gracefully curving ornament is actually a chair whose four legs come squarely down to the floor and support the kind of seat a person might sit on; or that this flower-like object is really a cruet from which one can pour liquids. But embellishment in Crébillon has still another function: it charms us into forgetting that his couples have only a single psychological dimension: they are sex objects, and nothing else. The young man is the merest gallant seducer, the young girl is only a coyly innocent charmer. And when she has charmed and he has seduced, pierced, the tale instantly ends while they disappear from sight, returning of necessity to their original void.

Le Sopha could not be more aristocratic in its form, style, mode, and tone. This is boudoir art at its most accomplished, and it is explicitly composed as an entertainment for a court that, bored and utterly lacking in resources of its own, needs this exotic tale by an Indian to provide even momentary distraction. Some critics may want to see social criticisms in this work. Perhaps the author is himself aware of the shallow uselessness of the characters he has created and of the class they represent; perhaps he is aware of the implications of the lack of inner resources, of an intellectual and moral impoverishment so extreme one has to go abroad for interest and vitality, of the vulgarity of the royal personages in the frame of the story.[6] Yet such disapproval must be inferred without any help at all from the author who is studiously looking the other way as he guides us through the elegant boudoirs, creations of the reader's own imagination, and ultimately as empty as the reader's own solitude.

II

Even in Crébillon, resistance or obstacle equals in part convention, or conventional morality. The girl in *Le Sopha* resists not only in order to seduce, but because she is defending her virtue or her reputation, that is to say, conforming to values that are entirely the creation of society (as opposed to impulsive nature). Whatever heat there is, is generated by the effort of the male to overcome these social strictures, here seen as sexual resistance. *Manon Lescaut* is more interesting in this respect because the obstacles encountered have a fuller psychological dimension; furthermore, they do not occur in the female herself – Manon does not resist – but are externally, socially given: the obstacle will be Tiberge and the honest loyalty he represents; or it is the father and the family values he stands for. And although these characters will often be thrust aside and knocked down by the Chevalier in his rush for Manon, nevertheless one never loses one's respect for the values they embody. We may even feel we respect them more, as they are so badly mistreated. Such a tolerant attitude towards hindrance is further evidence of this novel's essential conservatism: a more violent and *engagée* disposition might have shrivelled the obstacles encountered by the hero into caricatures, or even into material objects.

A fascinating case in point is *Le Portier des Chartreux* (1741), one of a handful of pornographic novels no one ever mentions, but which we can be sure everyone had read in the age of Enlightenment.[7] Its author (or authors) is (are) unknown, although some police records name a certain Gervaise de Latouche, and the suggestion is temptingly piquant, since this gentleman was an *avocat* in the Paris Parliament, an institution we are pleased to think of as composed of rather conservative lawyers and judges. The style of the work tells us it was written by a man (it could not possibly be a woman) of education and of some concern for social and religious issues: a mini-*philosophe*.

No one at the time it was written took the work seriously; it simply scandalized – just as the author intended: from the ironic dedicatory epistle to the Lieutenant of Police (because he likes dirty books so much), to the mock opening in which the author pretends to have repented his past sins (he is now very sorry about all the orgies), everywhere, in every scene, what energizes the continuous explosions of impudence and explicit sexuality are social conventions of every sort – especially prudery. The aim was to shock,

30

and the zesty, vibrant fun of the sexual encounters comes from the exhilarating excitement of breaking every taboo imaginable. Let us consider the first bedroom scene (pp. 4–8): the lusty male involved is a priest who is doing his best to desecrate his vows of continence; the female in the bed is supposedly the narrator's mother (actually she is not) who is gleefully breaking her marriage vows, her forbidden pastimes being performed right before the eyes of her delighted "son," who, for the rest, has his own obstacle to contend with, namely the separating wall that keeps him at arm's length from the busy couple. Our young hero, Saturnin by name, has found a loose knothole in the wall which he penetrates with his finger to watch Father Polycarpe penetrating his "mother" Toinette, while we readers penetrate the scene in our imaginations, being held back from the immediate experience by the wall of the words on the page. It all fits together even more cogently than in *Le Sopha*.

Actually, to think of Crébillon in connection with *Le Portier* is quite à propos, for the author of *Le Portier* obviously designed his book to say and describe in explicit terms everything that was never said or described in the language of the *roman galant* or any other derivative of French classicism. Crébillon cleaved unswervingly to his *beautés*, *charmes*, and *attraits*. For the narrator of *Le Portier* the fun came from telling about the color of the sexual discharge on the woman's *coquille* (also described in admiring detail) and the stiffness of Father Polycarpe's virile member as it returns to life for the second encounter. Crébillon discreetly calls on the reader to create the scene in the privacy of his own imagination, whereas *Le Portier* goes public and brashly does the whole scene out loud, deliberately using all the forbidden words, telling everyone's secret, lifting their skirts, while he strips the language as bare as Toinette's *gorge*, which in this book *always* means "breasts." This is realism. And here the term implies a putting aside of all the *pudeur*, the indirectness, the suggestiveness and subtlety that were the greatest appeal of the age of Racine. Nor is *Le Portier*, considered as a literary attack on classical conventions, lacking in astuteness: the *pudeur* of classicism was indeed, essentially, sexual *pudeur*; its language attempted to veil the very things *Le Portier* thrusts into daylight.

As the eighteenth century was becoming uncomfortably aware, the grandest traditions of literary classicism implied first of all that literary works would feature kings and queens, and aristocracy – if only because classical language itself had been systematically elevated and polished in order to be spoken by, or heard in, the delicate ears of persons of the highest rank. (Obviously Crébillon carries on this aristocratic tradition, too.) But here was another established classical mode, a sitting duck, waiting to be undone by the unscrupulous author of *Le Portier*. In the opening of his novel there is not an aristocrat in sight; we are in the world of people who work. The narrator is raised in a gardener's family and, in the first scene, Father

Polycarpe is able to enjoy the favors of Toinette so easily because the husband is off in the fields. Nor does the author for a minute apologize for putting before our eyes persons of the commonest lot: common or not, they all have something extremely interesting, fascinating, about them, which is sex, and, like "love" in Gilbert and Sullivan, sex in this novel levels all ranks; its thrust is literally democratic.

The hero's second sexual experience (the novel being a sexual *roman d'apprentissage*) is particularly revealing in this respect. His supposed-but-not-real sister, Suzon (with whom, incidentally, he is already falling in love, and with whom, after many vicissitudes, he will be united at the end of the novel) takes him to the house of her Godmother, who is referred to as *la Dame du village* and is the wife of a *conseiller* in a nearby town. The lady in question, socially far superior, older, and sexually more sophisticated than Saturnin, is instantly attracted to the young narrator, and he likewise finds himself drawn to her.

In the lively account of his first sight of the lady, Saturnin asks the reader to imagine a person of "medium height," with "dark hair," "white skin," a face generally "ugly" and a "ruddy" complexion such as the women from Champagne have, but with "watchful," "amorous" eyes and breasts whose proportions elicit wondering admiration. Already in just these few lines we have seen more of this woman's appearance than we did of Manon in an entire volume, and the description is far from over: we are told of her position lying on the couch, one leg raised and revealing the knee beneath her short skirt, the other leg going down to touch the floor. We seem to see every detail of the white and pink costume she is wearing, and, most important, one of her hands is placed beneath her skirt, for purposes the narrator instantly feels he recognizes (pp. 17–18).[8]

The scene is so gleefully pictorial, it might have been composed with the engravings, that were later made for the book, already in mind. But the visual emphasis also fits perfectly with the young, inexperienced narrator's outlook as he takes in the situation and adds it up according to the only item of interest, sex, and which instantly allows him to perceive the woman for what she really is: not the haughty *Dame du village* we expected, and not even some exotic odalisque lolling on Crébillon's pillows, but instead a rather unprepossessing woman with a plain, provincial face, and who is redeemed solely (though more than adequately) by spectacular breasts and the promise of still more interesting attributes down below. The description of her dress is actually preparation for an undressing, and as, in his imagination, Saturnin's hand moves in towards her, at the same time it instantly abolishes all the social differences that existed between them. There are no more class lines; the lady and the gardener's boy are one. Only sex can do this so swiftly and so completely, and with the rustic simplicity and natural-ness of Saturnin's expressions of enthusiasm, how far down the social scale we have come from the artful coyness of the *Sopha*'s "Ciel! que de beautés . . .!"

There are long interruptions in the narrative of *Le Portier*, but the sequel to the meeting of Saturnin and Madame Dinville is worth waiting for. She seduces him on the garden lawn by pretending to be asleep. The scene is quite droll. Sitting on the grass beside her supposedly slumbering form, the young narrator describes himself as torn between the desire to see and enjoy her, and his fear of waking her in the midst of the liberties he is taking. He watches her bare breast rising and falling beneath her fan. We see his timid hand advancing, hardly daring to press upon it, light as a bird's wing, then taking away the fan; his first timorous kiss. Next his attention turns to the skirt, which ever so delicately he starts to lift . . . and suddenly all seems lost; the lady is awakening, shifting her position; he draws back in fright – only to discover that now, thanks to the shift, the lady's knee is raised, her skirt is open, and everything is exposed to his delighted view, everything . . . (pp. 136–40).[9]

This passage has numerous aspects that might interest us in other contexts: the ironies generated by the double cat-and-mouse game in progress, the realism of the description reflecting the narrator's own watchfulness as he responds to Madame Dinville's titillations (this is irony, too). And there is still more irony in seeing the peasant boy struggle, working so hard, to use all the delicacy and tact he imagines a highly born lady requires, while the highly born lady just rolls over like any peasant girl and the rhythms of the passage bring on the climax just as we reach the last triumphant word designating her sexual organ. But still more to the point, this scene deliberately exploits all the qualities that were forbidden to authors in the grand tradition, such as Crébillon. It is anti-classical in its essence. It came into being as a sort of dare: it would be so explicit, so baldly sexual, so confounding of all ranks, so amoral, that it would sparkle with all the wit and fun boudoir art never could have. The attraction of the contrary here involves a literary statement, as well as a social and sexual one.

The nature of the contrariety becomes even clearer in the section of the text that follows (p. 140), in which the narrator describes the lady's sexual anatomy. Whereas the language of classicism grew dimmer, vaguer, more formless, or at least more indirect, the closer it came to explicit sexuality, here the exact reverse takes place: as we draw nearer to the sex organ, the more the author uses colors, forms, graphic indications of all sorts. We are told of the knee with its garter, and of the delicate little foot; we learn everything we need to know about the thighs.[10] The sexual organ comes in full color along with the blackness of the hairs surrounding it. There is even an odor. Now at last there are no more secrets, nothing left to hide.[11] Classicism has had its last prudish veil removed, and is waiting to be deflowered; and since the intensity of the vivid description is supposed to reflect the narrator's increasing excitement, we sense that for him, too, the seduction is now complete: Saturnin goes into action, and the author's aim is again to tell it all.

The form of the novel is variations on a theme; and, as one might expect in a pornographic work, the theme in question is copulation. The hero has sex with women of all ages – old, middlish, and young, fat and thin, blonde and brunette. Every conceivable posture, and some double-decker inconceivable ones, are tried. The discussions of the various aspects of sex in this pre-*Encyclopédie* novel are almost encyclopedic in scope. It delves into everything, producing apologies for buggery (p. 227), an apology for incest through the ages that lays particular stress on biblical precedents (whom else did Adam's children sleep with if not each other?) (p. 242), a powerful and very graphic lesbian scene (pp. 88–9) (it lacks Diderot's psychological depth, to be sure), an elaborate and eloquent apology for sexual freedom for women (pp. 40–1), protesting against their slavery to the male and bringing out their special need for greater sexual activity and diversity (pp. 252–6). Everywhere the message is the same: there should be no barriers to, or restrictions on, sexual pleasure. It should be enjoyed constantly, joyously, and in all forms. As several of the characters remark, sexual pleasure is a sort of divinity, which should be worshipped above all else (p. 244, etc.).

The blasphemy here is quite intentional, for religion and its confinements are very important generating forces in this novel, in the negative sense. Let us consider the monk. He is more active sexually than any other species of male (claims the hero) (pp. 2–3). The reason? Being shut up, denied the possibility of sexual enjoyment makes his need for it greater than anyone else's. This is why so much of the novel takes place in a monastery: nowhere else is sex so important. And so, it is not really surprising, on second or third thoughts, to find the lusty hero, Saturnin, whose sole interest is sex, not only in a monastery where sex is totally forbidden (pp. 203ff.), but signing up for a novitiate, on the way to becoming a priest – a species that, in theory, never has sex at all.

Using the same inverted logic (and contrariety is basic to the inspiration of this novel), it naturally follows that the ensuing secret orgies with the "niece" of Father Desfontaines and various monkish companions should be held, not outside the monastery, and not even in some neutral place, like the monastery garden, but in the most sacred spot of all, right in the church, so that the phrase "going to church" is converted, perverted to a sexual meaning (p. 215). Actually, the orgies take place in the organ loft, perhaps to facilitate the associations with *orgues, orgie*, and *organes* (p. 219). Meanwhile (as was mentioned), the hero, through diligence in his "theological" studies, is making his way up in the ranks, a spiritual ascension that will finally lead to holy orders as a priest. This ascent, with all the increase in moral and spiritual strictures it implies, engenders, through the principle of negative inversion, a topsy-turvy movement downwards, towards increasing sexual libertinage. In fact, the top of the spiritual ladder, his ordination as a priest, will gain him admittance to a new and more select group of monks (his initiation, incidentally, may have vaguely Masonic overtones) (p. 237), who descend to meet regularly with some nuns, on the lowest level, at a secret pool ("la Piscine"). There they indulge in every possible sexual activity (Saturnin even comes dangerously close to having sex with his real mother). The debaucheries are described in riotous and enthusiastic detail. Might this not seem like the climax of the novel? For so long Saturnin had been struggling to overcome the restraints and restrictions that limited the extent of his sexual pleasure. And now his priestly vows have resulted in everything he craved in unhoped-for abundance. The women are beautiful, available; no obstacles at all exist, to hinder his complete sexual fulfilment. . . . At which point the hero finds himself felled by total impotence (p. 257). He can do nothing.

Naturally, the nuns rally round in a concerted effort to arouse him, their seductions recalling the famous *Postures* of Aretino, and even anticipating the postures of Sade. Nature joins art in the most intriguing way in their attempted cures: they dispose themselves in a circle, Saturnin in the middle, one nun lolling on a couch exposing, and partly hiding, the vital parts in the most enticing fashion; another, knees raised, ready for "combat," panting and heaving in anticipation; others caressing each other lasciviously and passionately in anticipation of the pleasures he will give them. The postures are so wonderfully varied, they assure complete coverage of all possible allurements: exposures that are arranged face down, other exposures face up (pp. 258–9), the choreography continues unabated for several pages of densely worded description, and everywhere one finds the same technique of crowding the tableaux of the postures together to increase the intensity of the experience.[12] It never could be claimed that this author was a Baudelaire or a Diderot. However, the graphic dream-like effect does suggest an effort at a prose poem, and, oddly, the fluidity of the movement, as each tableau is replaced by the next, not only suggests a series of engravings, but even something like a film.

Perhaps it seems incredible that any human male could resist lascivious enticements on so grand a scale for even an instant. Yet everything the nuns do is in vain: the author in his wisdom has made his hero impotent and will keep him so. In fact he will not restore Saturnin to vigor until he changes tack entirely, abandons those obliging nuns of the pool and starts pursuing women who are not automatically at his disposal, but who will resist his advances in the name of virtue and religion. Then, and only then, will his libido renew itself.

To my mind the incident proves that the sexual potency of the hero, and the course of his novel, depend totally on what the hero is working against. Without impediments he cannot function; the novel would end. We may conclude that, despite the almost ritually repeated affirmations by various characters concerning the divine importance of sexual pleasure, this kind of pleasure is not enough in itself to sustain anything. It may not even be the main issue. For the sexual energy of this novel is fighting energy and its life depends on being pitted against the barriers erected by society.

Actually, the author is often conscious of this: he expressly wants his hero to be continually breaking through society's prudish confinements, working to liberate himself by being totally other in respect to the imposed social norms. He knows that the explosions of sexuality are directed against the whole fabric of society and this awareness marks a significant "advance" over the perspective of *Manon*. The subversion is deliberate.

Yet, on the other hand, the author is quite blind to the limitations of these impulses. He doesn't see at all the degree to which working against the confinements of the system entails, in his case, working from within the system. This is the lesson of Saturnin's impotence which the author intuitively brought on, but was unable adequately to account for. It would have taken a Diderot to understand that actually the hero doesn't want the total sexual freedom he is constantly striving for, and everyone is so busily preaching. His potency depends on his not having it.

There are lots of fireworks in this novel – blatant sexuality, blasts against the monks, blasphemy, etc. etc. – but they fizzle out, and ultimately we find ourselves in a world not too different from that of *Manon Lescaut*. I would even suggest that the mock repentance in the frame of the work – the hero heaving sighs of gratefulness that he has at last been rescued from the toils of sin – may not be quite so ironic as the author thinks. For in essence his novel is not a philosophic statement, or even a call for reform (much less for revolution). It is pure impudence, exuberant naughtiness, entertainment, momentary escape from sexual prejudice and prudery, escape, above all, from social pretentiousness. The pleasure and relief it brings are quite exactly those derived from loudly saying the four-letter word in the drawing-room, the chapel, or the police station. Its aim is simply to shock.

This is not to say, however, that *Le Portier des Chartreux* has no redeeming social or artistic merits. On the contrary, it has them in abundance: hilarious comic scenes with everyone in the wrong bed (reminding us of how much literature lost with the invention of electricity), astute social commentary in the drawing of portraits, drama, and at times a human warmth that is *rarissime*, almost never found in pornography of this period. Soeur Monique, whose history is inserted at various points in the main narrative, is presented as a woman of refinement and education. She has an affair with a man far beneath her socially (he has no education and cannot even speak correctly (pp. 68ff.)). Nevertheless the author persuades us that her love for him is true and deep, and that she loves him not merely for his considerable sexual prowess, but also for his honesty, kindliness, and gentle qualities. Not bad for this snobbish period when Marivaux got into hot water merely for composing a banal exchange of insults between a bourgeoise and a person of the lower classes, in *La Vie de Marianne*.

I admire the final sequence of *Le Portier des Chartreux* for similar reasons.[13] The hero at last finds the woman he is depicted as always having loved more than anyone else, Suzon (pp. 314ff.). Since Saturnin last saw her she had been forced to have sexual relations with a monk who got her pregnant and then betrayed her. Abandoned and destitute in Paris, she had turned to the only livelihood available, prostitution, so that Saturnin comes across her, quite by accident, in a whorehouse. Not that her condition makes any difference to him; their reunion is blissful. But Suzon is aware that she has venereal disease and at first refuses to have sexual relations with him. Only after much urging can Saturnin persuade Suzon that their love is far more important to him than contagion. They sleep together anyway (the last obstacle overcome).

Perhaps the rest is somewhat melodramatic: the guard bursts in; Suzon is taken off to prison, where eventually she dies of her disease, the hero being lucky to escape with only castration on account of his. Indeed, the account of these events may seem rather gauche if one compares them to Abbé Prévost's polished narratives. Yet there is a fine sort of honesty here in the author's willingness to tackle the major social problem of venereal disease, one that was almost never mentioned in respectable fiction, much less presented seriously. The hero and heroine achieve a new sort of dignity as they confront it together, a dignity, incidentally, that quite outweighs the irony involved in presenting the act of sleeping with a syphilitic whore as an act of virtue. No doubt the rejection of accepted moral norms (the attraction of the contrary) reaches a new extreme in the final section, and whereas this rejection, until now, has always been accompanied by a joyous sentiment of release, here it leads in the other direction, to contagion, mutilation, and confinement. In other words, the creative act of liberation – short-termed and self-limiting – is now bringing itself and the novel to an end.

The author of this work never raises the question of the function of the novel. If he had done so he surely would have stated the standard position held by eighteenth-century authors, that the function of the novel was to be a mirror of life, to reflect life truly. *Le Portier des Chartreux* is one of a handful of works from its time which convince us they succeed.

After the stark "realism" of this ending, Crébillon's boudoir gallantries seem off in another world. And this is exactly my point: the two works are in fact poles apart, and by design; each is deliberately thumbing the nose at the art of the other. I cannot claim that their contrariety is so extreme as to produce topsy-turvy mirror images; yet I would maintain that stylistically at least one does sense a liberation, as the author of *Le Portier* systematically denies and cancels out the sort of reticences deployed in *Le Sopha*. One might imagine another kind of liberation, too, on the part of Crébillon, as he so successfully eliminates the threat of vulgar explicitness, climbing up out of danger through stylistic elevation. In short, the contrariety is very much at work in these two productions. No doubt literary historians will continue to lump them together under the sign of "libertinage." But if they do, we must be aware of the incompatibilities the label disguises, a cleavage that is quite typical of the intellectual life of this period in France, and, if only because this split in particular derives from a clash between high and low styles, we may assume it gives symptomatic indications also of much deeper-lying social conflicts in the making.

III

So far I have been assuming that sexual energy and the energy of literary creation have been generated by reactions against social norms that are felt as hindrances: without the desire not only to break through these hindrances, but even to oppose them with contrary values, neither of these two novels could have existed. Nor is this kind of creative tension exceptional in fictions of this kind. Indeed if one surveys the whole panoply of famous erotic or pornographic novels of the period – from *Vénus dans le cloître* (1682) and *Le Temple de Gnide* by Montesquieu, from Crébillon's gallantries and Fougeret de Monbron, on to Nerciat, Mirabeau and Sade at the end – one finds in all of them that sexuality is linked to the breaking of barriers, psychological and/or social. In fact it very much appears that the single most indispensable ingredient of the *roman libertin* is the impediment.

And yet there was at least one exception to this rule in the eighteenth century; one work of quasi-explicit eroticism that was cunningly constructed so as to be full of sexual excitement, but at the same time to do without obstacles of any sort. This was a longish poem in nine *chants* by Marmontel, entitled *La Neuvaine de Cythère*.[14] Its author, who wrote it in 1764–5, never dared to publish it during his lifetime, and was extremely frightened when he thought it had fallen into the wrong hands and was being copied for circulation. We find the account of his terrified reaction in a letter by his friend Diderot (21 July 1765), and it is Diderot, too, in the *Salon* of 1767, who suggests jokingly the possibility that *La Neuvaine de Cythère* may be the manuscript one saw Marmontel holding in his hand in a portrait of him by Roslin.[15] Actually, the choice of this poem to appear in a painting would have been most apposite, for *La Neuvaine* is itself composed, in part, as a great series, in fact a whole gallery,[16] of paintings, the explicitness of the

38

erotic descriptions relating to the conventions of that art, rather than to nature.

Also veiling the bare realities is the mythological plot, the poem purporting to sing of the nine "prowesses" of Venus and her Faun lover (in reality an understatement; there are many more "prowesses" than that). This erotic mythology very much suggests that we are again dealing with boudoir art, if only because scenes from the life of Venus had been so frequently chosen as subjects by boudoir painters, the most famous series being by Boucher. (Another reason, of course, why it is so natural for the poem itself to be in the form of a series of paintings.) We might note, too, that the role of Venus was just the sort of role royal mistresses, such as Mme de Pompadour, liked to imagine themselves playing. In short, for many reasons the erotic mythology centering on Venus suggests an appeal that was first of all aristocratic.

Although we will return to them later, let us for the moment leave aside the very interesting introductory lines, the prelude, in order to hasten – even as the author himself does – to the main plot. Here is the opening scene:

> Dans un bosquet, dont l'amoreux feuillage
> En se courbant mariait son ombrage,
> Vénus dormait sur un gazon naissant;
> Le coloris, la fraîcheur du bel âge,
> De la santé l'éclat éblouissant,
> Et les rondeurs d'un élégant corsage,
> Et d'un beau sein le tour appétissant,
> Et cette croupe et si blanche et si belle,
> Et mille attraits dont il n'est pas decent
> De peindre aux yeux l'image naturelle,
> Se déployaient sur ce corps ravissant.
>
> Dans le sommeil un songe caressant
> Flattait son sein, voltigeait sur sa bouche,
> D'un doigt folâtre appelait le désir,
> Et d'un coup d'aile éveillait le plaisir.
> Vénus soupire: une nouvelle couche
> De vermillon colore son beau teint [. . .]
> Elle touchait à ce moment où l'âme
> De ses liens est prête à s'envoler,
> Et n'attend plus qu'une bouche où sa flamme
> Par un soupir se plaise à s'exhaler.
>
> Un jeune faune ardent, nerveux et leste,
> Le coq brillant des nymphes d'alentour,
> Très-éloquent de la voix et du geste,
> Et, comme un page, insolent en amour,
> Trouve à l'écart cette beauté céleste,
> S'arrête, admire, approche à petit bruit,

Dévore tout d'un regard immodeste.
– 'Ah! c'est Vénus; je reconnais le ceste,'
Dit-il; 'Amour, c'est toi qui m'as conduit.
'Reine des coeurs, charme de la nature,
'Vénus, je brûle, et crains de te saisir.'

Puis, d'une main soulevant la ceinture:
– 'Le voilà donc le trône du plaisir!
'Que de trésors! ah! brusquons l'aventure.'
Quelque novice eût trouvé le bonheur
Dans un baiser; le faune, moins timide,
Va droit au fait, et la reine de Gnide,
En s'éveillant, le nomma son vainqueur. $(27-72)^{17}$

Marmontel's palette may be generally more pastel, and his forms slightly less voluptuous, otherwise his description is a perfect *mise en mots*, and a *mise en mouvement* of the famous *Vénus endormie* by Correggio in the Louvre.[18] One remembers also Watteau's enchanting depiction of the same scene (wrongly entitled *Antiope endormie* in the Louvre catalogue),[19] and above all, the version of it attributed to Fragonard (in a private collection in Paris), which is so close to the indications of this poem as to suggest that one is actually the source of the other.[20]

Aesthetically the pleasure of the passage comes first from imagining in these words the celebrated pictorial moment when the Faun discovers the sleeping goddess in all her loveliness. We linger in contemplation of her; time stands still, just as it does in the paintings. But then, putting the scene in motion, the poem moves us beyond the fixed confines of a painting, into the sexual experience itself. The picture simply arouses; the poem both arouses and goes on to satisfaction. No doubt Diderot would have reflected at this point that the moment of action best suited for a painting may not always coincide exactly with the center of interest in a poem because of the inherent nature of the two arts involved – which is true enough. But today we notice, rather, that as this picture is set in motion, we feel as if we were going in the direction of something resembling a film, an effect that seems astonishingly modern.

May we take a moment at least to admire Marmontel's poetical skill in suggesting, through the languidly flowing rhythms of his lines, Venus' own sultry disposition? The muscled, ready-for-action Faun, on the other hand, gets a taut series of abrupt verbs, perfectly suited to his physique and to the impetuosity of his temperament. The reader on her/his own may wish to explore the possibilities of the amusing counterpoint one can imagine between the seduction of this *femme endormie* by the Faun, and the gardener's boy's approach to the allegedly sleeping lady in a similar posture on the grass, from *Le Portier de Chartreux*. One might even go back to the penultimate sequence of *Le Sopha*, since that woman was *endormie*, too. For present

4. Antonio Allegri, i.e. Correggio, *Vénus endormie*

5. Watteau, *Vénus avec un satyre*

purposes, however, it will suffice to note that linguistically Marmontel's poem falls at the precise mid-point between the other two authors: he conveys in words considerably more than Crébillon's quasi-eternal discretion; he does not go nearly so far as the blatant explicitness of *Le Portier*. At the same time, utterly different from either of the two other authors, and giving this poem its unique, slightly decadent quality, is the total absence of any apparent impediment, the softness. No doubt the Faun pays lip-service to the "fear" he feels as he approaches the goddess, and it is true that he catches her unawares. But nothing could be further from forcible entry than this action. On the contrary, Venus had been dreaming of the sexual experience the Faun obligingly provides her with. He simply gives substance to her own desires.

In the passage just quoted there is literally nothing to push against, indeed the copulation takes place so rapidly that, immediately after it happened, the author instinctively felt the need to back up and go through the action again, so that one could take in at least a few of the details. Sexually the enjoyment of the scene comes from Venus' being so ripe and ready – everything, incidentally, that had brought on Saturnin's impotence. We recall, too, that Crébillon's hero has had to contend both with the girl's partly feigned *pudeur* and with her physical virginity, also. But here, in this context, even the idea of "perçant" seems an exaggeration:

> Le trait perçant brûle d'être lancée
> Il le retient, l'ajuste, il le glisse
> Si doucement . . .[21]

The alliterated "s's" spell out the utter ease of the movement of penetration. The feeling is very close to that of floating, and in fact, in the opening of the next *chant* Venus and her lover *are* floating in her "char," copulation taking place effortlessly, simply because they are placed so close together, because of her posture. It happens almost of itself:

> Le frais du soir calmait l'ardeur du jour;
> L'azur du ciel et ses vapeurs humides
> De la nuit sombre annonçaient le retour,
> Lorsque le char dont Vénus tient les guides
> De l'air serein fend les plaines liquides.
> Mille zéphyrs voltigeaient alentour;
> Dans les cheveux de la mère d'Amour
> Ils se jouaient, et d'une aile folâtre
> Les étalaient sur deux globes d'albâtre,
> Dont les sommets, à la rose pareils,
> Du doux baiser sont les trônes vermeils.
> Ce corps charmant, que le grand Praxitèle
> Dans sa Vénus a si bien modelé,
> Et que Pâris avait vu dévoilé
> Lorsqu'il donna la pomme à la plus belle,
> Ce corps pressait sous le plus doux satin
> Les muscles bruns du faune libertin.
> En souriant, sa devine conquête
> Se renversait, penchait vers lui sa tête,
> Et l'animait du geste et du regard.
> De ses deux bras le mouvement cynique
> Excite en lui cette ardeur sympathique
> Qui du plaisir électrise le dard. [. . .]
>
> Le faune allait commettre un gros péché,
> Si de Vénus la tendre inquiétude
> N'eût à ses coups présenté l'attitude
> De son beau corps sur les rênes penché. [. . .]
> Très-décemment elle reçoit soudain
> Le trait de feu que le faune lui lance,
> Et du combat la douce violence
> Lui fait tomber les rênes de la main.   (122–76)[22]

Could anything be more typically eighteenth-century, and more typically French, than the first part of this passage? The pastel colors, the delicate *nudités* and rather sophisticated eroticism, the discreetly ornamental use of mythology, the utter femininity of the scene, everything combines in a harmony that belongs only to one time and one country. Again we are in the presence of a painting: *Vénus dans son char avec le faune*. One might recall

Boucher's lovely picture, *Le Char de Vénus*. Marmontel would also have been aware that Venus (or some other divinity) rising or descending in her "char" was one of the specialties of the machines of the Paris opera, where it was staged virtually every week with special lighting effects. In the poem, the landscape is composed entirely of softness (it is all an extension of Venus, of course): the cooling moisture of the vapors,[23] the liquid "plains," the play of breezes, wings, rose petals, satin, even the globes of alabaster, since they designate breasts, prolong the same feeling. No doubt the muscles of the Faun make a direct contrast with this; yet, surrounded by such masses of material ready to yield, the muscles seem rather unnecessary. No effort is going to be required. Nor is the thrust of the male going to dominate the action. Instead, it is the sexual climax of Venus that is focused on in the lines immediately following the quoted passage, as one watches her in a spasm of ecstasy, spreading her "doux parfum d'une vapeur divine" over the entire world, so that (as Lucretius and others proposed) everything in it feels love – a theme that will be embroidered upon in the ensuing "Hymn."

Insofar as the poem has any plot, it is, first, a series of moving pictures showing Venus in her various activities (swimming and making love in the water,[24] giving birth to Amour, taking part in Bacchic revels, in orgies, etc., etc.) mostly with her new lover. But, second, there is also a mini-sociological theme. Indeed, Venus, a divinity, is carrying on right under the eyes of all the gods with a non-divinity, an upstart, almost a commoner. Among others, Mars and Apollo are so scandalized and jealous, they get Venus' blasé husband, Vulcan, to provide them with thunderbolts with which to strike the Faun as he rides up in the air. At last it looks as if the plot is getting ready to thicken; perhaps we may even run into some of those energizing obstacles, something to give the Faun a chance to put his muscles to work. But again the plot refuses to turn problematic and the whole thing fizzles: Venus doesn't care a fig about her lover's genealogy. When the thunderbolts come she simply shields him from them with her body – which furnishes them with another pretext for, and incitement to, lovemaking. Most important, Jupiter doesn't care either. He thinks it is quite permissible for divinities to bestow their favors on whomever they wish, and eventually, at the end of the poem, he will confer divinity on the Faun, anyway:

> . . . je veux, dans ma famille,
> Qu'en liberté chacun aime à son choix.
> Faune ou mortel, dieu du ciel, dieu des bois,
> Tout m'est égal. Un amant qu'on écoute,
> S'il est heureux, l'a mérité sans doute. (428–32)[25]

For Jupiter there simply is no problem.

Obviously Venus will allow anyone to enjoy upward social mobility in her "char," provided he's lusty enough, and by the same token, commoners and common themes are installing themselves in this traditionally aristocratic art form with practically no disruption. In fact, a sort of social and literary revolution has taken place, but happening as easily, as effortlessly, as smoothly as the Faun copulates with the love goddess. Later, downward social mobility will be achieved with equal facility: in the final *chant*, Jupiter will descend to human levels of lovemaking, and stage a bickering scene with his wife, Juno, that makes him sound like any grumpy middle-class husband. The Faun's apotheosis at the end makes the revolution complete.

It is entirely possible to see the Faun as Marmontel himself, an author who has performed many creative acts, not only with various mistresses and finally his wife, but in producing all nine *chants* of this poem.[26] He was a commoner who, deftly manipulating this high-class theme, was installing himself with hardly a ripple in a traditionally aristocratic literary form. There *are* energizing forces at work here, pushing against the system, but they are not presented as stresses and strains, rather they are diffused in the lovemaking and also in the worldly-wise comedy of the pseudo-Homeric strife among the gods.

In this poem we reach a social stage decisively more "advanced" than that of *Le Portier des Chartreux*, for all that author's noisy obscenities, blasphemies and philosophical diatribes against monks. In fact, the absence of loud protest is what reveals how much more advanced Marmontel is: he is so secure in his principles he can afford to be serene, playfully impudent, utterly relaxed, nor will his hero retreat to the monastery at the end: his poem will finish in an orgy of universal copulation, the whole world making love.

One of the puzzles of the poem is religion, for, as the title says, this is a "novena," which automatically makes us think of the Virgin and of the multitudes of novenas in her honor. And in fact there are hints in the poem's account of how Venus gave birth to Amour, that the author was deliberately parodying the birth of Christ.[27] I would go even further. In my view all nine of the *chants* are inspired – negatively – by the Virgin, whose austere, perpetual frigidity brought on these sexy tableaux of the voluptuous goddess, doing constantly and on every possible occasion, the one thing the Virgin never did, by definition. The four "Hymns" interspersed in Marmontel's poem celebrate the incomparable pleasures of copulation *because* hymns to the Virgin celebrated the beatitude of a maid who was totally chaste. The poem is an antidote, a remedy, whose contrariness contravenes, negates, and replaces the ethics of those who worship the absence of sex. And even if one prefers a less literal interpretation, if one prefers *not* to see Venus as actually standing in for Mary (as I do), she certainly is deliberately supplying relief from, and an alternative to, all the sexual repressions and austerities associated with Mary's religion. Attracting in the opposite direction, Venus' sexual freedom is set against the religious spirit of the times. It is anti-Christian to its (admittedly soft) core.

The author never bothers to inform us of this directly: no word is spoken against Mary, and there are no diatribes against the Church's doctrine. Again I interpret this absence as marking a religiously more "advanced" stage: the author doesn't have to be on the defensive. Venus pulls her own weight, speaks for herself, and her activities are so absorbing, so filled with thrills, she just puts the Virgin and all her mistaken virtues out of the picture.

As was mentioned earlier, *La Neuvaine de Cythère* purports to describe the nine love feats of Venus with the Faun. In the opening lines of the poem, however, the poet – using a mock heroic style and a light touch difficult to render in English – tells what he is *not* going to sing of in his verses, and this rejected topic turns out to be *war*, and the prowesses of warriors in battle. Who would want to sing about that? he asks: burning, devastating the fields, killing, pillaging, raping, invading convents (there is more than a hint of Rabelais here), the author is simply not interested in what he calls the games of "terrible" Mars:

> L'art de détruire est sans doute un grand art:
> En frémissant c'est ainsi qu'on le nomme;
> Mais j'aime mieux avoir fait un seul homme,
> Qu'avoir vaincu, n'en déplaise à Folard,
> Tous les héros de la Grèce et de Rome;
> Cueillons le myrte, et laissons les lauriers.
>
> Chantons l'Amour, qui console le monde
> De tous les maux que lui font les guerriers [. . .]   (16–23)[28]

Just as Venus acted as a replacement for the Virgin Mary, she is acting, too, as relief from the god of war, and one suspects that this function is operating throughout the poem, even when not actually specified (thus the contrariety would often be implicit). As the poet has just suggested, the games of love, creative pleasures that they are, replace and make up for the harmfulness of warfare. Thus Venus' softness is being set in some basic, fundamental way against the hardness of soldiery. And since war, for this poet, is pure destruction with no redeeming social value, it is certainly not worth singing about. So much for the heroic tradition.

Marmontel's attitude is certainly a familiar one; in fact, he is simply linking up with the well-established philosophical campaign against wars of conquest, going back through Voltaire and Bayle to Renaissance traditions at least, the most notable forefather being, of course, Rabelais.[29] The outlines of this semi-pacifist tradition are clear enough, but has it been noticed sufficiently how much this strain of thought takes on an anti-aristocratic coloring as it comes into the eighteenth century? This should be quite obvious in Voltaire, whose plain, virtuous Quaker (in the *Lettres philosophiques* of 1734), so movingly eloquent as he inveighs against the destructive inhumanity of war, is deliberately put forward as an alternative to useless aristocracy. But everywhere that the principle was applied, the enlightened denigration of military prowess was working against the chief claim to fame of the military caste, the *noblesse d'épée*, diminishing their glory, perhaps even trying to disarm them.

I see this as very much belonging to the spirit of Marmontel's poem also. When in the final *chant*, the gods, weary of their boring elevation, and quite aware of all the fun going on, down on earth in Venus' grand orgy, descend en masse – Jupiter in the lead – to join in the universal copulation, one of the author's points is that, for the sake of amorous pleasure, they are laying down their arms. The god of war ("le dieu des combats") steps out of his warrior's role as he becomes a lover. Nor is there any doubt about the poem's egalitarian message:

> Le fils d'Alcmène et le dieu des combats,
> L'ardent Pluton, l'impétueux Neptune,
> Jupiter même, en prenant ses ébats,
> N'est plus ici qu'homme à bonne fortune,
> Dieux et mortels, dans le cirque amoureux,
> Sont tous égaux, car ils sont tous heureux.   (1841–6)[30]

The last word, "heureux," taken from the vocabulary of gallantry, means above all "success" in amorous activity, so that the poet's final message is that not social rank, not (heaven knows) religious austerity, and not victory in war is what counts, but solely and uniquely winning out in love, which, as we all know, conquers everyone, eventually. The gods and mortals are enjoying themselves so riotously in the universal orgy, everyone is having such a good time, that no one, neither the participants nor the reader would think of noticing that, in addition to the quasi-explicit eroticism, this daring author has dreamed up a dismantlement of the entire social and religious structure. The revolution has already happened; the new order prevails. (It is no wonder Marmontel became terrified when he thought his manuscript had fallen into the wrong hands.) Of course, at the same time, this poem is all purest fantasy, dream-fluff, spun sugar, utterly removed from reality. Jupiter, Juno, the other divinities are cardboard imitations taken from Homer; Venus and her Faun, the three charming graces, are the merest paintings that have been set in motion, playthings for the reader's idle amusement. Surely there can be no historical connection between this decadent boudoir piece and the great and at times cruel Revolution which often tended to center its iconography, naturally enough, on David's implacable males. Yet, actually, here the reader is in for a surprise. For according to the latest research on the iconography of the Revolution, the last word from the workshop of the great Hogarth scholar, Ronald Paulson, the principal goddess of that Revolution, "la déesse Liberté," whose statue, venerated and incensed by patriots, presiding benignly over official festivities, was actually a replacement for – and bore vestiges of – both the main goddesses of Marmontel's poems: Venus, first; but also her rival, the Virgin Mary. Even though coming from a different vantage point, we may speak in this connection, even as Professor Paulson does concerning certain paintings of David, of "latent content" and "prolepsis." This is to say that, despite the frivolous appearance, Marmontel's *Neuvaine* bore within it anticipations of very serious political realities.[31]

3

Inversions and subversions in the *théâtre de la foire*, or, the end of Piron's *Arlequin-Deucalion*

"Il s'agit de savoir si Piron a plus d'esprit que Voltaire." Piron wittier than Voltaire? Surely the unnamed speaker in Diderot's *Neveu de Rameau* cannot be serious.[1] Alexis Piron (1689–1773),[2] barely remembered by connoisseurs for two comedies (*La Métromanie* and *Arlequin-Deucalion*) plus a handful of epigrams, but forgotten in nine other volumes of works no one but the most determined specialist ever reads – how could anyone hope to match wits such as his against the author of *Micromégas* and *Candide*? The comparison looks especially dubious in 1761–2, the supposed date of the passage quoted from *Le Neveu de Rameau*, for by then Piron's career as a playwright had been finished for almost two decades, while Voltaire's career bloomed in just its finest and wittiest flower.

6. Claude Gillot, *Voltaire receiving Alexis Piron*

49

Yet oddly, the topic of Piron vs Voltaire had survived as a staple of eighteenth-century Parisian conversation (perhaps something like the earlier debates over Corneille vs Racine). The matter still aroused interest in 1761, even though the terms of the debate had become somewhat stylized: usually, Piron was given credit for his incomparable sallies of wit, his inimitable *boutades*, but these were thought to be flash-in-the-pan affairs, of little consequence in the long run; whereas Voltaire was considered more *suivi*, more enduring and deeper.[3] Collé in his Journal gives a slightly different edge to the argument by describing how in conversation (and Collé was remembering particularly a conversation he had overheard *en tiers* between Voltaire and Mme de Pompadour), Voltaire could be marvelously and continuously not only witty, but polished, easy, elegant, discreetly setting up subjects to make the other person appear more clever than she really was. Collé admits that the rather vulgar Piron was incapable of any of this, but for what he calls *feu*, and for inventiveness, Collé declares that no one could compare with Piron.[4] We may note, too, that this entry in his Journal comes from the same time as the presumed date of the passage from *Le Neveu de Rameau*, confirming that, even after the mid-century, the topic still had life in it.

Actually, Alexis Piron had established a reputation for himself, in the early years of the eighteenth century, which was formidable, and even after his theatrical career had ended he still managed to keep himself in the public eye, partly by his picturesque and slightly scandalous behavior, and partly by taking epigrammatic pot shots at his enemies and rivals. Need one add that chief among these targets was the illustrious author of *Oedipe* and *Mérope*? Witty epigram following witty epigram, the contest between the Virgil of France and the comic author from Dijon lasted for years. To be sure, Voltaire rather unfairly took refuge in an attitude of lofty disdain, pretending to ignore the sallies with haughty indifference. The ploy didn't fool Piron for a moment; the barbs continued, despite the silence on the other end. Even on his deathbed – so the story runs – Piron gave notice that Voltaire should not be so foolish as to think he was safe simply because Piron was descending into the tomb: there were 150 epigrams *en réserve*, just waiting to be let loose each time the Patriarch so much as breathed a word against him . . .[5]

No one doubts that Voltaire was more subtle and more accomplished. Piron had composed an epigram against Elie Fréron that was quite clever, although not entirely free of a certain slight awkwardness in wording, just a suggestion of clumsiness that was part of Piron's rather engaging personality. It was not a bad performance; in fact it was rather good.[6] But hark! The Master, the Patriarch himself approaches. Before we know it his bow is raised, and the perfectly balanced shaft gleams dead on target:

Inversions and subversions

L'autre jour au fond d'un vallon
Un serpent piqua Jean Fréron;
Que pensez-vous qu'il arriva?
Ce fut le serpent qui creva.[7]

Piron is forgotten, at least for the moment. But fortunately for him, other, less important occasions arose – doubtless disdained by the elegant Voltaire – when Piron could shine unrivaled. For example, when M. Turgot, Prévôt des Marchands, widened the Quai de l'Horloge, an act so beneficial to jostled Parisians that it called for commemoration, Piron had the floor, the pavement, all to himself:

Monsieur Turgot étant en charge
Et trouvant ce quai trop peu large,
Y fit ajouter cette marge.
Passans qui passez tout de go,
Rendez grâce à Monsieur Turgo.[8]

Voltaire would never have bothered to write that. An absurdity so modestly droll, belongs only to Piron, and Piron's drollery in turn belongs to a milieu very different from that of Voltaire. For, while the Patriarch had launched his theatrical career in a royal theatre, *chez les Comédiens du roi*, Piron had gotten his start at the Fair, *au théâtre de la foire*. There was no royal patronage here and working conditions for playwrights were terrible. Piron was lucky to have begun with marionettes.

In the early eighteenth century, *le théâtre de la foire*, or rather *les théâtres de la foire* were marvelously diverse; they did everything from trained animals, acrobatic and slapstick farce, to *opéra comique*, ballet, pantomime, and a multitude of parodies, including pseudo grand opera, and pseudo grand tragedy.[9] It is not always possible to specify the traits characterizing their originality, since they borrowed so freely from others (particularly from the *Italiens*) and were regularly plagiarized in turn. Yet one kind of *opéra comique* crops up frequently enough to be identified as belonging very much to their art, and it flawlessly exemplifies what I have been terming the "attraction of the contrary." *Le Monde renversé* by Le Sage, Autreau and d'Orneval, first performed at the Foire St Laurent in 1718, was the archetype of the species.[10]

Its title, *Le Monde renversé*, would instantly have been recognized at the time as belonging to a set genre, familiar through a virtually endless tradition in art (popularized since the sixteenth century in prints),[11] in music, in holiday festivities and all sorts of folklore rites, and in the theatre, too (in plays and dance). Apparently since civilization started, one of the games people have wanted to play – for a host of reasons ranging from

51

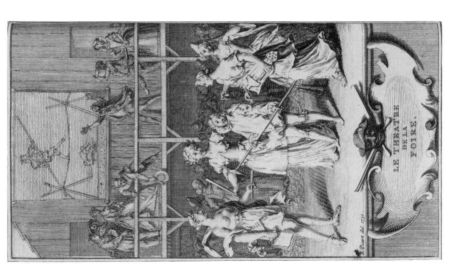

7. *Le Théâtre de la foire*, anonymous engraving, 1730, from *Le Théâtre de la foire ou l'opéra comique*

gravely serious to utterly frivolous – is the game which turns the world topsy-turvy, *le monde renversé*.[12] A number of the traditional inversions remain familiar today, especially those that involve the fundamental social inversion of the slave becoming the master. Thus, in popular engravings, the farmer is depicted riding grandly on horseback while the king walks ignominiously behind; or again (in, among other sources, a painting by Bosch)[13] the rabbit slays the huntsman and, blowing on his hunter's horn, brings the body home strung up; or again, men put on skirts and play women's roles, while women play men's. Sometimes inversions were staged as "real" events, saturnalia, taking place at carnivals or other festivities. Sometimes the inversions appeared less realistically as proverbs, songs, or drawings, that is to say, expressions of fantasies, whether angry, learned, quirky, or simply wishful thinking.

The plot of *Le Monde renversé* is pure wish fulfilment, deriving entirely from turning the world upside down: Arlequin and Pierrot find themselves in Merlin's realm where, contrary to everything they had experienced before, their wishes are granted the instant they formulate them. They have only to say the word "food" and a table appears, set with everything they could desire.[14] A mere mentioning of amorous inclinations instantly brings two ladies as beautiful as anyone could imagine, and ready to marry them on the spot. True, money is a problem here, but not because, as in the real world, the grooms need to be well off; in fact, for the opposite reasons: a topsy-turvy law decrees that anyone getting married should *not* be too rich. Arlequin and Pierrot hasten to assure their anxious fiancées that they don't have a penny, and the ladies are delighted. There follows a parade of characters, each one making as great a contrast as possible with the same figure in ordinary life: the philosopher is well dressed and good humored, never quarrelsome, and versed in poetry, dance, and music. He tells how, in Merlin's realm, merchants are scrupulous, judges incorruptible, commission agents honest. As for the theatre, all actresses are vestals, and all actors modest. Enter two characters named "Innocence" and "Bonne-Foi," whom Pierrot and Arlequin don't recognize: having lived all their lives in France and Italy they have never seen them before. Then comes the doctor, Hippocratine, who turns out to be a lady. She explains that here they never bleed or purge sick persons, but only well ones. Instead of the doctor taking the patient's pulse, the patient takes the doctor's. For the rest, she has only to stroke the patient under the chin and he is already on the road to convalescence – an idea so enticing that Arlequin and Pierrot have half a mind to become patients themselves. Instead, the two suitors get into a dice game in which they almost lose their fiancées, but Merlin intervenes in time, and the opera ends happily with the wedding.

One of the most engaging qualities of this altogether delightful theatre is the naïve simplicity that informs it. It speaks of life in a way that strikes one as innocent and authentic, so that it would seem a travesty to subject this creation to any sort of analytical dissection. And yet, the mere fact that so sophisticated an author as Le Sage had a hand in it invites a closer look. For indeed, if the libretto generates so much fun and gaiety by inverting all worldly values, the implication is that these values all badly need inverting: the construction of this charming utopia carries – however backhandedly – the conviction that the social system, the real experience of it, presents nothing but vices, miseries, injustices, dishonesties, frustrations – frictions of every sort, to such a degree that the only way to make life enjoyable is to convert it into something totally other. From the elementary problem of finding enough to eat, the more sophisticated vexation of marriage, money, buying and selling merchandise, law courts and medical practice (not to mention less consequential items such as the character traits of philosophers and actors), the opera assumes that these are all wrongs that need to be righted: perhaps it's the real world that's upside down. In sum, behind all the laughter, the conception of this utopia bespeaks a form of social discontent; its perspective is critical. Furthermore, as entertainment on the stage, the opera aims to bring actual remedy to the social problems it encompasses, canceling them out, one by one, with contraries, inversions, *renversements*. The more topsy-turvy the plot and the gayer the fun, the more blissful the relief; the more complete the utopia, the more effective the theatrical experience.[15]

In this *opéra comique* the genre achieves a kind of perfection; it never reappears in so pure a state. However, elements of this achievement do surface at the *foire*; in particular, one finds the same urge to make up for life's deficiencies by turning prevailing social values upside down. Surprisingly often the inversion turns ironic: in the island setting of *Le Jeune vieillard* (1722) it is not youth, but old age that is held in esteem. The "beautician" there has creams and ointments that will *create* wrinkles and gray hair, rather than cover them up. When the Princess discovers that her suitor, Adis, is not the old man he seemed, she is furious and threatens to destroy everyone . . .[16] *Les Animaux raisonnables* (1718) gives the inversion a still more interesting ironic twist: Ulysses gets permission from Calypso to break the magic spell that has turned his companions into animals.[17] They may become human again, on condition that they themselves desire to make the change. Ulysses is in for a shock. One usually assumes that humanity is superior to animality, but here we discover the reverse, and for reasons that are not as crazy as one might at first assume: the *ci-devant* Procurer wouldn't dream of becoming human again; he is far better off as a wolf, for he no longer has to pretend he has anything to do with justice. The former financier is, naturally enough, doing just as fine as a pig. The hen actually prefers laying eggs to having babies; besides, the rooster is far more amorous than her grumbling husband has ever been. The bull is thankful

9. *Les Animaux raisonnables*, anonymous engraving from *Le Théâtre de la foire*

for his two horns just as they are: if he returned to his wife in the real world, he might be wearing much bigger ones.

Just as in *Le Monde renversé*, there is discontent implied in the conception of this comic opera, and, behind the gaiety and fun, the financier–pig and procurer–wolf poke at some rather serious social problems. There are abundant instances in the theatres of the *foire* when this kind of criticism is produced by comic inversion. In *L'Isle des Amazones* (1721), women liberate themselves and proceed to do all the things they are never allowed to do in real life, like running the government, and running after husbands – in fact, capturing them by chasing them down in pirate ships. (One does note however that their law that no marriage may last more than three months is

10. *La Boîte de Pandore*, anonymous engraving from *Le Théâtre de la foire*

only observed in two out of three cases.) *Les Fra-Maçones* shows women breaking into the all-male Masonic Lodge and demanding membership privileges.[18] After considerable uproar they are eventually accepted. Admittedly the reversal is only half-complete in this instance. *La Boète de Pandore* (1721) makes the reversal run backwards, not creating a utopia this time, but suppressing one: the opera begins with an age of gold where everyone is sweet and innocent in a world where good faith and kindliness prevail. Then Pandora opens her cursed box, and everyone grows sour, mean, and selfish. Thus, turning the world topsy-turvy creates the real world with all its miseries and social strife.

A number of opera librettos stage a sort of social upheaval, sometimes just a frivolous one, as in *Arlequin Prince et Paysan* (1713), where the clown plays at royalty and makes a predictable mess of it, or in the later *Le Bal impromptu* (1761), where servants and masters change places for a time, although without any benefit to the former. (This piece is essentially in the aristocratic tradition, as were Marivaux's earlier experiments with the theme at the Comédie Italienne.) But with Sedaine's *Le Diable à quatre* (1756) the upheaval takes on a violence that shakes up the social system so much, one wonders whether the pieces really have gone back in place at the end.[19] Sedaine adapted his libretto from a French translation of an English play popularized by Garrick. This was his first theatrical effort, and his bold adaptation gave the work his own characteristic stamp. The *Diable* of the title is a mean and haughty Marquise who inflicts cruelties on persons she considers socially inferior: the maid relates that her mistress asked for a glass of water, only to throw it in her face when it was brought. The cook tells how, just as he was getting ready to serve a meal, she had burst into the kitchen and thrown the soup pot on the floor. Later we find the servants informally dancing together to the tune of a hurdy-gurdy played by a harmless old drunkard who is blind. Bursting in again, the Marquise stops the music and the dance by smashing the blind man's instrument. She was so rude to a doctor–magician who happened by, that he plots revenge: summoning devils from the underworld that same night, he casts a spell by which the she-devil Marquise changes places with a shoemaker's wife, so that she wakes the next morning to find herself in the cobbler's bed, looking just like his wife, and dressed in her clothes. Meanwhile the real cobbler's wife has been changed to resemble the Marquise. Thus there is a double inversion: the high becoming the low, and the low becoming the high.

Remaining true to her awful temperament, the Marquise tries to use her haughty airs on the shoemaker, who is so incensed by her behavior he actually beats her onstage, threatens to throw a bucket of dirty water on her when she seems about to faint, and forces her to her knees to apologize. As for the real cobbler's wife, perhaps one should have predicted that even in her newly acquired rank, her touching modesty and gentle kindliness would win her the affection and loyalty of all who had suffered under the Marquise's arbitrary cruelties. Thus the double inversion not only revolutionizes the classes of society by turning them upside down, but it brings justice at last: both women receive their due; guilt is punished and virtue gets its reward.

At the end of the opera the reversal is righted by another magic spell. But meanwhile this socially conscious author has powerfully suggested how wonderful the world might be if only the deserving downtrodden were raised to high social station, and he has been positively gleeful in his presentation of the debasement and physical punishment of the arrogant lady. After the performance is over, what remains with us is the pleasure of turning the tables on aristocracy. There is plenty of loud, coarse laughter in Sedaine, and it is partly to disguise the thrust of new seriousness and social *engagement* in *opéra comique*. If ever a literary work can be termed "proleptic" in the Revolutionary sense, this libretto can.

There is a final irony: the *approbation et privilège* for printing the opera is signed by Crébillon, *fils*, royal censor, who had, himself, regularly – on account of his questionable subject matter – been forced to publish under false imprints. He explains in his *imprimatur* that he could find no reason why this work should not be printed.

If so many of these librettos turn ironic, if the never-neverland doesn't completely succeed, this may be because the strongest talent of the *foire* authors was not in the creation of blissful illusion anyway, but in pricking balloons, in giving the raspberry, in doing what the French used to call "faire la figue."

Thus far we have been considering situations that really do present contraries, and found them an abundant source of comic inspiration for these authors. But *contrariety* was not the only kind of contrapuntal tension operating in the eighteenth century; far from it, and because one of these other counterpoints is so relevant for the *théâtre de la foire* it should perhaps be mentioned briefly here. I am thinking of the strong current that comes not from a contrary, but from a side, so to speak, an extraordinary lateral force that created an authentic groundswell during the eighteenth century. Primarily responsible for the commotion was a single theatrical character who, though Italian in origin, took on a rather French personality as he was constantly borrowed or stolen by the *foire* and as he came to speak French even at the Comédie Italienne. This was Arlequin, everybody's favorite clown, the most ubiquitous personage the theatre had ever seen, the star of literally hundreds of plays and librettos.[20]

Arlequin allegedly had a character of his own, of course. Everyone knew that he was greedy, licentious, light-fingered, rather unprincipled, not very bright, emotionally shallow, and thoroughly lovable. But what audiences wanted endlessly to see was this character playing the part of someone else. Needless to say, playwrights were glad to oblige.

He could take on any nationality (*Arlequin baron allemand*, 1712; *Arlequin tailleur anglais*, 1784); practice any trade (*Arlequin cabaretier et comédien*, n.d.; *Arlequin garçon marchand*, 1784; *Arlequin pâtissier*, 1781; *Arlequin astrologue*, 1727; *Arlequin barbier paralytique*, 1740). He could answer any calling (*Arlequin ermite*, n.d.; . . . *franc maçon*, n.d.; . . . *magicien*, 1739; . . . *sorcier sans le savoir*, n.d.; . . . *esprit follet*, 1739; . . . *invisible*, 1713; . . . *muet*, 1786; . . . *mort*, n.d.). He could turn up in any dramatic situation (*Arlequin avalé par la baleine*, n.d.; . . . *au sabbat*, 1752; . . . *aux champs élysées*, 1710). He could join the army (*Arlequin officier*, n.d.; . . . *colonel*, 1714; . . . *déserteur*, 1715, 1759; . . . *recruteur*, 1768; . . . *prisonnier*, 1747; . . . *assassin*, 1748). He could ascend the social scale to any height (*Arlequin heureux jardinier*, 1748; . . . *honnête homme et bon père de famille*, 1786; . . . *Gentilhomme malgré lui*, 1715; . . . *premier ministre*, n.d.; . . . *roi des chinois*, 1770; . . . *roi des ogres*, 1720; . . . *empereur dans la lune*, 1712). Nor was he a stranger to the "sciences" and what the Enlightenment called the "arts of imitation" (*Arlequin philosophe épicurien*, n.d.; . . . *peintre et musicien*, 1739; . . . *poète*, n.d.; . . . *génie*, 1752). He could be endowed with any humor or passion (*Arlequin misanthrope*, 1741; . . . *malheureux par ses richesses*, 1750; . . . *jaloux et guéri*, n.d.; . . . *squelette par amour*, 1775). He was as at home with the ancients as with the moderns (*Arlequin Romulus*, 1722; . . . *Jason*, 1746; . . . *Orphée*, n.d.; . . . *Mahomet*, 1714). He could practice the most unlikely occupations (*Arlequin juge et concierge des petites maisons*, 1731; . . . *pilote du vaisseau volant*, 1783), assume the most surprising identities (*Arlequin eunuque*, 1740; . . . *fille malgré lui*, 1713), and sometimes he did everything at once, as in the piece by Cadoret: *Arlequin enfant, statue, perroquet, ramoneur, astrologue, grenadier de Catalogne, squelette et notaire arabe*, 1750.[21] The list has barely begun.

There was automatic comedy whenever Arlequin appeared in one of his roles, because with his unmistakable black mask, diamond-checkered costume, and clumsy manners, his true identity instantly showed through whatever role he was playing. The result was a droll counterpoint that drastically undermined the pretended seriousness of the dramatic situation. (As I suggested, the tension here is contrapuntal by being subversively different, rather than contrary.) And what an extraordinary source of theatrical invention he proved to be: all the while the respectable Voltaires and d'Alemberts were moaning that the great days of comedy were finished, that the genre had exhausted itself, the authors of the *foire* were striking gold everywhere. For any personage, any plot, even any *thing* could be converted into comedy just by letting Arlequin play the part.

Here was an astonishing and important literary trend, of course, but the sociological implications are still more interesting: the almost literally ubiquitous nature of this clown suggests the *prise de conscience* by authors and audiences alike that everything in French society, in all of French life, had become a target for ridicule. From monarch to peasant, no class was safe from Arlequin's satire; from priest to financier to blacksmith, no calling or trade was secure; people wanted to laugh at all of them. Granted, there is a kind of innocence and good fun in most of these lampoons: Arlequin was an essentially good-hearted creature, and he endowed his librettos and plays with that spirit. Nevertheless, if one takes into account the extraordinary vogue of this kind of satire that fairly sweeps through the productions of the *foire* and the Comédie Italienne, it is difficult not to interpret the phenomenon as one of the innumerable symptoms of a society that is losing faith in every sort of traditional value – a society turning against itself.

Similar conclusions are in store when we consider another of the "sideways" counterpoints of the century, embodied in a theatrical form very similar to the Arlequin plays and often overlapping with them, but nevertheless having a life of its own, namely, theatrical parody. Here again it is not a question of a "contrary" so much as a subversive difference – as will be seen.

For both the *foire* and the Comédie Italienne the ultimate pretense, the ultimate fakery whose balloon was most needing to be pricked was the theatre: the Opéra with its insipid *féeries*, its boring, impossible mythology, its outlandish scenic effects.[22] And then there were the *Comédiens du roi*, otherwise known as *les Romains*, whose high-flown Alexandrines and idiotic plots *à l'antique* were sitting ducks for the authors of satire. In the eighteenth century the great age of theatrical parodies began.

Certainly the preceding century had seen a number of individual parodies, but nothing like the avalanche we find in the eighteenth. Lanson was mistaken in his famous article to speak of something over two hundred theatrical parodies in this period:[23] there were at least three or four times that number, seven to eight hundred, and many others that were lost track of, for frequently no one bothered to print them.[24] But when Rameau composed *Les Indes galantes*, the *foire* countered with *Les Indes dansantes*. *Inès de Castro* by Houdard de la Motte became *Agnès de Chaillot* by the *Italiens*. When Voltaire produced *Alzire*, the *foire* came back with *Alzirette*. Voltaire's *Mariamne* provoked *Les Quatre Mariannes* by the *Italiens*, and *Les Huit Mariannes* at the *foire*. *Mérope* brought on *Marotte*; *L'Orphelin de la Chine* led fatally to *Les Magots*, and so on, straight through the century. There were fifty parodies of plays by Voltaire; *Le Mariage de Figaro* alone actually inspired dozens.[25]

As Houdard de la Motte stated at the time, and as critics have been repeating ever since, the most frequently used comic strategy in these parodies is that of *burlesque*: the queen of the tragedy or comedy is turned into a waitress in the parody; the action is moved from the palaces and temples of ancient Greece to the "Grenouillère" of Bougival, or some other disreputable location not too far from Paris. Tragedy's noble Alexandrines become the lowest sort of speech-slang, including obscenities; simple, sometimes bawdy, ditties that everyone knows by heart replace Rameau's stately airs. The great classical conflicts that affected the destinies of whole nations are replayed as tavern brawls and marital squabbles. The anti-classical, anti-aristocratic slant of such parodies is fascinating, and Lanson and others were quite right to examine them from this point of view. No doubt the literary quality of most of them is, to put it mildly, a disappointment (the genre invited hackery and vulgarity), and yet, the parodies sometimes convey a sense of reality that is refreshing, especially when seen against the artificial contrivances of *tragédie* and *tragédie lyrique*, and occasionally they afford some of the most perspicacious dramatic criticism of the century.

Anyone who has suffered through the troubled plot of Voltaire's *Sémiramis* with its all-too-obviously-imitated-from-Shakespeare ghost emerging from the dark tomb where eventually the wrong person will be stabbed, mercifully bringing the innumerable unlikelihoods to an end, or anyone who has seen the Gabriel de Saint-Aubin drawing of it,[26] showing Sémiramis, Queen of ancient Babylon, with her French wig perched on top, and a

12. Gabriel de Saint-Aubin, "La Tragédie de Sémiramis comme elle a été représentée la première fois" (1748)

61

vast hoop-skirt billowing below, will be devoutly thankful for the clever parody by Bidault de Montigny.[27]

Bidault has imagined a group of characters named such things as l'Exposition, le Dénouement, le Récit, la Langueur, L'Ombre du grand Corneille, plusieurs Beautés, troupe de Défauts, la Pitié, and so on, who have assembled to discuss the tragedy's problems. It soon becomes clear that this meeting is a sort of metaphor for the experience of the play itself. Le Dénouement and L'Exposition have trouble deciding which should come first. L'Intérêt is late for the meeting; they wonder whether he will ever appear; whereas la Langueur is right on time, punctuality itself. Sémiramis announces she needs their advice because she is about to give herself to . . . the printer. Thunder is heard and the Ghost of the great Corneille rises from the tomb to rebuke her for her audacity. Eventually, Sémiramis herself has an accident in the tomb (where, in the play she is stabbed): she strikes her head against Vraisemblance, a blow, she declares as she staggers on stage, that may prove fatal. She makes a long speech describing her plight, to which the rejoinder of l'Intérêt seems quite apposite, though his *césure* leaves something to be desired:

Intérêt: Il convient d'abréger un peu quand on expire Madame . . .[28]

Finally, l'Intérêt avers that, given the robust temperament Sémiramis has inherited from her father, and with the help of such friends as la Pitié, she may survive after all.

Not only does the parody show up the defects of this particular play, it describes rather adroitly what we in the twentieth century have come to feel are the shortcomings of eighteenth-century tragedy in general: how often the dénouement is already visible in the contrivances of the exposition. (And how many times we have wished the author had put the end at the beginning, and spared us so many acts!) Plusieurs beautés, troupe de défauts: that is exactly why *Sémiramis* and most of Voltaire's other tragedies are never performed, and indeed the Shade of the great Corneille, visible so constantly in the rhetoric of Voltaire's Alexandrines, is what spoils them for us too.

But this parody also suggests another phenomenon found repeatedly in theatrical parodies of this time, one which appeals especially to our modernism: the phenomenon of theatricality reflecting upon itself. Again and again in these parodies one finds not a completed play (so to speak), but a sort of rehearsal or preparation of the play, a play about putting on a play, and whose function is specifically to bring into question the devices on which the dramatic illusion depends: theatricality turns problematic, while characters take on separate lives, stepping out of the tragedies written for them, adrift with their own motives and destinies, searching for other plots and other authors. And whereas at the real opera, or at the Comédie

Française, the enjoyment of the spectacle hinges on a suspension of disbelief, a desire to lose oneself and become immersed in the action, in the parodies of the *foire* the pleasure derives from the exact opposite: from the breaking-down of illusion, in the playing-up of contrivance, and often in a clear subversion of the form itself. Voltaire's *Mariamne* is a heavily dramatic affair, set in ancient times and portraying Mariamne's heroic courage in resisting the cruel jealousy of Herod. Piron, in his parody of this play, brings four (eventually eight) characters called "Marianne" on stage. They are dressed in regal attire and they strike noble attitudes, but beneath their queenly robes and postures the costumes and manners of Scaramouche, Arlequin, Pantalon, and Fabia are easily detected. Piron's answer to Voltaire's high tragedy was to put his heroine in drag.[29]

Curiously, it was part of the same public which went first to the Opéra or the Comédie Française to see the tragedy, and then turned up at the *foire* or the Comédie Italienne for the parody. We can be sure of this because so many of the parodies make no sense at all unless one has clearly in mind what was said or sung in the original. They were composed for an audience that had already seen and heard what was being parodied. That is, while on the one hand the noble, courtly traditions of *tragédie* and *tragédie lyrique* were still very much alive in the eighteenth century, and were actually taken almost as seriously as in the reign of Louis XIV, nevertheless a substantial part of this same public were drawn to see these noble traditions reduced to something silly, idiotic, risible, vulgar. Even in the case of the greatest tragic poems, such as *Phèdre* by Racine, for example, they were denigrated, laughed at, lampooned in parody after parody, on throughout the century. It would be difficult not to read a kind of social message in this double phenomenon of the desire to preserve, and in fact enhance, the heroic, courtly theatrical traditions, and yet to desecrate them at the same time. Surely these are further symptoms of a society that had begun to destroy the values it most esteemed, a society in decay.

If the theatres of the *foire* managed to survive, they did so in the face of almost constant persecution and harassment by the *Comédiens du roi* (and sometimes by the Opéra, too) who resented their insults and their competition, trying repeatedly to shut the theatres down, and sometimes succeeding. The ingenious response of the *foire* authors was to convert all the restrictions, harassments, and even foreclosures into comedy. Far from stifling their inspiration, repression only served to spur the authors to greater invention.[30] At times, one has the impression they actually preferred to fight with one arm tied behind their backs. When the regulations forbade them to perform *plays*, the *foire* staged disjointed *scenes* which the audience could assemble in their minds to form a complete plot. When they were forbidden to use actors that spoke, they performed *à la muette*, the audience singing, to popular tunes, verses that were rolled down from the ceiling on a scroll.[31] When regulations forbade performances acted by people, they used marionettes, or even, on occasion, children – a rousing success at the box-office.[32] In the same spirit, when the actor–impresario Francisque lost almost everything he owned in a fire in Lyons, the fire became part of the plot of the next play he staged in Paris.[33] When anything in dialogue was forbidden, they put on plays in monologue and used infinite ingenuity in circumventing the terms of the regulations: Sosie would talk to his lantern, which, being an object rather than an actor, didn't count legally; a tree trunk would speak; voices would come from the wings, and, as a last resort, there were always marionettes, which the regulations so frequently left out.

But how modern they seem, these theatrical inventions born of repression: plays broken into bits and pieces that dangle in isolation with no continuity at all save in the imagination of the spectator; operas played out in noiseless gestures, and whose singing has been bizarrely displaced: the actors open their silent mouths, the audience burst into song. And there was more: plays composed entirely of nonsense syllables that made rhymes and rhythms sounding like idiotic Alexandrines, gibberish the actors spouted while imitating the tragedians of the Comédie Française doing their most famous dramatic scenes; plays in which all the characters were life-size marionettes; a verse *drame* in which the normal proportion between punctuation and words had been reversed: the lines consisted mainly of commas, periods, quotation marks, and exclamation points, which were only occasionally punctuated by an isolated word or incomplete phrase. . . .[34] Not until the surrealists would such wildly imaginative experiments in theatricality and the absurd come back to the French stage.

One of the eighteenth century's worst moments of theatrical repression – playwrights were reduced to monologues and/or marionettes – produced one of the great masterpieces of the *foire*: *Arlequin-Deucalion* by Piron (1722).[35] This play is one enormous three-act monologue (with passages that come perilously close to cheating), and it embodies in its energy, imagination, and daring every aspect of the *foire* that we have been considering: in addition to acrobatic feats, and a mock trained-animal act, we find the main character, Arlequin, in a grandly virtuoso performance impersonating not only Deucalion, but every imaginable role from king to disgruntled husband, to amorous suitor, to drunken philosopher, etc., etc. – a veritable apotheosis of Arlequin. There is singing, dancing, a sort of marionette act, a parody of tragedy, a parody of opera, and there are miles of low comedy. There is literary criticism while the play deliberately breaks down the barrier between the illusion and reality, and, most to the point, there are speculations on the creation of a utopia through the inversion of normal values leading to social criticism that is stronger and more daring

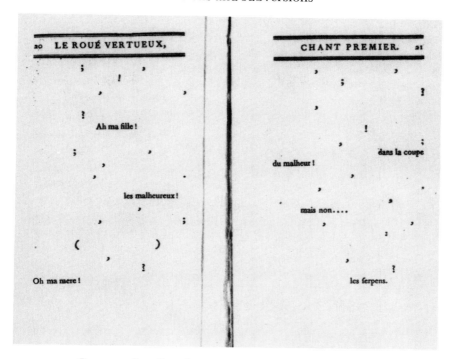

13. Two pages from Coquelay de Chaussepierre, *Le Roué vertueux . . .*

than anything the *forains* had staged before. In short, this extravagant comedy in its gaiety, its infinite diversity, and in its critical attitude towards the social system, subsumes the whole art of the *foire*.

Piron was almost totally unknown in the theatre when he wrote it, but with one stroke this play not only launched his career as a sought-after writer of comedy, but established his reputation as a playwright decisively for the rest of the century. There are many possible explanations for its resounding success. My own view is that the huge dimensions of the monologue, its inexhaustible inventiveness, the daring of its attack on social abuses, are due mostly to the repressive circumstances under which it was written: the intolerable, impossible restrictions that somehow provoked the author to strain all the rules – theatrical and social – to the limit of one grand surge of creative genius.

The plot, such as it is, comes from the classical legend of Deucalion that curiously resembles the story of Noah: the flood has destroyed all mankind except Arlequin-Deucalion who floats, astride a barrel, to safety on Mt Parnassus.[36] Eventually, at the end of the play, Arlequin will find a way to decipher an obscure pronouncement by the oracle enabling him to re-populate the earth. Humanity will be reborn. But for the moment he is quite alone, and since there is no one else to talk to, he begins a series of out-loud reflections to himself that during the course of the play will range over every conceivable subject from the nature of comedy to childbirth. Naturally enough, the first topic is the flood itself, and the reasons for its occurrence. No doubt, muses Arlequin-Deucalion, the gods sent it to punish mankind for its sins:

Ma foi, il n'y fallait pas une moindre lessive que ce déluge, pour laver la terre et blanchir l'espèce humaine! Une chose doit être bien nettoyée quand la mer a passé par-dessus. Voilá tous mes coquins noyés; si cela ne les corrige pas, je ne sais plus ce qu'il y faut faire. . . .   (p. 493)[37]

But the present situation has advantages for him, at least, if for no one else. Is he not monarch, so to speak, of the whole world? And then, he has gotten rid of his wife, not an unmixed blessing perhaps, but a blessing neverthe-less. He has all the food he needs for the moment. On the other hand, what will he do without women? How can he repopulate the world alone? Enter the muse of Tragedy, Melpomène, a beautiful lady whose speech, on account of the regulation forbidding dialogue, is somewhat restricted:

[Melpomène] serpente majestueusement sur la scène, sans prendre garde à Deuca-lion, faisant des mines passionnées, poussant des *ah!* des *hélas!* des *dieux!* des *qu'entends-je!* et gesticulant à grand tour de bras.   (p. 496)[38]

Arlequin at once proposes marriage, explaining that he is the last remain-ing human being and that it is a question of repopulation. This leads him to continue the reflections begun earlier, on the causes of the late disaster:

Mes frères et moi, il n'y a qu'un instant, nous étions rangés sur la surface de la terre, comme des pièces d'échecs sur un échiquier. Rois, reines, cavaliers, pions, et fous de toutes couleurs, étaient à leurs places. Les dieux s'en jouaient; nous allions et venions à tort, à travers, à leur gré. Je ne sais quel mauvais joueur d'entre eux eut un échec et mat qui lui fit perdre la partie. C'était sa faute; il voulut que ce fût celle des pièces, et, come ceux qui perdent aux cartes et qui les mordent de rage, dans la sienne il ramassa pêle-mêle et jeta tout, cul sur tête, dans cette boîte que vous voyez (en se montrant), pions, cavaliers, reines, rois et fous; je suis la petite boîte qui renferme un si bon onguent. Que de moi ressortent canaille et potentats! Prenez la clef, et rouvrez à cette malheureuse multitude. Marions-nous . . .   (p. 497)[39]

No doubt these remarks were supposed to pass for low comedy; how could the official Commissaire take them seriously when they were only part of Arlequin's absurd proposal of marriage to the muse of Tragedy? On the other hand, such objections to the doctrine of the Fall and Redemption and to the Christian interpretation of the story of Noah were exactly the ones being formulated – most unhumorously – by Voltaire at just this same time in his didactic poem *l'Epître à Uranie* (1722). The only significant difference is that Voltaire was more open in his attack:

[Dieu] créa des humains à lui-même semblables,
 Afin de les mieux avilir:
 Il nous donna des coeurs coupables,
 Pour avoir droit de nous punir:
 Il nous fit aimer le plaisir,
Pour nous mieux tourmenter par des maux effroyables . . .
Aveugle en ses bienfaits, aveugle en son courroux,
A peine il nous fit naître, il va nous perdre tous.
Il ordonne à la mer de submerger le monde . . .[40]

On and on Voltaire's impious résumé goes. There is no escaping its argument: the relentless irony, the pitiless clarity of his rationalism are designed to destroy Christian credibility totally and to compel the reader to reject these absurdities, even as he himself had done. Voltaire goes for the jugular.

Piron, in contrast, is more discreet, more modest – after all, it's just a clown speaking – and doubtless, in his deft handling of the traditional chessboard imagery, more "poetic" as well. Thankfully, he leaves the reader free to seek the bold message if he wants to, or be content to enjoy the comedy, if he does not. Nothing could be further from the purposeful didacticism of Voltaire's cultivated art than the good-hearted, unassuming warmth with which the style is infused. And in fact, its literary tradition lies in another direction entirely, for the author closest to Piron in style and attitude is certainly Rabelais, in one of his jovial moods. Piron may even be alluding to Rabelais toward the end of the passage quoted when he refers to the "boîte" containing the "si bon onguent."

And how the author of *Pantagruel* would have enjoyed Arlequin's fantastic account of his separation from his wife, Pyrrha (who survived after all), during the flood:

Quand j'eus dévidé tout le peloton de ficelle attachée au cerf-volant sur lequel je t'avais posée, en m'abandonnant sur les eaux, et qu'alors je t'avais perdue de vue dans les airs, je pris le parti, ne pouvant mieux faire, de me nouer vite le reste autour du col et de continuer à nager de mon côté, pendant que du tien tu continuais à voler au gré du grand vent qu'il faisait. Tu me servais de voile, et la bise qui te soufflait en poupe me faisait fendre les flots avec une rapidité de tous les diables. Après avoir voyagé de cette étrange façon tous les deux pendant la matinée, nous servant l'un et l'autre, toi, de force mouvante, et moi, de point d'appui, j'entendis sonner midi sous mon ventre à un clocher sur le coq duquel je me trouvais. J'étais à jeun et passablement fatigué. Ne voilà-t-il pas que j'aperçois, peu loin de moi, un tonneau roulant sur les ondes? A la vue d'un objet si intéressant, je fais les cinq sens de nature pour en approcher. Le courant l'entraînant à gauche, le maudit vent qu'il faisait te faisait voler à droite; l'instinct me tirait vers le tonneau. Je voyais l'instant où tu t'allais souiller du meurtre de ton cher époux; tu m'étranglais. Pour t'épargner ce parricide, j'ai tiré des ciseaux de ma poche, et, crac, je me suis mis à l'aise, en te recommandant aux dieux . . .   (pp. 502–3)[41]

No doubt it was just such *boutades* of low comedy that made respectable eighteenth-century critics wag their heads and wish that Piron's art were more "suivi." But for modern readers the delight, the inspiration of this passage lies precisely in its total gratuitousness: the whole description just soars aloft into surrealism, along with Pyrrha's kite, while the underwater church bells toll mid-day. This is improvised fantasy of the purest, most joyous kind, uncontaminated by any sort of usefulness, *vraisemblance*, or even sanity.

Consonant with such gratuitous moments, there is hardly any plot to this sprawling comedy. It relies entirely upon a planless improvisation that might go anywhere or do anything. From the classical legend of Deucalion we surmise that when eventually Arlequin manages to repopulate the human species, it will be in some unexpected, seemingly impossible, non-sexual way. We note, also, that surprises and seemingly impossible regenerations have constantly marked the jolting course of this comedy, which has survived solely through last-minute, on-the-spot improvisations that bring the action to life unbelievably, ex nihilo. Not just the ending, but the whole plot is miraculous re-creation.

Several stage devices play upon the element of surprise, of not knowing what is ahead: things drop down onstage from the flies; there are sudden entrances from the wings. Twice we find Arlequin opening a sort of grab-bag of surprises. Near the beginning, his *bissac* survives the flood, marvelously and unexpectedly containing enough food for three persons at least. Near the end (III, iii), the barrel on which Arlequin has been floating is now broken into and its contents are taken out, one item at a time. At this point there is an abrupt increase not only in the seriousness of the play's social tenor, but also in the importance of the personage of Arlequin. In keeping with the all-purpose nature of his character, implying that no aspect of society is safe from his satire, Arlequin now shoulders the burden of his universality, setting himself up as judge of everyone and everything in the whole world. It is as if (in the last moments of this comedy) he were exploiting all the potentialities of his character, such as they were scattered in the innumerable eighteenth-century plays that bore his name.

Reaching into his barrel, Arlequin brings forth the most amazing inventory: a book of heraldry that elicits remarks directed against the whole aristocracy, remarks so daring they caused one late eighteenth-century critic to label Piron a precursor of the Revolution of 1789;[42] a frivolous lawsuit over literary matters; a brace of pistols, prompting some sardonic reflections on the effect of such technological "advances" of the age, "progress" that makes it so easy for the nobodies of the world to destroy the high and mighty. Here Piron harks back to Renaissance traditions, especially to the earthy sagacity of Rabelais and Montaigne, but he also looks forward, like an uncanny prophet, to the agonies of our own death-dealing age. Just as he had done with most of the other items in his barrel, Arlequin throws the pistols out to sea. Out to sea also goes another lawsuit, and if Arlequin decides after all to keep the money bag (the next item) for himself, he throws away the last item, the marionette Polichinelle-Momus. Since this is a mere puppet, Arlequin can legitimately hold a dialogue with him, and thus he learns the secret of the oracle's pronouncement that will enable him to repopulate mankind. Unexpectedly, it is the puppet himself who asks to be thrown away; he's so tired of hearing his own silly chatter (*baragouin*) he wants to end it all. Arlequin is glad to oblige, and the puppet goes flying gleefully to his doom. It has been pointed out that Piron is making an ironic jibe at authors such as Le Sage who, under pressure from the regulations, had abandoned the impresario Piron worked for, and gone elsewhere to write marionette plays.[43] At the same time we note that from this moment on there are far fewer of the jolting surprises that characterize the rest of the play. Arlequin is turning into Deucalion, the repopulator, almost a divinity, and his discourse will become almost sober, the clownish side of him just barely remaining visible in his embarrassment at his new role. In effect, throwing away Polichinelle-Momus (i.e., slapstick-satire) signals the end of that aspect of his own character.

And now, in the climactic ending of the comedy, Arlequin and Pyrrha manage the repopulation by throwing down stones that turn into men and women. Interestingly, the new generation instantly exhibits all the bad characteristics of the old, so that the flood hasn't accomplished anything in terms of social improvement. And yet, this dramatic situation has given the author a pretext to take a fresh look at the social classes, and to pass judgement on them all. Each newborn "son" represents a different social class, and as Arlequin greets each one in turn we realize that the order of the greetings has significance; in fact, it establishes the author's own hierarchy of social values, which daringly inverts all of those found in the real world. Turning society upside down, Arlequin is creating a *monde renversé*. Hence, neither the churchman, nor the nobleman, nor the bourgeois is allowed pride of place: the last shall be first. The farmer (*le laboureur*) comes before all others, and in a rather emotional eulogy Arlequin salutes this eldest son as the most worthy, innocent, and necessary part of mankind, albeit the least appreciated by the other classes. In speaking thus, Arlequin gives him a special benediction bestowed on no one else. Second place is accorded to the artisan, who is to the farmer, declares Arlequin, as the age of silver was to the age of gold, or as utility is to necessity.

The third son is the nobleman, who comes swaggering insolently with his sword and plumes. Arlequin knocks his hat off, and tells him to be more respectful ("Mon gentilhomme, un peu de modestie. Tout ton talent sera de savoir tuer . . .," p. 515).[44] And Arlequin is still more insulting to the next son who represents the *noblesse de robe*, not even trying to hide his disgust, and openly declaring his regret he had not thrown the stone from which the "robin" came far out to sea ("Je te vois là des yeux fripons, un nez tourné à la friandise et des mains crochues . . .," p. 515).[45]

But it is the last son that requires closest scrutiny. He is not identified by class, as the others have been, and his bizarre costume is a puzzle:

[Le] cinquième garçon [. . .] a une large calotte sur la tête, une perruque à la cavalière en bourse, une longue barbe de capucin, un petit collet, un habit de couleur, une épée au côté, un paquet de plumes à la main, un bas blanc, un bas noir, une culotte rouge d'un côté, noire de l'autre, etc., etc., etc.   (p. 516)[46]

What are we to make of this? The wig doesn't fit with the stockings, the sword doesn't go either with the collar or the skull-cap, and the "paquet de plumes" doesn't belong anywhere.

Scholars have agreed (with good reason) that this figure represents the priesthood, and part of the evidence for their interpretation is that Arlequin himself seems to be reaching the same conclusion as he ponders the celibacy of this personage, the fact that he alone of all the sons has no mate:

Quelle étrange espèce est celle-ci? Je remarque même qu'il n'y a que quatre femelles, et que celui-là n'a pas son vis-à-vis. Ah! J'y suis! Il n'en a que faire pour se multiplier. La race n'en sera que trop nombreuse, sans que le mariage s'en mêle. Ainsi que Prométhée, mon grand-père, ils se perpétueront sans avoir jamais chez eux de femme en couches. J'ai connu de ces gens-là à milliers avant le déluge. Les uns nous en menaçaient de la part des dieux offensés, les autres nous chantaient les mœurs innocentes des premiers temps, et tous accumulaient les crimes et grossissaient l'orage. Ils y sont enveloppés aussi comme les autres.   (p. 516)[47]

How the Commissaire, who we know was present at performances of this play, can have let this derogation of the priesthood pass uncensored, we may never quite understand. Indeed, this attack against the first estate is to us unmistakable, and it is tempting to conclude that this is the whole point of the enigma: the figure represents simply the priest, and all the other elements of his costume are decoys to throw the authorities off the scent, or at least to mask the extraordinary daring of the criticism. We note that one gets only the briefest glimpse of this personage, hardly enough time to react, before the cuckoo's mocking song breaks in, and the final dance begins, bringing the comedy to a close.

On the other hand, this interpretation – correct so far as it goes – leaves much unexplained, and it may just be possible to see further into the enigmatic meaning of the various parts of the costume. For in one of Piron's later plays (*Les Enfans de la joie*, 1725),[48] a similarly clad figure appears and reveals at least something more about the oddities of his attire. From this later play we gather that the sword identifies a military officer (*noblesse d'épée*) who is ready to kill ("Avec l'épée, je tue"). The "calotte" gives us an "abbé," a priest, just as we thought, who with his "petit collet" seduces pretty women ("avec ceci je subjugue les belles").[49] The "paquet de plumes" indicates pens with which to write ruin ("avec la plume, je ruine").

No doubt I have been influenced by my study of the literature of the religious persecutions following the Revocation of the Edict of Nantes of 1685, but it is difficult not to notice that the disparate elements of this weird costume (except for the clownish ones, which I assume are a disguise to mask the boldness of the ideas), combine to make sense if one assumes that Piron is attacking not only the priesthood, but the entire Church in its cruelest role, as persecutor – *l'infâme* – at its most infamous. For, as the Huguenots and the whole world had learned thirty years before, it was the obscene yoking of spiritual powers with temporal ones, the Church with the military, that had brought on all the atrocities of the persecutions. Pierre Bayle had denounced the evils of this combination of powers in his plea for religious toleration, *Commentaire philosophique* (1686), nor did he fail to point an accusing finger at the scandalous lives led by the clergy who were as busy with their debaucheries as they were busy wreaking havoc on defenseless people of a different religion. Bayle mentioned, too, the pens, "plumes" (doubtless whole packages of them) engaged in writing apologies for these miserable campaigns.[50] And finally, there is evidence that precisely this issue, the linking of the secular powers to the religious powers, was of the greatest moment to Piron.

In 1730 Piron composed a very bold, and much neglected, tragedy entitled *Callisthène*. One must grant that as poetry it is quite desultory; it deserved to flop, as it did, after a mere eight performances. But the plot is astonishing: the action concerns a philosopher (Callisthène) who, virtually alone with his brave sister, stood up to Alexander the Great, setting himself, in the name of truth and morality, against all the monarch's tyrannies and ambitions for self-aggrandizement. There is a strong possibility that the arrogant despot's conduct in this tragedy was intended to suggest, covertly, the arrogance and tyranny of the Sun King. In any event, at one of the play's most dramatic moments, a sycophant named Anaxarque proposes that Alexander actually be worshipped in the temples as demi-god. Callisthène's reaction is furious; in fact, he declares that Anaxarque should be struck dead for such blasphemy. The reaction of Callisthène's friend Lysimaque is more rational and specific:

> Anaxarque, pour tous j'ose ici vous répondre
> Que le Trône et l'Autel ne sont pas à confondre.
> Le Monarque a ses droits, et les Dieux ont les leurs.
> Vous avez proposé le comble des horreurs.
> S'abstienne de ces Dieux la foudre vengeresse,
> Pour le crime d'un seul, de châtier la Grèce,
> Et l'indignation dont nous frémissons tous,
> Puisse-t'elle suffire à leur juste courroux! (III, vi)

Much more might be said concerning this courageous, if badly written, play and of the author's daring theories on tragedy, theories so radical they actually foreshadow those of Mercier (see below, chapter 11).[51] But the essential point for present purposes is that Piron's concern for the separation of powers came from deep and far-reaching religious and political convictions. It is not at all unlikely that his comedy also should contain a heavily disguised attack on the Church and nobility united in their cruelest roles, as persecutors.

But what an extraordinary comedy to compose in 1722! As the bitterly anti-revolutionary La Harpe was to point out later,[52] Piron's dramatic *renversement* amounts to an overthrow of the entire social structure, something like the great Revolution *en germe*. Nor can one ignore the deadly earnestness of this critique, as Arlequin knocks the nobleman's hat off, forcing him to show respect to his superior, the farmer; as he snarls insults and sarcasms at the disgusting representative of the *noblesse de robe*; as he denounces the moral turpitude of the priesthood.

This was strong stuff; there was nothing else like it in its time. Even his "rival," Voltaire, never launched such a broadside attack on the upper classes. Indeed, the Patriarch maintained a considerable stake in the society whose abuses he so courageously denounced. Whereas Piron turned buffoon, thus opting out of the mainstream. Viewed from the fringes, every part of the establishment becomes fair game; nothing is sacred, except perhaps the simple, earthy values Piron associated with the lower classes, and the integrity of his own engaging role as Arlequin.

Looking back over the other works that were considered in this chapter, we may certainly conclude that there was potential subversion at the *foire*, a great deal of it, taking many different forms: utopias, clowning, parodies, direct attacks, and so on. And yet, at least until the appearance of Sedaine in the late 1750s, subversion at the *foire* was always held in suspension as play-acting, ready to be dissipated, blown away in the spirit of song and laughter – even as it is in *Arlequin-Deucalion*. For, at the end of Piron's play, just after the last crescendo of criticism against the upper classes, the clown expressly and symbolically tells all the newly created sons and daughters to join hands with one another: all are united in the harmonious pleasures of the finale. Comedy prevails, or, to quote the last line of *Le Mariage de Figaro*, "Tout finit par des chansons."

Collé, in his lively journal, was surely right: Piron has qualities Voltaire never dreamed of: he is so much more inventive (and what an astonishing departure from classical traditions, this three-act, non-stop improvisation!), earthy, amiable, even prophetic. But then the witty, the elegant, the incomparable Voltaire, just like the not-so-witty-and-elegant Bayle before him, was one of those unique individuals destined by history to change the way people think.

4

Crispin's inventions

Even before Hegel had given the theme such a grandiose philosophical setting in his *Phenomenology*, numerous individuals in the late eighteenth and early nineteenth centuries had been aware of the special importance of the master–slave (valet) relationship for the literature of Enlightenment, and today it has become a commonplace of theatrical criticism to cite the developing drama one observes in the social oppositions, as one goes from Molière to Beaumarchais, that is, from the fascinating complexities in the tensions between master and valet as depicted by the greatest writer of the seventeenth century, to the end of the trail, which is the revolutionary impudence that explodes in *Le Mariage de Figaro* (1784). Unfortunately for literary historians, however, in between these poles the course is anything but steady, and "progress" toward the emancipation of the valet at the master's expense is anything but regular. In Marivaux there is positive backsliding, while the author dallies and toys with the possibility of raising the valets out of their menial positions, only to lock them finally into a social machinery whose functioning assumes they will be content to stay in their place as inferiors. In a playwright such as Le Sage we find a different sort of muddying of the waters: this author, fully aware of the social potentialities of the situations he creates, nevertheless appears to be taking perverse enjoyment in deliberately refusing to let his master–valet relationship produce the kind of contrary tension these elements would develop later – despite a grandly deceptive hint in the title that they would do just that. To be sure, with this clever and calculating author one must ever be on one's guard against being taken in. But before entering into the details of the matter, the discussion must move just a bit further upstream.

Playwrights seeking to subvert or enliven life's banalities in eighteenth-century France could draw on a whole battery of clown characters for their comedies – most of them Italian, and deriving specifically from the *commedia dell'arte* traditions. But two very famous clowns were French: Pierrot, who was so popular he has survived until today, albeit now endowed with romantic traits he did not originally possess. And then, Crispin, who originated in the seventeenth century, maintained a respectable following in the eighteenth, and is still remembered, chiefly because Alain René Le Sage immortalized him in one of his most accomplished creations at the Comédie Française (before his famous move to the *foire*): *Crispin rival de son maître*. This play, staged while Louis XIV was still alive (1707), is an amazingly bold work of social criticism, as scholars have already noted.[1] In terms of theatricality it is also extraordinarily interesting, as I hope to suggest.

What a sordid plot! Valère, the handsome, young, aristocratic suitor, is apparently motivated solely by money as he goes after the rich man's daughter, Angélique. At least this is what his valet, Crispin, says to him, and he doesn't protest in the slightest. For the rest, hounded by his creditors, Valère has already resorted to the most tawdry devices to get cash: using a wealthy Marquise's affection (lust?) for him to pay an alleged debt to his tailor, when actually he and the tailor are in league to bilk her for all they can; dishonest manoeuvers to borrow money against dubious collateral. ... Morally, he is no better than his own quite unscrupulous valet, so that it is hard to feel indignant when we find Crispin scheming with another servant-friend, La Branche, to betray Valère, and get rich themselves.

At this point the plot gets a little complicated, by modern standards. No doubt we should have been raised on the knotty tangles of the pretenders to the Spanish throne, *c.* 1701, as Le Sage's generation had been, or, at least, have spent our childhoods watching the fantastic complications of the comedies at the *foire*. To enjoy Le Sage's play, one has to be ready to swallow anything, and fortunately, as the play proceeds, the impudent buoyancy of the author's style lifts us effortlessly over all the plot involvements.

Thus far we have encountered only one pair of lovers: aristocratic, debt-ridden Valère, and rich, bourgeois Angélique; meanwhile the two valets, Crispin and La Branche, are busily scheming to get the money for themselves. Actually, they intend to capitalize on a situation so perfectly suited to their talent for creative improvisations one would think fate had deliberately placed it in their path: Angélique has had another suitor, in fact a fiancé, named Damis, who lived in Chartres. This pair had been as good as married: contracts had been drawn up; all that remained was the paying of the dowry. But then, suddenly, the fiancé reneged: Damis found himself forced into a shot-gun wedding with a noble lady from Chartres whom he had gotten pregnant (an occurrence that is repeatedly brought to our attention during the course of the comedy). In fact, La Branche had been sent from Chartres to bring the urgent message that the wedding with Damis had been called off because the groom was already married to someone else. The contracts were to be annulled, and the obviously large dowry would not be coming out of the coffers.

This was what set Crispin's fertile imagination to work: suppose he, Crispin, were to impersonate the erstwhile fiancé and pretend he had just arrived from Chartres to marry Angélique? The wedding was scheduled for that very day; La Branche even had the groom's wedding attire with him. It was merely a question of putting on the clothes and getting through the few hours before the dowry was counted out, at which point he (perhaps accompanied by his accomplice, though this is not so sure) would slip out of town and head for the border.

It is clear that this extravagant scheme – in the play's own terms – could never have succeeded, and Crispin's clownish make-up and costume constantly showing through the groom's clothing are reminders of the fact that the impersonation can't work. Obviously, Valère will recognize Crispin and tell everyone that he is not Damis; furthermore, Valère is a close friend of Damis who had informed him by letter of his marriage to the other girl in Chartres; besides, Damis' father is about to arrive in town to convey the news of the annulment in person; we note too, that Angélique didn't even want to marry the real Damis (whom she had never seen), and her objections are likely to grow far stronger when confronted with this vulgar clown who spends most of his time flirting with her mother. In addition . . . But why go on? The humor and dramatic interest of the comedy lie in watching the doomed, but sometimes inspired, efforts of the two valets to stave off the mountainous evidence pressing more and more weightily on the fragile surface of their unlikely bubble that by all the laws of reason should have popped long ago and exposed them for what they were: fakes.

What saves them time and again in the various crises that dot the action of the play turns out to be the laws, written and not written, of *vraisemblance*, a notion that, like so many literary phenomena in the eighteenth century, was turning unexpectedly problematic.[2] The word itself meant literally, of course, *giving the appearance, or illusion, of truth*, and everyone agreed that it was essential to any idea of theatricality. According to the grand classical tradition, it was assumed that *vraisemblance* reflected the truths of nature at the same time as it followed the rules of art, each having equal importance in the production of the whole. This combination of nature and art was thought to explain the extraordinary integrity we experience in the greatest dramatic poems of Racine and Corneille. In the eighteenth century, the concept was becoming unbalanced, shifting generally in the direction of all the rules, contrivances, and formulae that were thought to compose an "art." (Critics find these easier to talk about than the elusive qualities of nature; minor authors like to cling to them.) In extreme cases, playwrights seemed to feel that, natural or not, anything could be made believable (*vraisemblable*) provided the right rules were being observed.

No doubt the "doctrine" of *vraisemblance* had numerous components and definitions, and it might be approached from several different points of view, but judging by the *practice* of eighteenth-century playwrights, one of the ingredients thought to be most essential in producing *vraisemblance* was *consistency*.[3] Put bluntly, it was their conviction that if each line spoken by each *personnage* was entirely consistent with the character he or she was supposed to be, and also with the given dramatic situation (no easy task), this would infallibly produce the illusion of truth, i.e., *vraisemblance*, and at the same time the audience would be bound to believe in it. There is a real shift in emphasis here, if one looks back to the preceding century. Certainly, in Corneille and Racine consistency in this sense was assumed to be necessary, and classical authors were ready to justify their characters' behavior according to this criterion. But in the age of Voltaire the rules of consistency became to a greater degree the *means* by which the illusion was attained.

Today we are not always so impressed with the results: consistency spreads like some awful pall over Piron's empty tragedy, *Gustave-Wasa*, whereas in its day this work was highly respected, perhaps actually enjoyed, and certainly thought to be a well-sustained dramatic illusion.[4] Even if one takes the most successful eighteenth-century tragedy, Voltaire's *Zaïre*, one senses how much the author is banking not merely on the powerful set of characters he has created, and on the pathos of his heroine's plight, but on the seamless consistency of every line spoken: perhaps if the consistency is totally airtight, sheer lack of oxygen will keep the audience from rising in rebellion against the unlikelihoods of the basic plot.

O rage! O désespoir! O vieillesse ennemie!

moans the helpless father of Corneille's most famous hero, in a scene everyone who went to the theatre in the eighteenth century knew by heart.

. . . ô trahison! ô rage! / O comble des forfaits!

moans the equally helpless hero of *Alzire* (ii, 6) by Voltaire. As readers of Voltaire's tragedies had long been aware, examples of such much-too-close-to-be-coincidental imitations of Corneille or Racine are legion,[5] and one of the many reasons Voltaire was so eager to fit these hemistichs from famous classical plays into his own dramatic system was that, provided he could have the lines spoken in dramatic contexts resembling those created by the original authors, their efficacy was proven. Though their power might have dimmed slightly with the passing of time, these lines were magic formulae that could invariably be counted on to light up and sustain his own dramatic illusions with tested *vraisemblance*. Needless to say, Voltaire saw to it that they were so exactly, so marvelously suited to the theatrical situation he was creating, the audience had no choice but to go along.

Actually we have not wandered so far away from the topic at hand as it might appear, for in our comedy by Le Sage, the valets, Crispin and La Branche, are playwrights, too, of a sort, staging their own – very unlikely – illusion for the other characters. Just as in a tragedy, the fiction on which

Crispin's inventions

these two "authors" rely is that if only they can present their deceit in a way that has internal consistency (thus producing *vraisemblance*) the other characters have no choice but to believe in it; their "audience" will automatically be hoodwinked. The trick is to find just the right words at the right time. If they can, the valets will have total control over the illusions they are creating, no matter how objectively absurd the whole contraption may appear to us – the very real, sophisticated spectators who see behind everything, of course.

Surrounded by so many sharp pins of reality ready to prick the bubble of their deception, their task is not easy. Let us consider, for example, Crispin, appearing for the first time in the groom's finery, nervously engaged in finding suitably flowery compliments with which to greet his pretended parents-in-law-to-be, just as the real groom would have done:

Ma joie est extrême de pouvoir vous témoigner l'extrême joie que j'ai de vous embrasser.
(scene 9)

he declares to the father of the bride, barely making it to the end of the sentence, coming close to bogging down permanently in his compliment. One more "extrême joie" or "joie extrême" and he would have looked like a fool. Of course his mistake was in throwing all the logs on the fire at once: "joie" already goes pretty far, and "extrême" is by definition perched on the outer edge and leaves no room for further advance. Perhaps he will be doomed to spend the rest of the scene revolving round and round with the same immutable adjective welded, bonded, cemented to the noun that says it all. But fortunately for him, no one ever notices his near blunder, first, because he diverts attention by flirting with the mother of the bride, and second, for the very good reason that, even though he almost gets stuck with them, he has found two words that were just exactly right for the situation, so that no one has any choice but to believe they emanate from the person for whom they are so well suited: a real groom.

Also helping him through this difficult moment was another critical element working in his favor, namely, the fact that he knew quite precisely the kind of words he was expected to say, the kind of syllables he was to pronounce. This was an advantage he sorely missed, a moment later, after La Branche had left him alone with the bridal party, in order to arrange for the horses to assure their getaway (it always tempts fate, to count the chickens before they are hatched). Suddenly the father of the bride inquires about the lawsuit the real groom's father has been deeply involved in. Lawsuit? Crispin finds himself obliged to manufacture syllables relating to a complicated situation he never heard of. Since La Branche is not there to help, he has to brazen it out, and wisely realizes that the best way to get rid of this uncomfortable topic, and put it behind him, is to pretend the suit is over. He simply announces that the suit has been won – and the strategy works like a charm. Not only the father of the bride, but the mother, too, declares herself most satisfied to hear the good news. Crispin is just in the clear when unfortunately he makes the mistake of not leaving it at that. Perhaps he feels it is a little early to drop this obviously consequential topic, or perhaps he suffers a spell of overconfidence. Whatever the reason, he finds himself improvising further reflections on how much it meant to his father to win, how much money it had cost, but then (fatal garrulousness, that, given the crook saying the words, is just asking heaven for trouble), justice is such an excellent thing, it's worth any price. . . . Whereupon, he utters one syllable that looks so innocent it couldn't hurt anyone, but which suddenly rears up and throws his whole feigned identity into jeopardy: he refers to the alleged opponent in the lawsuit as "[le] plus grand chicaneur [. . .] de tous les hommes." "Men???" But the real opponent in the real lawsuit was a *woman*. The real father made that very clear, so what is he talking about? Suddenly all is crisis.

Actually the situation is not hopeless, if only because Crispin has learned, albeit through a dangerous blunder, a magic syllable – *femme* – that he can attach to his phrases, and that will brighten everything with *vraisemblance*. All he needs is a verbal extension cord; even "homme" will light up, too, as we see:

Oui, sa partie était une femme, d'accord, mais cette femme avait dans ses intérêts un certain vieux Normand qui lui donnait conseils. C'est cet homme-là qui a fait bien de la peine à mon père [. . .] (scene 10)

The point is that, provided one observes the main law of *vraisemblance*, "homme" is just as serviceable as "femme." In fact, since both of them are the merest illusions anyway, they are actually interchangeable. Any word would do: even "chien" might have been used instead, if only Crispin had known enough about the "real" lawsuit to make it fit. The play's verbal surface is so thin, meaning is so lacking in depth and weight as to skim off into meaninglessness.

In this connection, if one wanted to pick out the single most important trait of this comedy, perhaps one might choose slipperiness, for, even in the language of the play, the syllables are constantly sliding in and out of place, just as "homme" slides in for "femme," and then Damis, the suitor from Chartres, slips in and out of the wedding (and into bed with another girl at the last moment), while Crispin tries to slip into his place, and into Valère's place, alternating giddily between fake suitor and valet. Aristocratic Valère slides far down the social scale in his sordid conduct, as we saw (his name almost rhymes with "valet"), while the real valet, La Branche, sliding up the scale, describes his recent *fourberies* using a *précieux* language that makes him sound positively upper class. And frictionless substitutions are everywhere in this well-oiled comedy: naturally the two valets can change places whenever they wish, one taking over for the other, but even the mother of the bride – whose youth obviously belongs to a distant past – can stand in for her daughter, blushing prettily at the fake groom's compliments, and acting positively nubile when he assures her he would have preferred her instead.

In the supple manipulations of *vraisemblance*, one of the most daring strategies is invented by La Branche to get himself out of an especially tight corner (scene 14) – a problem, incidentally, that the audience could see coming for some time. We had already learned that Valère was supposed to be personally acquainted with Damis, who had informed him by letter of his sudden marriage to the other woman in Chartres. Naturally we expect that Valère will tell Angélique that Damis is already married – so she is free to marry him, Valère. Naturally, too, the father of the bride will be informed of the other wedding, and will confront La Branche with the facts and denounce him as the deceiver he is. This is the tight corner mentioned above.

Faced with the father's accusation, La Branche first pretends that, far from admitting guilt, he cannot even understand what the father is talking about. This rather weak ploy fails; indeed the father threatens to summon the police commissioner, a clear and present danger that inspires La Branche to reach new heights of invention: just who was it, he asks the father, told him about Damis' marriage to the girl in Chartres? Valère? But of course, that explains everything: Valère is himself in love with Angélique and wants to marry her. He dreamed up the false story and forged a letter to make it seem plausible. Enter Crispin, who plays along, adding that Valère did it all to get the dowry. Everyone knows about Valère's debt; the creditors are pounding on the door. Meanwhile, there are roars of laughter from La Branche (What a devil, that Valère!), grand hilarity from the father (Imagine that young fellow thinking he could put something over on a clever person like me!); and rather nervous spasms of laughter from Crispin (Ha! Ha! Ha! But it was a close call, and the news about Damis' wedding may cause trouble yet!).

La Branche's strategy flawlessly conforms to the laws of *vraisemblance*. First, his story all hangs together because there is so much allegedly certifiable "truth" in it. Most of the events "really" happened that way: indeed there is supposed to be a suitor; in fact, there are supposed to be two suitors pursuing Angélique. There is a forged document making it all seem possible, too (just like the text of the play by Le Sage). The father is being hoodwinked into a false belief (not unlike the audience in the theatre), just as La Branche stated, and Valère is depicted as being in debt, and hence very interested in the dowry. Of course, much of the "truth" of the story applies to themselves, the valets, rather than to Valère; it is essentially the tale of their own *fourberie*, "falsely" attributed to Valère, that La Blanche is relating. But actually it doesn't matter to whom, if anyone, the events "happened." It suffices that they have the ring of truth. Since the *vraisemblance* is flawless, the success is assured: the indignant father on the spot wants to advance the hour of the wedding, so as to thwart Valère and his creditors all the sooner. But the supreme masterstroke comes from Crispin, who even manages to convince Valère that the letter from Damis doesn't actually say what in fact it actually says. Illusion is so rampant, no one can know any more where the "real" truth lies.

To give another example: in a later scene (18), the two valets are discussing their getaway plans (a fateful topic that has already brought on one mishap, as we saw). Has La Branche procured the horses? He has. Crispin suggests that the Flanders road is the one they should take. Meanwhile La Branche stares off distractedly into the distance. No doubt he is looking in the very direction of their escape, imagining Crispin and himself on those galloping horses, money bags clanking with coinage, going so fast they're already just a speck in the distance . . . When suddenly the dream of their departure reverses itself and comes back toward them, walking on two rather elderly feet, coming right onstage. The speck in the distance La Branche has been staring at has turned into M. Orgon, La Branche's employer from Chartres, Damis' father, who has come to Paris expressly to break off his son's marriage in person. Obviously if the father of the ex-groom meets the father of the bride, the game will be up, and the two valets perform prodigies of ingenuity to keep each out of sight of the other. But their efforts are useless; they are beaten before they start: the two fathers' names are Orgon and Oronte, no one can keep that straight, or apart. They belong together, in fact they are virtually identical, so that it's the most natural thing in the world when, at the end of the play, Orgon slips into Oronte's place and takes the other man's wife off to the dance.

But the most curious illustration of slipperiness comes in scene eight, where La Branche tries to hand over to the father of the bride a forged letter supposedly written by Orgon in Chartres. This bit of *écriture* is a key piece in the construction of the illusion the valets are creating because it allegedly identifies and authenticates Crispin as the groom to be and gives a plausible explanation for Orgon's absence from the wedding of his own son. (He allegedly has the gout, which also is supposed to explain why the letter is written in an *écriture* so trembly it can hardly be deciphered, much less compared with any other specimen of his handwriting.) But oddly, at this critical moment, La Branche, three times in a row, either hands over, or almost starts to hand over, to the father wrong letters – letters addressed to other persons, for other purposes. It's a droll scene, to be sure, when the father, expecting an envelope addressed to himself, bearing his identity, is suddenly brought up short by:

Crispin's inventions

A Monsieur Craquet, médecin dans la rue du Sépulcre

which brings on the inevitable joke about a doctor making his residence in
the same quarter as his patients.

Again, La Branche pulls out a wrong envelope:

A Monsieur Bredouillet, avocat au Parlement, rue des Mauvaises Paroles

And there is still a third:

A Monsieur Gourmandin, Chanoine de . . .

Critics have been somewhat embarrassed by this part of the scene.[6] The
jokes on the envelopes are rather low comedy – one-liners; they interrupt
the action, and they are certainly gratuitous.

But perhaps that is just the point, for these letters don't belong in this
comedy at all. They suggest, in fact, other fictional possibilities, other plot
situations, other texts, écritures, that, had the envelopes been opened and the
letters actually read, might well replace the fictions at hand. Again there's a
slightly uneasy feeling about the momentary slippage, about a play whose
main plot is so loosely tied into place, whose characters are so inherently
light-weight – wobbly and inconsequential, like the weak-headed mother of
the bride – it wouldn't matter very much if they sailed off into other
situations and other identities. It begins to seem as if everything in this play,
from the syllables, words, and sentences, to the characters, the exposition,
and the outcome, might change places with something else, and this implies
a curious system of values working throughout the comedy in which everything is equal.

Perhaps not quite everything. For one factor at least seems to be standing
against the leveling forces in this brilliantly conceived comedy: after all, the
valets have deliberately created false roles for themselves. Crispin is not the
fiancé he claims, and La Branche, too, knows who is lying. Surely the one
element that cannot be abolished or interchanged is the basic opposition
between the "real" characters supposed to be concerned with real wed-
dings and real sons and daughters, and these mystifying clowns who
knowingly put on masks and hoodwink for purposes that are quite different
from the motives they feign.

This may seem like solid ground, yet even here the distinctions break
down (ultimately there are no distinctions in this play, even the one
between male and female is in jeopardy): for when the bubble finally bursts
and both valets' vraisemblance-producing syllables run out, when the jig
really is up and the culprits are forced to admit their guilt and tell the truth
about themselves, we suddenly find that, on the flimsiest of pretexts (it's all
supposed to be a gesture of gallantry toward the giddy, vain mother of the
bride) the valets have been not only pardoned by those they have deceived,
but instantly welcomed into the fold as business *partners*, friends, allies,

virtual members of the family. So that, at the end, the deceivers collapse into the deceived, and from the celerity and ease with which it happens one can only conclude that there never had been any real differences between them in the first place. Indeed nothing remains standing, the whole play has deconstructed – not that we have any time to think about it. For already the characters are going off to the wedding festivities, the curtain at the Comédie Française is falling, and the applause of the (at last) real audience reminds us that it was all fakery, anyway, fraudulence, clowning. The whole text is a forgery to make us believe in ersatz imitations, a pack of cards.

If one were still writing amid the critical modes of the 1960s or 1970s it might make a fitting conclusion to this discussion to observe that Le Sage's consciousness of the void beneath the words, constructing and deconstructing the scenes, makes his art seem astonishingly modern. But now that it is the 1980s, the emphasis naturally shifts: we move beyond the problematic confinements of language to note how many of the play's most ingratiating qualities depend on its origins in a time quite unlike our own, and also, how well this playful approach to illusion and theatricality at the Comédie Française was preparing Le Sage for his starring role as impudent librettist at the *foire*.

5

On Voltaire's *Mérope*

In contrast to playwrights of our own era, Voltaire preferred to start his tragedies with the loftiest affairs of state: with royal marriages that have taken, or are just about to take place, with political power that has been consolidated or is changing hands, with peace being restored, or war being declared, in short, with matters imperial. As a result, the human drama that follows has the grandest possible setting, and the psychological entanglements of the characters – the hatreds, jealousies, loves and loyalties – are seen not merely as personal involvements, but as part of a national situation as well. This insistence on the unbroken continuity between the psychological and the political is a classical trait, of course, Corneille and Racine having brought it to perfection. It is also clear that the phenomenon was a natural outgrowth of the aristocratic traditions of tragedy: if the principal characters are all royal, their affairs are, by definition, affairs of state, as any courtly audience would have understood. This point of view implicitly denies the cleavage which Rousseau and others in the eighteenth century were exploring, and which seems indispensable to us in the modern age, between the private individual and the public one: in classical tragedy, privacy is literally unthinkable, since everything, ultimately, belongs to the public weal; it is all onstage, just as the tragedy itself is. There are no corners in which to hide.

Voltaire's *Mérope* (1743) looks like an exception to the rule.[1] Though at the beginning the traditional confidante relays the usual, rather heavy dosage of affairs of state (peace has been restored, but Queen Mérope will have her hands full if she wants to keep her rightful place on the throne, for the tyrant Polyphonte is threatening to take over),[2] yet, strange to relate in a classical tragedy, Mérope appears to be turning her back on the whole business. She doesn't care a bit about the urgent situation that so clearly calls for energetic action if she is to preserve her right to rule. Mérope's concerns are of another nature entirely (or so it seems); it is not her status as Queen that matters, but solely and uniquely her role as MOTHER:

> Je suis mère . . .   (I, i, 36)

she declares in solemn, passionate tones, and instantly everything else –

thrones, wars, governments, successions, politics – dwindles to inconsequentiality by comparison.

It hardly needs to be pointed out that Voltaire was exploiting here a new trend in the eighteenth century as he so dramatically brought to the fore the sentiment of maternity. In fact the passions and lofty politics of traditional tragedy seem to be giving way, in Voltaire's play, to new and very intense sentiments *of a family nature*, and their appearance here in 1743 is particularly interesting because it precedes the great tide of middle-class sentimentality that would later flood into so many forms of literature and art.[3] In other words, the excitement surrounding the idea of motherhood at the opening of *Mérope* belongs to a general shift in social attitudes.

On the other hand, Mérope's maternal role here is rather peculiar in that, at the beginning, it seems to be playing itself out in a void. During the late civil wars Mérope's only surviving child, her son Egisthe, disappeared, having been taken off into hiding by the faithful Narbas. That was fifteen years ago (numerous characters remind us of these "quinze ans" during the course of the play). Since then, scarcely a word has been heard about him; just one letter from Narbas, received over four years ago, attested to the fact that the son was even alive. How can it be that this child, who vanished while a mere babe, whom Mérope scarcely knew, could still preoccupy her so much that she is willing to let an empire slip through her fingers rather than break out of her fixation about him? Mérope's own answer is that although Egisthe disappeared literally from sight, her heart has never ceased to see him, in remembrance:

> Mon cœur a vu toujours ce fils que je regrette;
> Ses périls nourissaient ma tendresse inquiète:
> Un si juste intérêt s'accrut avec le temps.   (I, i, 41–3)[4]

While normally we think of time dimming people's memories, here obviously an opposite effect occurs, and there is a special reason for the increase where one would expect diminution. The famous "quinze ans" have endowed Egisthe with one quality beyond price to Mérope: manhood, and, being a man, he is now old enough to *reign*. This is the key to all Mérope's behavior, so that, contrary to our earlier impression, there is no opposition between politics and maternity for this Queen. She is vitally concerned for the fate of the empire, but she wants it for her son, who is now of age to ascend the throne. Nothing else matters. Why does he not appear?

How instructive, in this connection, to compare Voltaire's play with the two main "sources" he himself admitted were standing in the background of his tragedy. One of them was a popular Italian tragedy, *Merope* by Scipione Maffei (1713), and Voltaire openly declared that his play was simply an adaptation of the Italian version, to make it conform to French tastes.[5] Maffei had written a number of maternal scenes similar to those that would characterize the *Mérope française*. Yet Maffei's play does not begin by putting Mérope's maternal instincts in the forefront of the action. In fact, Queen Merope is battling on a number of psychological fronts as she faces the tyrant Polyphonte in Maffei's opening scene (the Italian play begins with this confrontation). Her emotions are not simple, but diverse, and one of the main ones is the utter loathing she feels for the man she faces because she knows him to be the murderer of two of her sons, defenseless children, slaughtered in the most brutal fashion. In contrast, Voltaire's heroine does not yet know the identity of the slayer of one (sic) of her sons, and she is freer to give herself entirely to her positive motherly feelings as she converses with her confidante. This concentration on maternity would have had a modish appeal to Parisian audiences, as was suggested earlier. Such a simplification of psychological motives was also very much part of the French tragic tradition, allegedly deriving from Racine. By comparison, the texture of the Italian play seems slightly richer, and less uniform.

The other main "source" of Voltaire's tragedy was Racine's biblical play, *Athalie* (1691), which featured a lost "son," too, Joas, who had been hidden out of sight in the temple of the Israelites for eight long years, but was destined to overcome all the strategies of the enemies seeking to destroy him, and reign, just as Mérope's son would. According to Racine, God's Grace was the miracle that kept his hero alive amid so many perils, for it was the divine plan that this boy should survive and lead God's chosen people.

Voltaire professed high regard for Racine's play; however, he was not so certain that religion was one of its merits. He even hinted that the play was a masterpiece despite all the piety.[6] Naturally, when he came to compose *Mérope*, it never occurred to him to put in anything that would suggest Catholicism. On the other hand, his "son," Egisthe, though lost from sight in the desert, survives, almost miraculously, too, and from the opening scenes we sense that his quasi-supernatural survival emanates somehow from his mother.

> L'empire est à mon fils ...   (I, i, 53)[7]

she declares, even though she has almost nothing but his absence and his silence to go on. Pronouncements such as these are really acts of faith, themselves almost supernatural, and they convey to us the conviction that, somehow, what kept Egisthe alive was simply the power of Mérope's determination that he should live (even as his memory had sustained her). It was her will that, so to speak, grew him to manhood (even as she had grown him in her womb), and that, like a magnet, draws him to the throne where he will reign (even as Joas had done, for Racine). His appearance onstage will be, in effect, her creation, even as originally she created him at birth. Perhaps this also implies that in composing *Mérope* Voltaire did not so much omit the role of Grace, as convert it into something else: the irresist-ible power of mother love. Needless to say, this in turn relates to a third source of power, which is the author's own creative act: Mérope's long-sustained determination forms the substance of Voltaire's play; his creation *is* her creation of a son–king.

Mérope's resolve that her son will reign goes back (fifteen years) to a specific event that set the course of her destiny forever. She recalls it (i, i), speaking with her confidante, in a very accomplished description (Voltaire was a master of this kind of *récit* – which had innumerable classical prece-dents, of course). In her mind's eye, Mérope sees again the nightmare: the palace is filled with the sound of voices crying out to save the king, his wife, his sons. There is blood on the walls, the portals are in flames, women are being crushed under the weight of the smoking panels, the slaves are fleeing, and all around her, she says, are tumult, fear, torches and death. Amid this general disarray, the figure of her husband, King Cresphonte, appears, bathed in his own blood, filthy with dust. And now the moment that will determine the rest of her life: he turns his dying eye upon her – but English can never do what the French does:

Tournant encor vers moi sa mourante paupière,[8]

and he expires even as he embraces her:

Cresphonte en expirant me serra dans ses bras.   (i, i, 70–1)[9]

The instant Cresphonte dies, our attention turns to the children, two sons, mere babes, and apparently twins. They too are bloody as they lean, propped against their father, and they try to lift their arms as if in supplica-tion to be saved from the assassins. Only one of them, Egisthe, will escape alive, thanks to the protection of Hercules, and to the faithful Narbas who spirits him away. But meanwhile, Cresphonte's last look, the dying eyelid, has bequeathed to the Queen a sacred trust, and the almost miraculous saving of the infant, baptized in his father's blood, makes clear which way her duty lies.

We are still in the opening scene of Voltaire's tragedy, but already casting a shadow over the action is the villain of the piece, Polyphonte, whose name was pronounced for the first time shortly before the lines we have been considering. We know, too, that he is Mérope's rival for control of the empire; in fact elections are about to be held and Polyphonte's chances of winning look excellent. According to Voltaire's version of the play, we have not yet learned – nor does Mérope know – that Polyphonte is also guilty of the assassination of Mérope's husband; for in fact Polyphonte did murder Cresphonte, though he managed to keep the deed secret. (Was that what Cresphonte's dying lid was trying to tell her?) Nor was it mere chance that tradition made the names of the two men – Polyphonte,

Cresphonte – so rhymingly similar: Polyphonte will attempt to replace Cresphonte not only by winning the election, but by persuading the widow to become his queen in marriage. The plot of the whole play will begin to turn around his efforts to replace his murdered victim both as king and as husband.

During much of the action Polyphonte behaves as if he had the upper hand, and he will make a blustery show of strength that at moments intimidates Mérope (though it never affects Egisthe who, like Racine's Joas, never wavers). Yet clearly the tyrant is unacceptable as a replacement for Cresphonte, and neither Voltaire, nor Mérope, nor Egisthe, nor the audience will have any part of him. Even if one could believe his lying words about how much service in combat he has performed, and how proud he is to have earned the throne by his own deeds, he would not be an acceptable mate for Mérope, if only because, as she harshly reminds him again and again, he does not have Cresphonte's royal blood in his veins – only Egisthe has that.

It is no doubt the "call" of this blood that brings Mérope so close to recognizing Egisthe when he at last appears, even though he has been given another name for his protection, by the faithful Narbas. Nevertheless, the instant she meets him (II, ii) she comes within an inch of finding his true identity, simply because her (maternal) feelings are so stirred and she is so strongly drawn to him by instinct. Paradoxically, this aroused mother also comes within an inch of killing her son (III, iv) when she gullibly believes the story spread by the false tyrant, that this young man, far from being Egisthe, is Egisthe's murderer. Of course this was traditionally considered one of the two most exciting scenes in the play: the moment when Mérope, who has been longing for her son for so many years, rushes toward him with dagger raised, bent on murder. . . . Such drama! Such irony! To think that she is only acting out of love for the son she is about to kill! Unfortunately for us, Freud has ruined most of the fun of such moments, since mistakes such as this one by Mérope are just the sort he has revealed to be secret desires, usually unmentionable, heavily disguised. We will not enter into the tangle of complicated motives opened up by such a psychiatric reading. For present purposes it will suffice to infer from what actually transpires in this scene that Mérope's mother love, for all its intensity, has a dangerous, even lethal side to it, and that for just an instant, as she raised her dagger against Egisthe, Mérope was acting on behalf of the tyrant and in effect doing away with his rival. We are supposed to believe that the unthinkable almost happened: if it hadn't been for the faithful Narbas' miraculous appearance out of nowhere at the last second to stay her hand, the plot might have gone off the rails entirely, or, worse, gone into reverse, so that the tyrant came out on top.

This uncomfortably close call makes us doubly grateful for the other most famous scene (IV, ii): Mérope had been trying to keep Egisthe's identity a secret, fearing quite rightly for his life if ever the tyrant spotted his rival. But by one of those quirks of fate Voltaire invented as often as he could for his tragedies, it turns out that Polyphonte, claiming he believed the young man in question was Egisthe's murderer, but also sensing something rather suspicious in Mérope's flustered behaviour, orders the guards to kill him. Cornered, and with no other recourse, Mérope now goes into action. What a gaudy moment it must have made in Mlle Dumesnil's original performance. Voltaire describes[10] how she flung herself, actually running across the whole length of the stage under Polyphonte's gaze, tears in her eyes, brow grown pale, sobbing, arms outstretched, and how at last, as Mérope interposed her own maternal body between her son and the weapons of the guards, she gave the unforgettable cry –

Barbare! Il est mon fils.   (IV, ii, 960)[11]

– one of the only lines in eighteenth-century tragedy that everyone agreed was destined for immortality. This is a recognition scene, of course, and a double one: Egisthe recognizes the woman who just moments before had tried to stab him as his mother, and their reunion carries with it all the bliss and pathos sentimental eighteenth-century audiences could wish for. But the identification of the lost son has revealed him to the enemy and placed him at the tyrant's mercy, just as anguished Mérope had been dreading. Polyphonte, with his usual bluster, promptly announces that he will have Egisthe put to death unless he agrees to be legally adopted as Polyphonte's son, to subject himself to Polyphonte's governance, and to see Polyphonte marry Mérope and rule with her on the throne. In other words, the price of existence for Egisthe is the agreement that Polyphonte shall do everything his late father once did.

Of course Polyphonte's demands are extravagant and his scheme won't work. Egisthe will never submit; we have already seen enough of his manly pride to know that. And so, in act V, when the "wedding party" straggles off to the temple where Polyphonte thinks he will marry Mérope and receive Egisthe's submission in pomp and splendor before the whole populace, we in the audience are left waiting with the kind of dread and expectation we feel in Corneille's *Polyeucte*, just before the hero, receiving an extra large dose of heavenly Grace, bursts out into violence and starts smashing all the pagan idols – offstage, of course. The blood and violence in *Mérope* are offstage, also, and for us it happens only in the mind's eye, as we listen to Isménie's breathless *récit* (V, vi). But what an extraordinary drama she paints, what a grandiose, horrific spectacle is evoked in Voltaire's slightly cramped Alexandrines, with their all-too-familiar rhymes.[12] Just as in Mérope's earlier description of the death of Cresphonte, the scene will be full of crowds crying out in dismay (the thunder of their voices can even be

barbare ! il eſt mon ſils.

Merope Act. 4. Sc. 2

14. J. M. Moreau, le jeune, scene from Voltaire's *Mérope*. Engraving (1783)

heard by the audience). But as Isménie tells the story, we see, first, sad Mérope, her head crowned with flowers for the ceremony, advancing toward the altar glittering in the light of torches. Suddenly there is a movement, someone is darting forward – Egisthe, of course, and before anyone can stop him, he seizes not a dagger, not a sword, not even a spear, but the axe (*la hache*) kept at hand for religious ceremonies, and strikes Polyphonte to the ground. Treacherous Erox, too, is laid low, when he tries to take vengeance. But now, Polyphonte revives enough to wound Egisthe, and, bizarre touch, their flowing blood mingles in a single stream. Polyphonte's guard, loyal to the tyrant, springs into action and would have killed Egisthe were it not for Mérope who again shields her son from their weapons and bravely reveals herself to be his mother and their Queen. Her loyal friends rush to her aid, and suddenly all is confusion, in fact the scene simply dissolves into a great blur (again reminiscent of Cresphonte's death) of running crowds, of altars overthrown and their débris scattered in the streams of blood, of children crushed in their mothers' arms, of soldiers, priests, and friends dying on top of each other. There is trampling on the bodies of the fallen, while great surging masses of people are hurtled from one end of the temple to the other, back and forth, again and again. Finally, the vast throng swallows Mérope and her son from sight, so that at the end of the *récit* their fate remains uncertain. (They have survived, of course.)

What a pity that the music and verse forms of decadent romanticism were so far off in the future, and that Voltaire insisted on snipping his lines so primly into Alexandrine lengths. The forceful qualities of the scene barely have a chance amid so many traditional constraints. Nevertheless, despite these confines, Voltaire is going as far as he ever would go to achieve an effect that cannot be accounted for by the precepts of classicism such as he understood and preached them: the deliberate blurring of outlines, the wild movement of the hysterical crowds, the mindless massacres, the streams of blood, all this takes us into an insane world closer to the surrealists than to the Age of Reason. Above all, Egisthe's bloody axe – it will actually be brought onstage for the final scene – strikes a lurid note and gives a nightmarish tone to everything that follows. How one longs for Richard Strauss' indecent harmonies and shrieking crescendos! They would have done so much to bring out the unnatural horror of this scene, and Strauss would have relished, too, all the "sordid" Oedipal implications that are quite visible if one takes the trouble to peer behind the clipped hedges of Voltaire's Alexandrines. For of course with that bloody axe Egisthe has murdered the man who was trying to marry his mother and become his father. As he killed him, Egisthe was baptized in the false father's blood, even as he had been in that of his real father, and this rite has prepared him to assume all the King's roles. To make things perfect, the tyrant's corpse, covered with a bloody robe, will be brought onstage for the

15. Gabriel de Saint-Aubin, "*Mérope*, acte 5e"

final scene, so that Egisthe claims his mother for himself and prepares to mount the throne with her, in full view of the man he is replacing:

Allons monter au trône, en y plaçant ma mère . . .   (line 1401)[13]

This is the climax: Egisthe now rises with his mother, his Queen, in a kind of apotheosis of their relationship, while, for those of a Freudian persuasion, the moment reveals implications that would seem undeniably Oedipal, at least on a symbolic level. No doubt we must assume that Voltaire was not actually conscious of all these implications, yet he must have felt especially pleased with himself as he boasted everywhere that he had succeeded in writing a tragedy in which there was no love interest at all, from which love was totally absent. To make doubly certain no one missed the point, he got the Reverend Father Tournemine to back him up in a prefatory epistle.[14]

All the pieces of this accomplished tragedy fit into place, except two. The first is easily explained: Voltaire confuses his own French version with the Italian version when he occasionally has a character refer to *two* sons of Mérope who were killed (a third having escaped).[15] Actually he had reduced the number to *one* son killed, a second having escaped – another instance of simplifying for French audiences what could be more complex for Italians. But the second mistake is truly incomprehensible: we all know that Egisthe and faithful Narbas have been gone for exactly fifteen years. There can be no question about this number. Isménie, Mérope, Polyphonte, Narbas, and Voltaire himself (in his preface) have all confirmed it.[16] Even Maffei wrote of the *quindici anni*.[17] How then are we to explain that faithful Narbas, who never lies, and who elsewhere refers to the *quinze ans*, also declares, concerning Egisthe –

Je l'ai conduit, seize ans, de retraite en retraite . . .?   (III, v, 801)[18]

Sixteen years! The word *seize* is not a rhyme position, which might justify the alteration; nor does it have either more or less syllables than *quinze* to make the Alexandrine correct; the use of the right number would not have created a cacophony with the surrounding syllables, nor is Narbas given to stretching the facts. Nothing in the immediate context accounts for the error. But then, the rules of *vraisemblance*, for conscientious authors, *are* a sort of slavery: to compose five acts (1402 lines in this case) in which every single word belongs perfectly with every other word is a discipline without mercy. Perhaps one should expect that a few syllables will go astray. Such is human nature. And yet for this reader the inexplicable, inconceivable *seize* also suggests the one small slip which according to legend even the smartest criminals make, and that gives their strategies away. Evidence has come to light implying that the *seize* may be an unconscious borrowing from a famous tragedy by Corneille, a tragedy for which Voltaire had composed elaborate commentaries,[19] criticizing it on various counts, one of them being the unlikelihood that so many years, *seize ans*, should have elapsed between the hero's murder of his own father and his reappearance in Thebes, where he married his mother. In other words, *seize ans* had been one of the disapproved features of Corneille's *Oedipe*.[20] In the most literal sense, Voltaire's slip was Oedipal. To my mind this curious flaw is a tip pointing to the fact that nothing in this so-called tragedy-without-love is quite what it seems, and that Voltaire's determined efforts to make his play conform to aristocratic propriety – the relentless high style, the exclusive concern with royal destinies, the refusal to admit anything that might be extraneous to the main action – actually bears a contrapuntal relationship to the daring underside of his dramatic enterprise.

Indeed, the "forme" acts as a cover-up for the "fond"; but more than this, the constantly implied denial of any indecency (a denial we find implied in both the style and the structure of the work) is probably what made the "indecency" possible in the first place. Rather like Abbé Prévost before him, the author could never have allowed himself to create such a sensational plot unless he accompanied it with endless testimonials (both stylistic and formal, and directed as much to himself as to the audience) guaranteeing that all such thoughts could not be further from his mind. Thus, through a rather perverse operation of opposite motivations, the denial permits the existence of its contrary[21] – just as in eighteenth-century music, the exquisite purity of the melody on top may actually depend for its life, and even for its character, on the coarse rumblings, the raucous rattles of the bass line, down below.

In *Mérope* all the disparate elements, the decencies and the indecencies, still fit together, and yet, seen from a historical vantage point, Voltaire's play appears to be pointing towards an inevitable fracture between moral values and formal ones in the theatre. Actually, I don't think subsequent playwrights chose to exploit this division very much. On the contrary, the aim of the new bourgeois theatre was to lower the high level of style associated with traditional tragedy, and at the same time, to "elevate" the moral tone. As a result, Voltaire's ambiguities (duplicities?) simply ceased to exist.

6

On the background of Rousseau's First Discourse

One of the most surprising and neglected of Rousseau's poetical works is the little opera libretto entitled *The Discovery of the New World* (*La Découverte du nouveau monde*)[1] written when the author was still under the influence of Mme de Warens, sometime between 1739 and 1741. In the *Confessions* Rousseau states that he also composed music for parts of it,[2] but this has not survived, and we are left with the words alone, which tell quite a story.

The scene of the opera proper (I omit the prologue, which presents special problems)[3] is set among the American Indians of the Isle of Guanahan in the Antilles. As the opera opens we see onstage the native Chieftain who has come to the Sacred Grove to pray among the idols that, Rousseau informs us, are set up on rough-hewn tree trunks. From the Chieftain's monologue we learn that the populace is in an uproar; even he, the intrepid leader, has become afraid. People have been hearing and seeing omens of some dire peril to come: the sacred idols have been bellowing predictions of doom, and a bloody star has appeared in the sky, bringing fear. Enter the Chieftain's beloved wife. She too sings of the anguish that has gripped everyone, and begs her husband to abandon the panicky populace: if they flee they may at least save their own lives. But the brave Chieftain not only rejects her suggestion, he is deeply offended at such cowardly advice: he will never forsake his people even if it means being separated from his wife. And now the dramatic tension increases: priests appear, there are choruses and even dances of alarm. Rumors say the land is about to be invaded. Finally the High Priest, his eyes piercing the night of time, utters a solemn prediction:

> Cacique infortuné
> Tes exploits sont flétris, ton règne est terminé;
> Ce jour en d'autres mains fait passer ta puissance.
> Tes Peuples asservis sous un joug odieux
> Vont perdre pour jamais les plus chers dons des Dieux,
> Leur liberté, leur innocence.[4]

In his vision, he now addresses the conquerors:

> Fiers enfants du Soleil, vous triomphez de nous
> Vos arts sur nos Vertus vous donnent la Victoire . . .[5]   (p. 827)

From the wings, a chorus sings in disarray of the appearance of winged monsters (i.e., sailing ships) on the sea; one hears cries of alarm offstage, and the Chieftain, despite his wife's imploring protests, rushes off to save his people. Thus our sympathies are entirely with the endangered Americans as the act ends.

Nothing could be more unexpected, more dramatic, more startling than the change from the end of act I with its rumblings of doom, the stage empty, save for the pathetic figure of the Chieftain's wife bewailing her fate in solitude, and the opening of act II. Suddenly the stage becomes crowded with brightly costumed men and women of Spain who disembark from their ships to the sound of trumpets and drums. We can imagine the brilliance and grandeur of the opening chorus – presumably in D major – that Rousseau planned for this moment, as all the Spaniards sing:

> Triomphons, triomphons sur la terre et sur l'onde,
> Donnons des Lois à l'Univers.
> Notre audace en ce jour découvre un nouveau monde.
> Il est fait pour porter nos fers.[6]   (p. 828)

Enter Christopher Columbus (!) bearing a sword and the standard of Castille. Clearly he represents Civilization with a large C. In verses that defy decent translation he sings of these climes that enrich nature, but have been unknown to what he calls "humans," and too much neglected by heaven. Planting the flag of possession in the earth, he sings an apostrophe to the land he is now declaring the territory of Spain:

> Perdez la liberté; mais portez sans murmure
> Un joug encor plus précieux.[7]   (p. 829)

Turning to his countrymen and women he tells them to celebrate this day: may their pleasure lead to the path of glory. May their enchanting pastimes (again the verses defy translation) shine forth on all sides, dazzling the eyes of this savage people. These last lines are taken up by the chorus. Meanwhile there is festive dancing, and more singing by a Spanish girl whose verses suggest that captivity may not be such a bad thing after all, since the "yoke" and "fetters" will be those of love.

And indeed, the next moment, Columbus' first officer, who has been singing some rather nasty lines about spreading terror and ravaging the countryside, catches sight of a lovely American girl and is instantly smitten by her beauty. The would-be conqueror now finds himself the prisoner of her charms:

> Que serviront icy la valleur et les armes?
> C'est à nous d'y porter les fers.[8]   (p. 831)

95

16. J. M. Moreau, le jeune, engraved illustration for Rousseau's *La Découverte du nouveau monde*

Suddenly we realize that the system of values we accepted in act I has been turned topsy-turvy: the enemy is no longer the enemy: they are desirable friends: bondage is no longer evil. Imagining the beautiful costumes, the singing, the elegant dances, we realize that these "arts" which are expressly designated as instruments of subjugation may actually be rather enjoyable. There are compensations for the loss of that innocence so highly prized in act I. Even liberty, which had been dramatically spoken of by the High Priest as the first of the dearest gifts from heaven, begins to seem less important. Columbus has claimed that the yoke of Spain is more "precious." And now it turns out that this leader of the Spaniards has a character that is positively faultless: though he subdues the natives (in a noisy scene in which Rousseau imagined that the sounds of musketry would mingle with those of the orchestra), he spares them as much as possible, and praises them for their bravery. As for the leader of the Americans, when Columbus sees his indomitable courage, his pride, his forthrightness in refusing to ask for mercy, the Spanish leader is so impressed he declares himself vanquished by virtues so extraordinary. He gives the Chieftain permission to take back his wife, to rule again from the throne; he even asks him to accept his offer of friendship. And now it is the American's turn to declare himself vanquished by such generosity (shades of *Cinna!*); he accepts the throne, the wife, the friendship, and becomes a Spanish subject on the spot.

Naturally, the opera ends in songs and dances to celebrate the arts that make such conquests possible, the delightful chains of love, and, in the final chorus which everyone sings, the conquests of Spain:

> Répandons dans tout l'univers
> Et nos trésors et l'abondance.
> Unissons par notre Alliance
> Deux mondes séparez par l'abime des Mers.[9]   (p. 841)

Even for Rousseau this is an incredible performance, and one might well be astonished, or even indignant, that the man destined to become the staunchest defender of noble savages against the corruptions of civilization could ever have penned this apology for colonial conquests, this whitewash of the cruelest exploiters of the New World.[10] But before one dismisses the work out of hand as some youthful aberration, we might pause to notice that the main issue Rousseau raises in his opera, the clash between natural freedom and civilized bondage, is never really resolved in the libretto: it is simply covered over by the colorful spectacle and drowned out in the lively music. No doubt the ending of the opera was supposed to be a happy one, but actually, if one peers beneath the surface of the spectacle, one finds that the opera has a rather cynical message: Rousseau is saying that, no matter how much the primitive people may prize their freedom and simplicity, the fact is that Columbus has landed, and civilization is going to prevail. As for the natives' original values, they will simply be seduced into not thinking about them. Thus, ironically, the Discovery of the New World of the title is not merely the discovery of unexpected virtues in these savage peoples, it is above all the latters' discovery of European civilization. The main plot tells how the barbarians were tamed and learned to accept, in fact to love, their conquerors.

II

Daniel Mornet asserts that Rousseau never wrote a line that was not autobiographical, and this *tragédie lyrique* is no exception: for indeed we find exactly this same plot – the civilizing of the virtuous savage – told repeatedly in Rousseau's early autobiographical poems[11] (as if he had no other story to tell), and the "savage" in question is always Rousseau himself. When Rousseau ran away from Geneva in 1728, he thought of himself as an untrained primitive. Again and again in the early poems he uses words like "moeurs sauvages," "grossier," "raideur sauvage," or just plain "sauvage" to describe his manners and appearance at that point in his life. Like the tree trunks in the Sacred Grove of the American Indians, he was rough hewn, and totally ignorant of the ways of the world. And yet, in one way at least – as we learn from the early *Epître à Parisot*[12] – this ignorance and simplicity were a source of pride in the young Rousseau, for his primitivism emanated from the simple Virtues of *Geneva*, a word that always resounds (at least momentarily) like a trumpet in the early pieces. In other words, I am proposing that in the opera the Antilles are a sort of analogue for the city of Calvin. And first among the Genevan virtues, just as with the American Indians, was *liberty* (and here I am again following what Rousseau himself states in his *Epître à Parisot*). Geneva was a Republic, whose citizens themselves claimed to be sovereign. Nor did they envy nations such as France for all their military might and the glitter of their luxury and arts. Such things, the Genevans declared, only masked their enslavement by disguising their shackles. And so the Genevans, like the Americans before Columbus, were content with simplicity: their magistrates wore plain clothes without any ornamental gold thread, for they thought their distinction should derive not from their outward appearance, but from *virtue*.

And now, in the *Epître à Parisot*, comes the crisis that in the opera occurred at the beginning of act II: having left Geneva, this rustic savage finds himself in a situation where simple virtue and love of liberty no longer serve, a situation that exactly parallels that of the Americans confronted by the firearms of the Spaniards. What should Rousseau do now? Enter, not Christopher Columbus exactly, but perhaps a feminine counterpart, Mme de Warens, the Goddess, the very embodiment of Civilization, even as the

Spanish ladies of the opera had been. She teaches him to value the fruits of the intelligence, not to mention those of the heart. From her he learns his errors, and resolves to correct his behaviour (*moeurs*). Even as the American leader gave up his liberty in order to be a Spanish subject, so Rousseau foreswears forever what he terms "those ferocious [Genevan] maxims" which he calls "precocious fruits of native prejudice whose bitter yeast nourishes the pride of Republican hearts." And now the climactic lines:

> J'appris à respecter une Noblesse illustre
> Qui même à la vertu sait ajouter du Lustre.[13]   (p. 1140)

Christopher Columbus would be a prime example of this kind of perfection.

But then, as if Rousseau felt his words were inadequate to explain a change of character so total, or as if his conscience were not quite easy about his new social outlook, he goes on to declare that it would have served no useful purpose for him to play the role of Don Quixote in society; his "raideur sauvage" would have made him a sorry figure. And so, his elected Mother guiding him, he learns to love humanity, to respect those who are highly born, to put up with their "hauteurs," while trying to equal them in virtue.

We may pass more quickly over the final stage of his gentrification: his friend Parisot teaches him to become less *grossier*, to enjoy the charms of polite society (which he terms *un climat moins sauvage*). His heart becomes tender (*sensible*); love teaches him to sigh, and he discovers the pleasures of lovemaking, bons mots, elegant verses, and lively conversation. (We may note that those accomplished Spanish ladies in the opera promised just such pleasures for the natives when they landed.) The appreciation of the fine arts rounds out his education. The poem ends on a rather personal note of anxious questioning as to what the future has in store for him.

In this poem, as in the opera, there is a tension between Genevan impulses toward severity in manners, simplicity in dress, Republican pride, liberty, and virtue on the one hand, and the new sophisticated life he persuades himself to undertake on the other.[14] According to this account, it was not so much that the Genevans were wrong, as that their principles had no relevance to the situation in which fate had placed him. It was not reasoned argument that persuaded him to change his ways so much as the gentleness of his Mother–Mistress guiding him along the new path and urging him to love his new lessons. Just as in the opera, the change was essentially a matter of seduction, and at the end of the poem he is not very confident that it will work.

The same kind of personal crisis is reflected in another autobiographical poem, the *Epître à M. Bordes* (1740 or 1741),[15] a curiously provincial imitation of Voltaire's *Le Mondain*, in which Rousseau with his rough-hewn rhymes and uncertain diction tries to do for Lyon everything the great

Voltaire had done for Paris. This is an *apologie du luxe* even as Voltaire's poem had been, and Rousseau takes care to explain that Industry and Commerce are advantageous to mankind because they strengthen the bonds of society while carrying adornment (*la parure*) and magnificence everywhere in the universe. He praises Lyon for its industries, particularly the Lyon cloth-makers for their skill in weaving ornamental gold thread. There are also more general praises:

> Ville heureuse qui fait l'ornement de la France,
> Trésor de l'Univers, source de l'abondance,
> Lyon, séjour charmant des enfants de Plutus,
> Dans tes tranquilles murs, tous les arts sont reçus . . .[16]   (p. 1132)

Just before the end, in an astonishing comparison he likens the citizens of Lyon in their opulence to a people of kings. . . .

Here, even more than in the *Epître à Parisot*, there is a stress on luxurious adornment and refinement. Yet, as in the other early poems, this emphasis is not without conflict. In the first part of the poem Rousseau had spoken of himself as a "proud Republican" with a rustic Swiss lyre, unwilling to debase himself by flattering proud persons of wealth. He wonders whether he should not celebrate simplicity and poverty, the virtues that contented our ancestors who, he adds, were "simples dans leur parure." He finally decides not to celebrate these virtues in his poem, because, given his present situation, it would be impossible to do so without hypocrisy. Abruptly the eulogy of Lyon begins.

Just as in the opera and in the *Epître à Parisot*, the second part of the poem does not really resolve the question raised by the first; it merely makes the problem invisible, overwhelming it in dazzling glitter.

III

Does it not seem odd that in one poem Rousseau would point with pride to the *absence* of ornamental gold thread in the clothes of the Genevan magistrates, and nevertheless have composed another poem celebrating the weavers of Lyon precisely for their skill in weaving ornamental gold thread? And yet this kind of blatant, outrageous contradiction characterizes almost everything Rousseau did in this period. The framework of the present chapter does not permit an analysis of all the relevant texts from the *Confessions*, but I will propose as a working hypothesis that the one rule of all Rousseau's conduct was a determination not only to reject his Genevan training but to embody the exact *opposite* of Genevan values. His conversion to Catholicism is the most obvious example of this anti-Genevan principle at work, and we may note too that, far from choosing some Jansenistic form of Catholicism that would have been closer to the religion of his birth,

Rousseau's worldly, Jesuit-tending Catholicism was at the opposite pole from Geneva's religion.[17] Calvin's stern God the Father was replaced by a gentle, rather seductive Holy Mother Church, symbolized in Mme de Warens. And here the polarity carries into the smallest details: the Calvinists forbade orchestral instruments in the temple; therefore Rousseau himself played the flute in the Catholic services at Annecy.[18] The Calvinists removed all pictures and ornaments from their places of worship; therefore when in Venice Rousseau circulated around the churches of the city making it a point to admire the ornamental pictures he found there.[19] Nor is this phenomenon confined to religion, for the anti-Genevan principle crops up everywhere: as we have already seen, the Genevans were Republicans; therefore Rousseau schooled himself in the ways of aristocracy, learning to wear a wig, to frequent persons of quality,[20] and he put on clothes made of fine cloth into which ornamental gold thread was woven. Genevans forbade all performances of stage plays, operas, and ballets as detrimental to public morals; therefore Rousseau embarked on a career as an author of stage plays, operas, and *comédies-ballets*. Given such oppositions, is it too far-fetched to note that one of Geneva's most fearsome enemies was France; therefore Rousseau moved to Paris?[21]

Obviously much more might be added concerning the origins of this attitude in Rousseau, of this extraordinarily far-reaching example of the attraction of the contrary, and its ramifications in his life,[22] but for present purposes the point is that when Rousseau tried to make a career for himself in Paris, it was still this anti-Genevan principle that motivated his activities: he was still adhering to the program initiated with Mme de Warens, although we are not informed as to whether he had kept up his flute playing. Now, as we know from the poignant account of these events in the *Confessions*, Paris quickly became a professional disaster for Rousseau, as the Academy of Sciences rejected his theory of musical notation, as the great Rameau publicly humiliated him, denouncing him as a fraud, and worse. His dismissal by the ambassador to Venice was but one of a series of defeats. We know too that Rousseau found it increasingly difficult to take part in the games of manners one was supposed to play in the Parisian *salons*, games that masked and tried to deny the painful realities he was experiencing. We may also assume (although Rousseau says absolutely nothing at all about this in the *Confessions*) that, if only because of the company he had been keeping, the Parisian years had prepared him for the realization that his conversion to Catholicism had been a mistake, a realization that must have had the deepest kind of psychological resonance for him.

Thus for many reasons we may infer that when Rousseau took his famous walk along the road to Vincennes, the walk that became the inspiration for his First Discourse, everything he had been building for himself under Mme de Warens's tutelage was ready to crumble. In the *Confessions* he relates that the moment of truth came upon him totally unexpectedly, out of the blue, sweeping all before it: "Je vis un autre univers et je devins un autre homme" (p. 35), he said, the language recalling conversion according to St Paul, and also the idea of "rebirth" or "regeneration" as the Calvinists conceived of it.[23] This is to say that the first meaning of this powerful experience was that Catholicism was now behind him. But "I saw another universe" suggests, too, a vision, as if Rousseau became for a moment a prophet or seer with some special insight he had not had before, and of course this vision actually became part of the First Discourse, written out as the prosopopeia of Fabricius. Clearly, at the time it all seemed very novel to Rousseau; and yet, as Kenneth Clark pointed out concerning the visions of William Blake,[24] what seems to the visionary to be the contemplation of something entirely new, may in reality be the memory of something very old. Certainly this is the case with the prosopopeia of Fabricius, which in essence represents simply a return to Genevan values. And, just as earlier he had systematically rejected and denied everything Geneva stood for, now, in the prosopopeia, the process is exactly reversed: in his visionary fantasy he imagines this virtuous Roman commanding his countrymen to smash and destroy all the anti-Genevan values Rousseau had been cultivating so assiduously in himself:

Ce sont des Rhéteurs qui vous gouvernent? C'est pour enrichir des Architectes, des Peintres, des Statuaires et des Histrions, que vous avez arrosé de votre sang la Grèce et l'Asie? Les dépouilles de Carthage sont la proie d'un joueur de flûte? Romains, hâtez-vous de renverser ces Amphithéâtres; brisez ces marbres; brûlez ces tableaux; chassez ces esclaves qui vous subjuguent, et dont les funestes arts vous corrompent.

(p. 15)[25]

Architecture, painting, sculpture, eloquence, music, *especially* the flute, all are swept away as insignificant, unworthy, debilitating, corrupting, effeminate. This imaginary iconoclasm is quite compatible with the spirit of Calvinism, which had stripped its temples bare of just such ornaments as Rousseau mentions here. But it is curious to see him contradict so many of the very words he had written earlier, as if he were determined to take them all back, one by one. In the *Epître à M. Bordes* he had likened the citizens of Lyon to a people of kings on account of their glittering opulence. But now, in the First Discourse, day has become night:

Quand Cynéas prit notre Sénat pour une Assemblée de Rois, il ne fut ébloui ni par une pompe vaine, ni par une élégance recherchée. . . . Que vit donc Cynéas de si majestueux? O Citoyens! Il vit un spectacle que ne donneront jamais vos richesses ni tous vos arts; le plus beau spectacle qui ait jamais paru sous le ciel, l'Assemblée de deux cents hommes vertueux . . . (*ibid.*)[26]

Two hundred men? Perhaps it is just coincidence that a Council of Two Hundred was one of the governing bodies of Geneva. But in any case, this was just how Rousseau had depicted the Genevan magistrates seven years before in the *Epître à Parisot*, only at that time he was determined to reject these values in favor of Catholic ones. From the same poem it is clear that the Genevans had known all along about the evils of luxury, and had understood too how the arts of civilization served as instruments of enslavement, just as Rousseau says in the crucial third paragraph of the First Discourse:

les Sciences, les Lettres et les Arts, moins despotiques et plus puissants peut-être, étendent des guirlandes de fleurs sur les chaines de fer dont ils sont chargés, étouffent en eux le sentiment de cette liberté originelle pour laquelle ils semblaient être nés, leur font aimer leur esclavage. . . .

(p. 7)[27]

And of course this passage is an exact résumé of act II of his opera, which had shown with music, dancing, and spectacle how indeed the arts became instruments of subjugation.

No doubt Rousseau wrote the First Discourse for the Academy of Dijon and, for that matter, for humanity, but above all he wrote it as a lesson for himself. As Professor Starobinski has remarked,[28] Fabricius is talking first of all to Jean-Jacques Rousseau, and if Fabricius can take a tone so uncompromising in the absolute values he proclaims, it is because Rousseau is not exploring new territory, however it may have seemed to him at the time. On the contrary, he and Fabricius had known what to say almost from the beginning of his lifetime. Having gone for years in one direction, the attraction of the contrary now reverses itself, pulls backwards, and negates the negation. Because the grooves of this second reversal were already graven so deeply in Rousseau's mind and heart, this was to prove one of the most successful intellectual revolutions of the century.

In his letter to Malesherbes,[29] Rousseau relates that he wept copiously during his vision on the road to Vincennes, even though he was not aware of his weeping as it happened; nor does he give any explanation for it. No doubt some of these were tears of relief: after all the anguish and defeats along the false road to Paris and French civilization, this noble Roman he had summoned up in his imagination had told him he should, and must, go home.[30]

Much effort has been spent trying to find the logical coherence of the First Discourse and to reconcile the divergent statements one finds in various parts of it.[31] Actually, there is no logical continuity.[32] It begins with an *éloge de la civilisation*, and then, right in the middle of the second sentence of paragraph three (in the part of the text quoted above), precisely at the word "despotiques," it turns abruptly into a diatribe against civilization. The change is unprepared, so swift we barely have time to take it in. But from this moment on, we must be alert to the fact that the key terms in Rous-

103

seau's vocabulary have undergone a mutation, acquiring new, and often opposite, values. In the opening paragraph man's search for knowledge through the light of reason is a fine and noble pursuit; two paragraphs later it becomes evil. Letters and arts are good things in paragraph two; they become dangerous instruments of despotism and enslavement in paragraph three. "Sociability," the desire to please others in society, is apparently an "advantage" even in the last lines of the second paragraph. Just a few words later it will be poisoned, turning into another symptom of mankind's fatal decay.

The most profitable way to interpret this cleavage is to assume that we are viewing the explosion itself: the crisis that so shattered Rousseau on the way to Vincennes is actually reiterating itself in the opening text of the Discourse. First he evokes, with incomparable eloquence, the excitement he himself had felt as he surveyed the progress of enlightenment. These were the emotions he had written of in the early autobiographical poems *Le Verger de Mme de Warens* and the *Epître à Parisot*, which is to say that in the opening of the Discourse Rousseau is faithfully reflecting that time in his life when he was enthusiastically civilizing himself through the study of the sciences and arts. The next section, after "despotiques," reflects with equal fidelity the new understanding he had acquired, while the abruptness of the change from one to the other translates the violence of the event itself as it happened to him.

We have already noted that the early poems bear witness to a conflict in Rousseau between his admiration for the arts of civilization and his lingering nostalgia for Genevan simplicity. The new phase shows the same tension, but in reverse proportion: Geneva is now clearly the winner, despite a certain sentimental attachment to the values he is rejecting. This implies that in reading the Discourse we should be prepared not only for emphatic rhetoric as in the prosopopeia of Fabricius, but for ambiguities that may tip in different directions from moment to moment. For example:

Puissances de la Terre, aimez les talents, et protégez ceux qui les cultivent. Peuples policés, cultivez-les: Heureux esclaves, vous leur devez ce goût délicat et fin dont vous vous piquez; cette douceur de caractère et cette urbanité de moeurs qui rendent parmi vous le commerce si liant et si facile; en un mot, les apparences de toutes les vertus sans en avoir aucune. (p. 7)[33]

No doubt the tone of the passage is heavily ironic, expressing a fundamental hostility toward the cultivation of the arts and sciences. Moreover, the passage forms part of Rousseau's reasoned diagnosis of the political causes of the decadence of civilization. And yet one senses, through all the irony and hostility, the hint of an attraction for the "douceur de caractère," for the "commerce si liant et facile";[34] and in fact, one paragraph later, Rousseau even lets himself go so far as to wish that the lovely exterior of society really did correspond to the true disposition of people's hearts. Of course, he soon returns to his uncompromising diatribe against civilization and all its works: ornament is denounced as inherently unhealthy, deceptive, vicious; and we finish the paragraph at the other end of the scale with the athlete who scorns all clothing and fights in the nude.

For Rousseau there was an analogy between the idea of stripping off the clothes that adorned him to find the naked warrior beneath, and the stripping off of centuries of decadent civilization to find primitive man, man in his truest, most natural form. This theme will be greatly expanded in the Second Discourse, but is there not a hint of it already in the text at hand?

On ne peut réfléchir sur les moeurs, qu'on ne se plaise à se rappeler l'image de la simplicité des premiers temps. C'est un beau rivage, paré des seules mains de la nature, vers lequel on tourne incessamment les yeux, et dont on se sent éloigner à regret. Quand les hommes innocents et vertueux aimaient à avoir les Dieux pour témoins de leurs actions, ils habitaient ensemble sous les mêmes cabanes; mais bientôt devenus méchants, ils se lassèrent de ces incommodes spectateurs et les reléguèrent dans des Temples magnifiques. Ils les en chassèrent enfin pour s'y établir eux-mêmes, ou du moins les Temples des Dieux ne se distinguèrent plus des maisons des citoyens. Ce fut alors le comble de la dépravation; et les vices ne furent jamais poussés plus loin que quand on les vit, pour ainsi dire, soutenus à l'entrée des Palais de Grands sur des colonnes de marbres, et gravés sur des chapiteaux Corinthiens. (p. 22)[35]

This imagined journey back in time had an exact equivalent in Calvinism (to which Rousseau was doubtless deliberately referring in the passage quoted): the desire to strip away the centuries of decadent accretions to find the bare truth of the Gospel, the notion that religion was essentially internal – an affair of the mind and heart – and only corrupted itself by turning outward into graven images and pompous ceremonies, these were the fundamentals of Calvinism.[36] And of course the reason why the iconoclasts among the Reformers in the sixteenth century threw out the pictures, broke the statues and forbade orchestral instruments, including flute players, in the Temple, was their belief that these things seduced the eye, perverted the mind, and obscured the truth. If one joins the passage just quoted to the prosopopeia of Fabricius it becomes clear that this noble Roman is merely breathing new life into a very old tradition.

And yet, the almost visceral hostility Rousseau expresses against the arts of civilization – so Calvinistic in its resonance – contains strong elements of personal defensiveness: having once been led down the wrong path, he is determined not to be seduced by the arts again, even though he cannot deny the power of their attraction for him. Here we find not only a tension between two parts of his life, but between two sides of his character. It is a matter of choosing an allegiance, perhaps even an identity, at this critical juncture in his development, and if he often sounds contentious in the First

Discourse, this suggests the precariousness of his new position, and the existence of tensions and conflicts that he would not, and could not, ever resolve entirely. No doubt this was another reason why Rousseau let the opening statements in favor of the sciences and arts stand as they were, even though they contradicted the next part, and why Rousseau, later on, in his diatribe against the *philosophes*, makes an exception for a small elite, those special geniuses who may benefit mankind. Perhaps Rousseau's fundamental ambiguity also explains why he addressed his Discourse against civilization to a most civilized Academy, in a most eloquent and civilized language, and why, just two years later, he could celebrate the charms of rustic life in that most civilized and un-rustic of art forms, opera.

Yet, despite all the contradictions that would remain with him forever,[37] the die was cast. In Paris, he reformed his dress, doing away with everything that might be called *parure*, or suggest aristocracy: fancy wig, sword, gold embroidery.[38] Refusing to heed Diderot's objections, he decided not to present himself for a king's pension. He not only signed his name "Citizen of Geneva," he returned to that city in person, reinstating himself in the Protestant Church and giving himself over to the intoxications of Republican enthusiasm. On the way occurred the famous last visit to his former Mistress–Mother, Mme de Warens. In the *Confessions* he finds himself at a loss to explain how he could have abandoned her in such distress, and wonders how he will bear the weight of this guilt for the rest of his life.[39] Yet looking at the event in the context of the revolution that preceded it, Rousseau's departure from her seems as inevitable, as predetermined, as his attraction to her had been in the first place. In both cases, it is like watching a stone sinking down to the level nature had ordained for it.

And even as his early feelings of love for her had behind them not only the passion of awakening sexuality but also an urgent need for maternal affection, so now the departure for Geneva had behind it not only the impetus of a journey toward a home he had lost, but also the awesome force of another psychological development that really should have occurred much earlier in Rousseau's life, and whose long delay would endow it with special violence and energy. For just as in the chronological development of ancient civilizations, archaeologists usually find some critical moment when a people's exclusive veneration of female deities shifts abruptly to make way for the dominance of Gods who are male, so too, according to the expectations of traditional European society, should a similar shift occur in the male child as he frees himself from maternal domination and comes to identify with the figure of the father.[40] With Rousseau the long delay of this process brought about the explosion that is the First Discourse: the violent prosopopeia of Fabricius, the brave warriors and naked athletes who parade so proudly in Rousseau's pages, at the expense of decadent courtiers, manifest his determination – however illusory – to free himself from the charms he associated with maternity. Even before Rousseau abandoned her on the way to Geneva, Mme de Warens had already been sacrificed in the First Discourse – to something that for Rousseau was the process of life: his blinding vision beckoned to him as a coming of age.

In a word, despite all the passages of reasoned argument, despite Rousseau's almost treatise-like handling of his paradox concerning "progress," this work is not philosophy, but the most intimate sort of autobiography whose message is quite as personal as any to be found in the *Confessions*; in fact, it is telling part of the same story. The First Discourse came into being on account of the peculiar development of Rousseau's life; it grows directly from the quirks of fate and oddities of character that made him such a unique individual. The true paradox is that these quirks, perversities, and peculiarities could produce a Discourse whose message was, or would be, almost universal: Rousseau's call for masculine pride and Roman virtue, his sweeping denunciation of the corruption of wealth and privilege, and of the enslavement they breed, above all the inflammatory tone in which these ideas were spoken, the indignant rhetoric to which no one would remain indifferent, this would be the voice of the nation, of destiny, a time-bomb whose content would explode in the Revolution. How a phenomenon whose origins were essentially so private could become so spectacularly public can never be fully explained; such things belong to the mysteries of the artist. And yet, it is clear that Rousseau's unique power and eloquence stem directly from the intensity of his involvement with his subject, and, in Rousseau's case, this very much implies that he is speaking of himself. Moreover, it may be that if Rousseau's appeal has been universal, his popularity has come, not *in spite of* all the contradictory, ill-assorted elements of his Discourse, but *because of* them.[41]

It comes from the reader's awareness that these arguments against the progress of civilization are being spoken by a man who himself has felt so keenly the attractions of civilization that he almost loses his way as he tries to argue against them, someone still so dazzled by the great minds of the past that he cannot bring himself to write them off, an author whose description of the progress of humanity since the Renaissance captures the excitement of the Age of Philosophy with a poetical eloquence unsurpassed by any writer during the century. It is the diversity and intensity of the contradictory experiences reflected in the Discourse that makes it even today such a compelling work, and if many individuals of Rousseau's time found him persuasive and his message important, perhaps this was because he had suggested to his readers something of the enormous personal crisis he himself had traversed, in order to sustain his arguments.

7

On the figure of music in the frontispiece of Diderot's *Encyclopédie*

What a heavenly way to allegorize the order and arrangement of all the sciences, arts, and trades for the frontispiece of the *Encyclopédie*![1] What a crowd of beautiful females! Such pretty faces, such ample forms, such enticing *décolleté*! Billowing clouds support the figures from below, like restful pillows. All are clad in loose drapery, their expressions look placid, perhaps even a little vacant, as befits the relaxation of their attitudes. One sees no men in the central portion of the tableau, and the scene has something of the easy intimacy one imagines especially when women are by themselves, undisturbed by the intrusive presence of the male. The appearance of the whole strikes one as distinctly ornamental, and as the eye descends from the upper part, it passes over the seated figures, one after another, as over so many flowers in a garland.

The artist has not tried to give much individuality to the physiognomies of the persons in this harmonious ensemble.[2] Indeed they would not have much separate identity at all were it not for the artist's having unobtrusively bestowed upon each one some appropriate accoutrement that identifies the figure's allegorical meaning. To make doubly sure the point is not missed, he has also written out a key which explains the engraving in plain prose.

The scene, we are told, is taking place beneath the temple of Truth, whose architecture is of the Ionic order, a fact that some scholars consider important because this architectural style was frequently associated with the Freemasons. It suggests that, in the artist's mind at least, the concept of this encyclopedia may have been connected in some special way with the idea of Masonry.[3] The central figure in the engraving, who is also the most elevated and most brightly illuminated one, is Truth (*la Vérité*). Appropriately enough, she radiates a light that parts the clouds (of ignorance) and dispels them. Nearest her, wearing a crown, stands Reason (*la Raison*) who, rather energetically, lifts the veil of Truth, while, lower down, Philosophy draws the veil away. (Does it not seem typically eighteenth century, and charmingly French, that the search for truth should be thought of as an allegorical striptease?) Meanwhile, flanked by Reason and Philosophy, we find Theology on her knees, who, the key informs us, is receiving her light

17. C.-N. Cochin, fils, *Frontispice de l'Encyclopédie*

from on high. If we look closely, we can also note that she is holding the Sacred Scriptures rather negligently down by her side. Nor does the key make any mention of the fact that Philosophy has put one arm out in position, ready, if necessary, to restrain Theology, while energetic Reason is about to press an iron bit – a piece of equipment usually reserved for indocile horses – into her mouth. Clearly the Age of Enlightenment had no intention of ever letting religion get out of hand again.

Following the figures down on the right, we come upon History, the various sciences (and what a delightfully erotic, piquant touch, that the naked bosom of Botany should be so perilously close to the thorns of a cactus), with the mechanical arts on the lowest level. But for present purposes the interesting figures are rather on the left side, because here we find the figures that embody the arts. Highest among them stands Imagination carrying the garland with which she will adorn the Truth. All the other figures on this side are supposed to owe their art to her. They form quite an array, as can be seen in figure 18. Immediately below come figures representing Poetry: in the middle sits the Epic, majestic in her pose, with an eight-stringed lyre in one hand and a sort of trumpet – perhaps a short salpinx – in the other. On either side of her we find Comedy and Tragedy; they too carry symbols to identify them. Pastoral Poetry, off to one side (doubtless in the country), peeps from behind with crook and syrinx, and Satire, also placed on the side, holds a barb that is prudently not directed toward any of the figures in the tableau.

Equally impressive is the group in the next line, the other "arts of imitation": Sculpture, chisel in hand, somehow supports a marble bust on her lap; then Painting, sleeves rolled up, holds paint brushes. Cochin has made her a commanding presence in his tableau, placing her near the centre and giving her a tiara to wear. We see her full length, literally from head to toe, and note that she is gazing straight at Philosophy, a most appropriate gesture in a philosophical picture such as this. The special importance attributed to Painting here is undoubtedly due to the fact that Cochin himself was a painter, but it also reflects the long-standing tradition that Painting was placed first among the arts of imitation.[4] The row comes to an end with Architecture with her ruler, level, and compass. So much, then, for the arts of imitation? Well, not quite. For if one looks closely enough in figure 18 one may discern, rather near the centre of this group, another figure, whose chin and neck are partially obscured by Architecture, whose chest is rendered invisible by the figure of Painting, and whose posterior is blurred by the strings of a harp: here at last is Music.

But how puny, how insignificant she looks, not only compared to the grand figure of Painting, but even compared to Satire's charming profile! Among these arts, only Pastoral Poetry receives such niggardly treatment, and she at least has been allowed a complete chin. Can Cochin have been so

18. C.-N. Cochin, fils, detail from the *Frontispice de l'Encyclopédie*

insensitive to the charms of music? Is he trying to suggest some attitude of disparagement toward an art so noble, and, more important, so highly admired by the philosophers of the *Encyclopédie*? I think not. I suspect rather that he was trying to express something about the nature of music and its relation to the other arts that may not be evident at first glance to us, but which was probably more obvious in 1764. The rest of my comments will explore some of the implications of this problem.

I

Our starting point will be d'Alembert's discussion of music in the Preliminary Discourse of the *Encyclopédie*.[5] This familiar text is useful because of its exceptional clarity, and because the ideas put forward here were held by other Encyclopedists,[6] including J.-J. Rousseau. We notice with surprise that music is the final topic in the long first section of the Discourse: it comes only after the author has discussed everything else, in the wake of all the arts and sciences. Even in respect to the other arts of imitation, music occupies the terminal position. D'Alembert hastens to explain that this situation does not imply that music is inferior to the other arts, but simply that music was the last of the arts to learn to exploit its true resources. It was d'Alembert's opinion (and this apparently was what it had taken music such a long time to realize) that music such as we normally think of it today, that is to say, practical music considered in itself as melody, counterpoint, harmony, dissonance, rhythm, etc., had virtually no interest or value; music only counted when it imitated, or "painted," something else. D'Alembert is quite explicit about this: "All music that does not paint anything," he says, "is simply noise." One suspects that he looked upon non-imitative music, "raw" music, so to speak, the way the sculptor looked upon "raw" marble before it was chiseled into shape, or the way the painter considered the shapeless blobs of color on his palette. The comparison d'Alembert himself draws is between non-imitative music and sonorous words that have been stripped of their "order and connection"; in other words d'Alembert likens "raw" music to verbal nonsense, to words that when brought together do not signify anything.

But just where, one might wonder, does this leave all the non-programmatic instrumental music that was so popular in the eighteenth century, those famous sonatas by Alberti, Galuppi, and Locatelli, just to mention three Italians who perfected the genre? D'Alembert is not impressed; in fact, he has no patience, and dismisses them with disdain: "I count as nothing the prodigious quantity of sonatas the Italians have given us. All this purely instrumental music, without plan or object [of imitation], speaks neither to the mind nor to the soul, and merits that one ask of it, following the remark of M. de Fontenelle, "*Sonate, que me veux-tu?*"[7] Fontenelle's remark, translated literally, means "Sonata, what do you want of me?" However in this disparaging context I assume it expresses above all d'Alembert's disdain that music which might have made sense by imitating something should prefer instead to create nonsense. In Americanese one might translate Fontenelle's remark: "Sonata, what *is* your problem?" D'Alembert then goes on to explain that composers of instrumental music will only produce vain noise, so long as they do not have in mind something to be painted.

As to what kind of painting, d'Alembert's answers are well known to musicologists. He means painting of the passions, first of all: the sentiments of the soul, joy, anger, sorrow, etc., and he argues that composers have not gone far enough in exploiting this kind of imitation; they should extend their art to encompass even more elementary sensations.[8] Though d'Alembert's theory might apply to a number of different kinds of music, he may have been thinking especially of vocal music in his discussion of the painting of the passions, since the combination of word and music was the most obvious means for the expression of this. Yet the verb *"peindre"* also had a musical meaning that would apply more specifically to instrumental music. I quote from one of the innumerable anonymous pamphlets produced during the "Querelle des Bouffons." This one, entitled *Réflexions sur la musique françoise en particulier*, has sometimes been attributed to d'Alembert, even though both the style and the content indicate that it cannot possibly have been written by him:

Les sons peuvent peindre tout ce qui est capable de faire du bruit; le tonnerre, les vents, les mugissements de la mer, le bruit des armes, le chant mélodieux des oiseaux, les cris des animaux, la chute d'une cascade, le doux murmure d'un ruisseau, etc. . . . Mais comme ces idées sont souvent jointes à d'autres, . . . elles les réveilleront nécessairement toutes les fois qu'elles seront bien rendues. Ainsi, si un Musicien réussissait à imiter les affreux mugissements de la mer, les éclats du tonnere, les sifflements des aquilons, l'horrible fracas d'un vaisseau qui se brise sur des rochers, qu'il fît entendre les cris des matelots éperdus;[9] il n'est personne en qui cela ne réveillât l'idée d'un naufrage, qui ne crût voir des vagues, des rochers, des malheureux en proie à la fureur des ondes. La liaison que les idées ont entre elles, nous fait apercevoir un aimable réduit champêtre dans l'imitation du chant des oiseaux, du murmure d'un ruisseau, d'un léger zéphyre, ou du bruit que font des branches agitées: on se croit transporté dans une prairie émaillée de fleurs. Qu'on y ajoute une musette, on voit un berger aux pieds de sa bergère, leurs troupeaux confondus bondissent sur l'herbe: tantôt on se représente un coteau riant, d'où l'on voit jaillir une fontaine qui se précipitant dans le vallon, va arroser mille fleurs.[10]

A little later, the author tips his hand: "Je n'ai jamais entendu jouer l'ouverture de Pigmalion [de Rameau], que je ne me sois cru dans l'atelier de Le Moine. Je voyais cet habile Artiste, le ciseau à la main, façonner un bloc de marbre; il en sortait une Vénus."[11]

Obviously this anonymous author, and d'Alembert also, are thinking primarily of opera in their theory of imitation in music, and this is logically so because in opera, as nowhere else, music is called upon constantly, and in so many ways to paint a scene, to imitate a gesture, to describe in sound an emotion that a character is expressing in words. But for present purposes the point we must notice is that when imitation in music applies to opera, the imitation in question is not the imitation of nature, as it usually was in the other arts, it is instead the imitation of poetry – itself a form of imitation, of stage gestures, of scenic effects, all of which are imitations. In other words, in opera, music imitates not nature, but art.

II

Is there not something almost mathematical about the way the noted geometer, d'Alembert, simply takes the theory of imitation currently used to explain the other arts, and applies it literally to music, regardless of the consequences, even if it means dismissing as vain noise all music that does not imitate? One notes too – as Cassirer and others have explained – how typical of the eighteenth century it is for a philosopher to seek some unifying principle that will tie everything together, as d'Alembert has done with this topic. And it is precisely because d'Alembert is so representative of his time that he is useful to us: he as much as anyone in the 1750s can be said to speak for the French Enlightenment, a touchstone for his age.

This is where J.-J. Rousseau makes such a surprising contrast with d'Alembert. I mentioned earlier that Rousseau shared d'Alembert's ideas on music as imitation, which indeed he did.[12] Yet Rousseau never quite fits the role of spokesman for other people. His own unique, intrusive, indiscreet personality bulked far too large for him ever to efface himself and disappear as a representative of someone else. Thus we find that in his *Encyclopédie* article "Sonate" (1749)[13] he states almost exactly the same doctrine expounded by d'Alembert, but with just one or two slight differences in terminology, and a radically different tone of voice, the whole matter becomes unexpectedly dramatized, turning into a very personal statement. In the interest of clarity and brevity, I will paraphrase him rather freely, as follows.

Since music is imitation, he declares, it is essential to know just what is being imitated. Such is the function of words which, joined to the touching sounds of the human voice, convey the message ("objet imité") to the heart where it can produce its full effect. In contrast, purely instrumental music without words or program can never move us so powerfully. And now the reader notes that the mere mention of instrumental music makes Rousseau's temperature start to rise. He weighs all Mondonville's follies on the violin against just two notes (or perhaps we should say "words") sung by Mlle le Maure,[14] and finds the scales tipping dramatically in favor of singing. As for all those sonatas (and presumably, like d'Alembert, he was thinking primarily of the Italians) he feels people have been overwhelmed by "rubbish." In phrases heavy with sarcasm he suggests that in order to be more comprehensible, perhaps instrumental composers should do as the clumsy painter did, who, finding that no one understood his pictures, wrote beneath them, "This is a man," "This is a tree," "This is an ox." "I will never forget," Rousseau goes on, "the words spoken by the famous M. de

Fontenelle, who, finding himself at a concert, exasperated by the endless sound of the instruments ["excédé de cette symphonie éternelle"], cried right out loud in a transport of impatience, '*Sonate, que me veux-tu?*' "

This of course is exactly the same anecdote related by d'Alembert. But how different is the sense of Fontenelle's remark, preceded as it now is by so many exaggerated, emotionally charged words. Instead of d'Alembert's disdainful dismissal, the remark in Rousseau's version gives voice to an enormous frustration, a "transport of impatience," as if Rousseau were convinced that the wordless music was trying to say something to him that he could not quite decipher. Behind his angry outburst one senses the whole force of Rousseau's hatred of the obscure, of his overwhelming desire for clear understanding that would remain with him until the end of his life.[15] We can note too that his emotions have distinctly Protestant overtones, since the Calvinists believed that the unique function of music was to serve as a vehicle for the Word, just as Rousseau has stated, albeit in a secular context. This verbal emphasis is another trait that separates Rousseau's version of the anecdote from d'Alembert's account; for d'Alembert, the point was that non-imitative instrumental music was simply nonsense; it signified nothing. Whereas Rousseau assumes there *is* a message, but that it has become garbled; hence he finds himself standing before a mystery and demanding a revelation: "Sonate, que me veux-tu?" means "What are you trying to *say* to me?" – as if Rousseau were demanding an answer. This attitude is not one that we associate readily with "Enlightenment" (or what we are pleased to think of as such) because it goes directly counter to the rational poise the term implies. In Rousseau we are seeing the kind of dynamic imbalance that was to characterize the psychology of the Romantics. I will also mention that, considered as a formal plan, the idea of some mystery, or implicit idea, that is forced to make itself manifest suggests literary forms later developed by Rousseau himself, most obviously in *Pygmalion*, but also – although more discretely – in the *Rêveries du promeneur solitaire*. It may even suggest certain musical forms – Schumann's piano fantasy, op. 17, would be an example – of the Romantic era.

All this is to say that whereas for d'Alembert the theory of imitation in music was a doctrine to be formulated as accurately as possible, a key to our understanding, a bond that would unify and simplify our conceptions, to Rousseau, in contrast, the theory becomes a vehicle for the very personal demands he himself would make of music, a creative, problematic concept that looks toward art forms of the future.

III

As an appointed spokesman for the doctrines of Enlightenment d'Alembert's main function was to provide answers and clear explanations regarding the arts, sciences and trades, and in an area so controversial as music this knowing attitude may occasionally be something of a limitation. Let us turn from d'Alembert's sonorous, meticulously balanced phrases to the works of Diderot, who was so much more imaginative and yet at the same time reveals a questioning attitude that seems astonishingly modern. "Imitation in music" was only occasionally and in passing a set doctrine, a formula for Diderot. More often it was a question, a matter for exploration and experiment. Diderot realized, for example, that "imitation" implied that one of the senses could be used in place of another; that it was possible to do in sound for the ear something that would evoke an image for the eye. There was a kind of transmutation, aural–visual, taking place. But might one not even reverse the process, awakening via the eye, sounds that would be heard in the ear? Diderot was fascinated by the experiments of Father Castel,[16] the half-crazy Jesuit who spent years trying to design a harpsichord that would play colored ribbons when the keys were touched. Eventually Diderot would find himself using the image of the harpsichord, with all its resonating strings, to represent our consciousness, the strings being plucked sometimes from without, as we experience something via sense impressions, sometimes from within, as experiences awaken memories, and memories in turn become experiences.[17] How pedantic and unimaginative d'Alembert seems compared to boldness such as this.

As was mentioned earlier, at moments Diderot very much accepted the notion of imitation in music. For example, throughout much of the early *Lettre sur les sourds et muets* (1751) Diderot assumes that the function of music is to imitate. And then, in *Le Neveu de Rameau*, the author actually puts the theory of imitation to work, exploiting it as a literary device in a manner so daring as to create virtually a new dimension in art.

During the course of the dialogue, the Nephew has been occasionally staging musical pantomimes: he has given an imitation of a harpsichord player supposedly performing a sonata by Alberti or Galuppi, for example,[18] and even though there was no harpsichord present, his gestures and facial expressions copied those of a real performer so perfectly that Diderot almost imagined that the performance had been the real thing. Just a moment before, the Nephew had pretended he was a violinist playing a sonata by Locatelli, and again Diderot's dazzling description is so lifelike that even today we can still imagine that we are not only seeing, but hearing him.[19] Toward the end of the work the pantomimes reach their culmination as the Nephew tries to stage a whole opera.[20] The music consists of bits and snatches taken from what seems like every opera ever written in the eighteenth century (plus some church music that is thrown in for good measure), and which are all jumbled together pell-mell. The Nephew himself sings and acts all the parts, plays all the roles, imitates all the instruments, jumping from one thing to another so rapidly the mind fairly boggles as it tries to keep up. And then at one of the climactic moments of this enormous pantomime we suddenly become aware that Diderot's words on the page (themselves already a form of imitation) are evoking the figure of the Nephew, whose voice imitates orchestral instruments, imitating stage machinery (and/or a painting by Vernet) that imitates a shipwreck, among many other things. This adds up to four layers of imitation, in fact five, since, in pretending to put on an opera, the Nephew is giving an imitation of his celebrated uncle. In other words, in this passage we find an imitation, of an imitation, of an imitation, of an imitation, of an imitation:

Que ne lui vis-je pas faire? Il pleurait, il riait, il soupirait; il regardait, ou attendri, ou tranquille, ou furieux; c'était une femme qui se pâme de douleur; c'était un malheureux livré à tout son desespoir; un temple qui s'élève; des oiseaux qui se taisent au soleil couchant; des eaux qui murmurent dans un lieu solitaire et frais, ou qui descendent en torrents du haut des montagnes; un orage, une tempête, la plainte de ceux qui vont périr, mêlée au sifflement des vents, au fracas du tonnerre; c'était la nuit, avec ses ténèbres; c'était l'ombre et le silence; car le silence même se peint par des sons. Sa tête était tout à fait perdue.[21]

This is not nature; this is all opera: opera music, opera atmosphere, opera scenery, opera acting, opera machinery.

From the words "un temple qui s'élève" to the end, the narrator is speaking specifically of orchestral music (as opposed to vocal music), and which in this passage is usually imitating scenic effects – just as in the anonymous pamphlet quoted earlier. Fortunately, some of these scenic effects have been preserved in the plates on opera machinery in the *Encyclopédie*, and even though they lack the color so essential to the success of operatic impressions, these engravings give at least some idea of the visual imagery being conjured up by the Nephew as he sang these musical imitations. For example, the narrator mentions a "cool and secluded spot with murmuring waters." At the opera this would have been imitated first of all in the music played by the orchestra, but it would also have been shown onstage, as in figure 19, a detail from an engraving that, in the original plate, also revealed some of the machinery needed to create this effect. In the quoted passage these "murmuring waters" are abruptly contrasted to waters that "descend in torrents from the mountain tops." This was another scenic effect made possible by machines, as is evident in figure 20, which depicts just such a cascade as Diderot mentions, and in which one can see the mechanical roller that made the waters seem to descend.

In the quoted passage, the violence of these waters leads by association to a storm, in fact to a tempest complete with shipwreck and the cries of those about to perish. Here Diderot and the Nephew would have been remembering the orchestral and choral music of Campra's *Idoménée* and/or Rameau's

19. Radel, "Décorations d'un désert" (detail)

20. Radel, "Détail d'une fontaine dans les rochers, avec son moulinet pour la faire mouvoir"

21. Radel, "Port de Mer avec naufrage"

Indes galantes,[22] as the anonymous author of the "Querelle des Bouffons" pamphlet had been, but they probably had in mind also the ships and shipwrecks that were something of a specialty at the opera. Figure 21 shows what is labeled "Port de Mer, avec naufrage," and figure 22 depicts some of the machinery that could make a boat rock perilously on the waters. The machinery here may even be in shipwreck position, since the angle at which the machine-boat tips is approximately as steep as that of the boats one sees in the famous "Shipwrecks" of Vernet,[23] paintings with which Diderot was particularly familiar because he had described them on a number of occasions in his *Salons* dealing with Vernet, sometimes using words very similar to those we find here.[24]

In *Le Neveu de Rameau*, Diderot also speaks of the "fracas de tonnerre." Since thunder had so many uses in opera, dramatizing storms and punctuating the gestures of the more powerful operatic divinities, there were several pieces of equipment that could produce it, one of which is shown in figure 24.[25] Although I have not been able to find any completely satisfactory illustration for the "temple qui s'élève" mentioned earlier in the passage,[26] one may assume that the orchestral music for the rising temple would have been appropriately solemn in tone. One might also imagine a

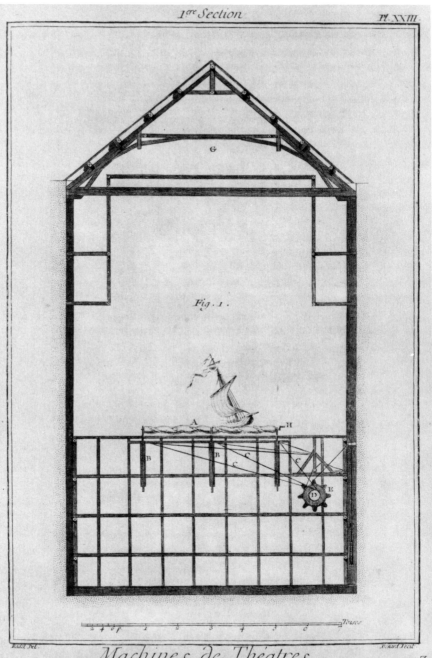

Fig. 1.

Radel Del.

Benard Fecit.

Machines de Théatres.

Coupe sur toute la hauteur et la largeur avec les Rues de Mer équipées.

Z

22. Radel, "Coupe . . . avec les Rues de Mer équipées"

23. Joseph Vernet, "Les Suites d'un naufrage" (detail), engraved by Catherine Elisabeth Cousinet

24. Radel, "Détail du chariot du Tonnerre"

rising musical motif to imitate the upward movement of the machines on stage.

To return one last time to the quotation from *Le Neveu de Rameau*, we may note that the disjointed, fragmentary character of these images, their extraordinary intensity, give the passage a quality that makes Diderot think of insanity. Today we would be inclined to speak, rather, of poetry, perhaps even of surrealism, and one of the subliminal elements that produces this magical, hallucinatory effect – and which makes Diderot's passage so different from the pleasant prose of the anonymous pamphlet we saw earlier, and which may even have been one of Diderot's "sources" – is the series of layers of transmutations, of alchemy, of "correspondences" as one of the senses is transformed into another, that is, transformed still again in our imaginations. In just these brief lines the Nephew has used song and movement to mimic the whole range of human emotional possibilities, from the slightest feelings to those that are most intense and gripping, from easy tranquility to unbearable pain and despair. And then, having in the violence of his projections, exhausted everything that *is*, he even comes to imitate non-presence: the *absence* of light (*l'ombre*), the *absence* of noise (*le silence*). But the extraordinary synthesis of the penultimate phrase reaches out still further toward the ultimate, as the narrator explains that a non-noise, too, can actually be *painted* in *sound*. This is the furthest literary outpost of the doctrine of imitation in music, in the whole eighteenth century. It is so far out, it verges on collapse.

This brings us to the final text by Diderot that we will examine in the present context. It comes from the *Lettre sur les sourds et muets* of 1751, the same year as d'Alembert's *Preliminary Discourse*. Throughout this entire work Diderot has been assuming that the function of music is to imitate. But then, just before the end, he suddenly finds himself brought up short by the objections of a correspondent.[27] She asks, with disarming simplicity, how Diderot accounts for the fact that, contrary to his theory of the necessity of music to paint images, there are some pieces of music in which neither Diderot, nor anyone else, ever found any pictures (Diderot's words are "peinture hiéroglyphique," implying poetical images), but which give everyone great pleasure.

Diderot's answers are characteristically contradictory. First, he meets the objection head-on and tries to explain it away. Though he does indeed concede that such music may give pleasure, he points out that the enjoyment is rather like what we feel when we see a rainbow: it is a purely sensual experience and the pleasure it gives is far less than it would be were the charms of harmony joined to the truth (*la vérité*) of imitation. If only the stars could retain their original brightness when painted on canvas they would seem more beautiful than they did in the firmament, because in painting, the reflective pleasure that derives from imitation would be combined with the direct and natural pleasure of sensation. Diderot is sure that his correspondent was never so affected by natural moonlight as she was by one of Vernet's [painted] nights. . . .[28]

In the virtually irresistible clarity of its logic, this is a most tempting argument. It not only demonstrates that music which imitates is superior to that which does not, but shows most persuasively why art can be superior to raw nature, a belief that should have endeared Diderot to all the greatest artists who have lived ever since – at least until the end of literary "symbolism." And yet, perhaps because the idea is too dogmatically stated, perhaps because Diderot realized it was incomplete, imperfect, partially false, he does not let the matter remain there:

Au reste, la musique a plus besoin de trouver en nous ces favorables dispositions d'organes, que ni la peinture, ni la poésie. Son hiéroglyphique est si léger et si fugitif, il est si facile de le perdre ou de le mésinterpréter, que le plus beau morceau de symphonie ne ferait pas un grand effet, si le plaisir infaillible et subit de la sensation pure et simple n'était infiniment au-dessus de celui d'une expression souvent équivoque. La peinture montre l'objet même, la poésie le décrit, la musique en excite à peine une idée. Elle n'a de resource que dans les intervalles et la durée des sons; et quelle analogie y a-t-il entre cette espèce de crayons et le printemps, les ténèbres, la solitude, etc., et la plupart des objets? Comment se fait-il donc que des trois arts imitateurs de la nature, celui dont l'expression est la plus arbitraire et la moins précise parle le plus fortement à l'âme? Serait-ce que montrant moins les objets, il laisse plus de carrière à notre imagination, ou qu'ayant besoin de secousses pour être émus, la musique est plus propre que la peinture et la poésie à produire en nous cet effet tumultueux?[29]

It would be an understatement to say that the author has just changed his mind: having previously declared that music ought to involve our faculty of reflection via imitation, Diderot now turns about face and discovers how much music relies on sensation, pure and simple. Forgetting his previous sponsorship of rational comprehension, he now heads off in the opposite direction to realize that music's unique effect upon us derives from its mystery, from the unknown. Its indefiniteness becomes a source of poetry.

The contradiction between the two directions of thought is inescapable, and one might as well resign oneself to it: to try to run these disparate arguments together on the same level distorts everything.[30] Nor is this the only instance of opposite attitudes emerging side by side in Diderot's work; in fact such bare antagonisms regularly intrude, especially at moments like this one, when rational argument had clearly been winning the day. The appearance of this "contrary" certainly indicates we have reached a further, later stage in the development of his thought, perhaps also a deeper one. Yet the advent of this new perspective does not mean that the old one has been canceled out or disproved: arguments are never terminal in Diderot; his thought is always emerging, evolving, subsiding, changing form as the author lives and breathes. In the passage at hand, the second argument depends on the first for its existence: the careful enunciation of the intellectual advantages of imitative music produced – through some curious, backward-working mechanism buried in Diderot's psyche – the awareness of the opposite, of the importance in music of the purely physical, non-intellectual, intuitive. Indeed the importance of this phenomenon – the attraction of the contrary – in Diderot's thought is what makes him the unspoken hero of the present study.[31] We note, too, that in the text under consideration the two perspectives belong together eternally, as creator and created. Nor does it really matter that, considered as attitudes, they form a contradiction. Aesthetic truths often do, and to eliminate one perspective in favor of consistency would surely have diminished the universality of Diderot's thought, the unique value of which lies precisely in his desire to embrace all the possibles.

We will return one last time to the figure of Music in the frontispiece of the *Encyclopédie*: it seems clear that the painter drew Music retiring so modestly behind the other figures in order to suggest Music's role as imitator. She belongs to others more than to herself. Her position, partially obscured by the other arts of imitation, indicates that she is being thought of primarily as an imitator of these arts, in other words, that she represents specifically opera more than any other musical form. Finally, seeing her warm, but slightly reticent smile, may one not imagine in her something of Rousseau's awareness of how personal a matter music may become? Perhaps the obscurity of her position suggests too those elusive qualities of mystery which, as Diderot had come to see, are music's greatest sources of power.

8

Secrets from Suzanne: the tangled motives of *La Religieuse*

In Diderot's *Neveu de Rameau*, the ne'er-do-well nephew of the great composer speaks of his celebrated uncle as being alive, well, and just as disagreeable as ever, on page 8;[1] whereas if we turn to page 15 we find the same nephew in the same conversation on the same afternoon referring to the same uncle as dead and buried; there has even been time for him to pick through the deceased's portfolios, looking in vain for unpublished compositions he could plagiarize. Of the innumerable contradictions in Diderot few are so extreme as this one; the case is flagrant. And yet, even so, several explanations relating to the composition of the dialogue may account for the discrepancy: Diderot may have written parts of it while the great Rameau was still alive, and other parts after his death (in 1764), and then neglected to patch over the differences. Or (a more likely hypothesis in my opinion), he may have been remembering bits of talks with the Nephew that had actually been held at various periods, diverse memories that finally merged into a single literary conversation. In any case, the example may underscore a point that has been slightly obscured by critics who like to stress the work as an inner dialogue (which, to be sure, it is): that the stuff and matter out of which the dialogue grew into whatever one chooses to call it, were real conversations with a real person. It is not quite conceivable that, independent of such external *données*, an author would dream up a dialogue in which he deliberately failed to make up his mind about the existence or inexistence of this famous person, a main touchstone for the great issues of his satire.

This flagrant discrepancy was, so to speak, indeliberate, and it could only happen because each moment of the dialogue comes into being on its own terms,[2] which in this case turned out to have nothing to do with the consistency of the whole. Certain contexts made Rameau alive, others made him dead. To resolve the contradiction might have calmed the nerves of jittery critics, but, *à coup sûr*, it would have dried up those essential juices bringing life to every precious syllable of this work, whose ecology is partly self-sustaining.

Such moments of discrepancy are perfect examples of *invraisemblance* in the theatrical sense of the term, and in general this work exhibits an exhilarating disregard for the rules of consistency that are basic to dramatic likelihood (one of the many reasons one should never even try to take an overview of it). *Le Neveu*, in this sense, is the exact opposite of a tragedy by Voltaire, or, better yet, of the *drames* of Diderot himself, with all their ponderously conceived characters inching their way through the turgid plot, scrupulously obeying the laws of dramatic causality that have been weighted down even further by their exasperating concern for virtue. Only the miracles of Diderot's genius keep them alive, just barely breathing. But how they make one long to throw open the windows and let the breezes blow, to snip all the cords binding the characters to their own seriousness, to rid them of their sense of class duty and morality, to set them free of their knotty relationships with one another. If it were possible to undo one of Diderot's *drames* in this way, the result might be a work quite similar to *Le Neveu de Rameau*, where there are fresh breezes at every moment, and which is constantly breaking out of its confines, creating new relationships as it dissolves old ones.

The *drames* and *Le Neveu de Rameau* represent the extreme poles of Diderot's art, the latter being one of the freest forms he ever created, the former among the most constricted. In the middle comes *La Religieuse*.[3] Certainly there is constriction in this novel – beginning with the subject matter, for in fact it is all about women locked in the confinement of convents. Yet there is the opposite, too, since it tells the story of one nun's struggle to get out: deconfinement. Its form is similarly two-faced: in part it is a *mémoire*-novel,[4] a genre that theoretically allows the author to go anywhere he likes for as long as he wishes. It assumes an audience that is hungry for intimate details and not too fussy about where they come from. At the same time, this *mémoire*-novel is rather special because it pretends to be persuading the Marquis de Croismare to come to Paris and rescue the poor nun who is writing him her pathetic story. This implies a novel that is tailored, confined, to the tastes of a given person it must not offend, whom, in fact, it must seduce.[5] Finally, it is also a philosophical text, a demonstration proving that convents are inherently evil institutions because they are contrary to nature, and this implies a further slanting of the material.

Generations of scholars have been pointing out that the novel is riddled with inconsistencies.[6] To mention just a few of the more sensational ones: Diderot gets his heroine's age seriously wrong according to the facts of his own chronology. At times she, Suzanne, is aware of events she could not have been aware of – or the reverse: Suzanne claims ignorance of crucial situations of which we know she has already been informed. Perhaps some of these discrepancies are due to the long period of gestation during which the novel developed into its present form; some of them may reflect a certain disarray as the work oscillates between a free form and a more constricted one, and there are other sources of disarray, too, as we shall see.

By comparison, the flagrant contradictions of *Le Neveu de Rameau* are actually less noticeable, probably because that dialogue demands we surrender ourselves to it, so that we generally lose track of boundary lines as we float along with the discourse. *La Religieuse*, on the other hand, being an effort to persuade, involves evidence that will score points[7] (with the reader, with the Marquis de Croismare). The polemics force one to keep track, and we become very uncomfortable when the pieces obviously don't fit. Just why does Suzanne, narrating the story of her childhood (pp. 83–4), pretend she is *still* unaware she was an illegitimate child when (1) she had long since surmised as much from the attitude of her parents and other telling bits of evidence, and (2) she had expressly been informed of the facts by Le Père Séraphim (p. 84, n. 6; p. 105)? One can only assume wilful blindness on her part,[8] as if she could, simply by willing, blot out her awareness and restore the question that has been answered to its pristine state of unansweredness. But the phenomenon also implies an absolutely bizarre blindness on the author's part:[9] he can cause events to happen to his characters (here, informing Suzanne of her illegitimacy, and elsewhere there are many other instances), and then, refuse to take cognizance of them. Events occur, yet at the same time they do not occur because the author deems it not decent, or wise, or opportune (who can fathom all the motives?) to register them. The facts are known, yet they are distinctly not known, not recognized: they are a secret which Suzanne and the author are keeping from themselves. I am tempted to claim that the whole novel may be a secret – from the heroine and her author.

Let us consider an example, from one of the novel's lesbian sequences:

La nuit suivante, lorsque tout le monde dormait et que la maison était dans le silence, elle se leva. Après avoir erré quelque temps dans les corridors elle vint à ma cellule; j'ai le sommeil léger, je crus la reconnaître. Elle s'arrêta; en s'appuyant le front apparemment contre ma porte elle fit assez de bruit pour me réveiller si j'avais dormi. Je gardai le silence. Il me sembla que j'entendais une voix qui se plaignait, quelqu'un qui soupirait; j'eus d'abord un léger frisson, ensuite je me déterminai à dire *Ave*; au lieu de me répondre, on s'éloignait à pas léger. On revint quelque temps après; les plaintes et les soupirs recommencèrent; je dis encore *Ave* et l'on s'éloigna pour la seconde fois. Je me rassurai, je m'endormis. Pendant que je dormais on entra, on s'assit à côté de mon lit, mes rideaux étaient entrouverts, on tenait une petite bougie dont la lumière m'éclairait le visage, et celle qui la portait me regardait dormir, ce fut du moins ce que j'en jugeai à son attitude lorsque j'ouvris les yeux; et cette personne, c'était la supérieure. Je me levai subitement; elle vit ma frayeur, elle me dit: Suzanne, rassurez-vous, c'est moi. . . . Je me remis la tête sur l'oreiller et je lui dis: Chère Mère, que faites-vous ici à l'heure qu'il est? qu'est-ce qui peut vous avoir amenée? pourquoi ne dormez-vous pas?

(pp. 237–8)[10]

Just before the beginning of this passage, the person called "elle" in the first sentence has been positively identified by the author and Suzanne as the Superior; but then, with the "je crus la reconnaître" that knowledge is being deliberately blurred (of course Suzanne recognized the Superior; who else would be prowling the corridor of her cell late at night?). And strangely, the more evidence there is – now, in addition to the sound of the footsteps, Suzanne can hear the Superior's voice sighing – the more the facts are presented as uncertain ("j'entendais *une* voix"). Even the Superior's sex becomes vague ("quelqu'*un* qui soupirait"), whereupon the Superior fades into total anonymity, becoming again and again the faceless, sexless, "on" whose identity Suzanne is no longer supposed to know. So much so that when the Superior appears through the opening of the bed curtains, Suzanne is actually frightened ("elle vit ma frayeur"), just as though the intruder had been an unexpected stranger. The first words Suzanne speaks resemble those of someone still under the shock of a surprise. The process is now completed: Suzanne's recognition of (desire for) the Superior has turned into a secret from Suzanne and from the author; even the reader is supposed to play ignorant and pretend to believe it was all simply an effect of her being asleep.

The quoted passage comes from one of the scenes of seduction between women that give this novel its special tonality. When Suzanne comes to her first convent (pp. 85ff.), the principal strategy used by the nuns to overcome what are called her "répugnances" is precisely seduction, mainly verbal: they tell her how pretty she is, hover over her, coo and admire her, and she and Diderot remember and treasure each detail of their compliments (pp. 89–90). These "caresses," joined with the nuns' propaganda against life in the real world, are so effective that by her own admission Suzanne has moments when she even yearns for the time of her final vows. To be sure, she finds that, as the actual date approaches, her "répugnances" are on the rise again. And then, there is the crucial event, bringing on a seemingly irrevocable about-face: a nun, usually kept under lock and key, and who had been driven mad by the convent, escapes from her cell. All the drama of the moment is packed into Diderot's first dense sentence:

Je la vis. Voilà l'époque de mon bonheur ou de mon malheur, selon, Monsieur, la manière dont vous en userez avec moi. Je n'ai jamais rien vu de si hideux. Elle était échevelée et presque sans vêtement; elle traînait des chaînes de fer; ses yeux étaient égarés; elle s'arrachait les cheveux; elle se frappait la poitrine avec les poings; elle courait, elle hurlait; elle se chargeait elle-même et les autres des plus terribles imprécations; elle cherchait une fenêtre pour se précipiter. Le frayeur me saisit, je tremblai de tous mes membres, je vis mon sort dans celui de cette infortunée, et sur-le-champ, il fut décidé dans mon coeur que je mourrais mille fois plutôt que de m'y exposer. (pp. 92–3)[11]

The first three words of the passage are what Diderot might have termed a "hieroglyphic," containing the message of the whole; in fact the structure of the passage is conceived as a progressive revelation of the various implications of these three short syllables. After briefly making sure the Marquis de Croismare is paying full attention, we find first, naturally, the

actual physical description of the mad nun, in rather lurid detail, and this
sight is at once so horrifying and so emblematic of all life in the convent that
it brings on the urgency and determination of Suzanne's decision. The first
three words have other layers of meaning, too, as we shall note.

Of course, the main thing Suzanne saw as she stared at the mad nun was
her own face in a mirror: the wild creature might be *herself*. And it was this
shock of recognition that brought on the energetic decision to do anything
in the world rather than suffer the same fate. In other words, for Suzanne
the sight is above all a warning. For the reader, on the other hand, this
portrait of the mad nun serves also as an omen, a foreseeing of quite
precisely the destiny in store for Suzanne, although actually not in ways we
could have predicted. Here again there is ambiguity: the mirror doesn't lie;
we know already what Suzanne's fate will be; we even know from this
portrait how she will look. Nevertheless, for us the course of her destiny will
prove full of strange surprises.

The frightening portrait of the mad nun leads us to expect terrible
treatment of Suzanne if ever fate forces her into a convent. Yet when fate
does just that, the treatment she receives is far from terrible. Indeed she
finds herself living under the most benign reign of a Mother Superior she
adores, of whom she is the favorite, and with whom – largely verbally – she
is having a romance. Neither Suzanne nor the author is willing to take full
cognizance of this, but even so the text leaves little doubt:[12]

[. . .] on eût dit que l'esprit de Dieu l'inspirait. Ses pensées, ses expressions, ses
images pénétraient jusqu'au fond du coeur; d'abord on l'écoutait, peu à peu on était
entraîné, on s'unissait à elle, l'âme tressaillait et l'on partageait ses transports. Son
dessein n'était pas de séduire, mais certainement c'est ce qu'elle faisait. On sortait
de chez elle avec un coeur ardent, la joie et l'extase étaient peintes sur le visage, on
versait des larmes si douces!   (pp. 118–19)[13]

Here Suzanne is claiming that her own experience was merely a shared and
communal one, as if she were only feeling what everyone else felt. Yet, later
in the novel, as she looks back on her relationship with La Soeur de Moni, it
turns out that she indeed remembered something uniquely hers, and that
makes the impersonal "on" of the preceding passage, once again, seem
quite deceptive:

[. . .] mon âme s'allume facilement, s'exalte, se touche, et cette bonne supérieure
m'a dit cent fois en m'embrassant que personne n'aurait aimé Dieu comme moi; que
j'avais un coeur de chair et les autres un coeur de pierre. Il est sûr que j'éprouvais
une facilité extrême à partager son extase, et que dans les prières qu'elle faisait à
haute voix, quelquefois il m'arrivait de prendre la parole, de suivre le fil de ses idées
et de rencontrer, comme d'inspiration, une partie de ce qu'elle aurait dit elle-même.
Les autres l'écoutaient en silence ou la suivaient; moi je l'interrompais, ou je la devan-
çais, ou je parlais avec elle; je conservais très longtemps l'impression que j'avais
prise, et il fallait apparemment que je lui en restituasse quelque chose, car, si l'on

discernait dans les autres qu'elles avaient conversé avec elle, on discernait en elle qu'elle avait conversé avec moi.   (pp. 147–8)[14]

Perhaps they are sharing a "religious" experience as Suzanne says they are, but even without a Freudian analysis of the images, it is clear that the main experience Diderot is depicting is that of love – passionate love on a basis of equality between two members of the same sex. One woman can substitute for the other because she already knows, and loves, the other's thoughts and feelings. She can have them, too, and so together – it doesn't matter which is in the lead – they mount toward a sort of ecstasy.

Blissful risings such as we see in these passages do *not* characterize generally the relationship between these two women. On the contrary, Suzanne describes herself as unable, unwilling, to rise to the religious, or emotional heights, striven after by La Soeur de Moni (p. 119). Suzanne remains, so we are told, earthbound, and with disastrous effects on her friend and would-be romancer. Suzanne drains and destroys the Superior's faith and all the thrilling emotions that went with it (pp. 119–20), and if La Soeur de Moni proceeds to pine away and die so inexorably in this section of the novel, the implication is very much that the grief-stricken, inconsolable Suzanne has, through her own inability/unwillingness to let go and share her friend's experiences – perhaps even to make them real for her – caused her death.[15]

The demise of this Mother Superior – so touchingly described (pp. 125–7), such a milestone in Suzanne's life – marks the end of one part of the novel. It is above all in the next section of the work that I'm not convinced the author always took in the words he had written on the page. Ostensibly this section demonstrates how inherently wrong the confinement of a convent is, and how to thwart nature in this way turns women into inhuman creatures, beasts.[16] But what his words actually say is that, faced with a new Mother Superior and unwilling to accept the change, Suzanne decides on a plan of behavior that will deliberately turn the new Superior, and everyone in her obedience, against her irrevocably.[17] Suzanne herself sets her own downward course by doing everything possible to thwart, insult, and slander the new Mother Superior (incredibly, Suzanne even uses lesbian insinuations, p. 131), demonstrating openly how much she scorns and despises her, fomenting discontent among the other nuns and urging disobedience, raising legal obstacles. . . . Of course they all come to hate her, but that was precisely what Suzanne had in mind:

Je n'omis rien de ce qui pouvait me faire craindre, haïr, me perdre et j'en vins à bout.
                                                                                      (p. 131)[18]

Why this sudden need to destroy herself with punishment ("me perdre")? No doubt the author was telling himself that it stemmed from Suzanne's unswerving loyalty to La Soeur de Moni, along with her irrepressible desire for freedom, and her unwillingness to compromise. Yet in view of her flamboyant provocations, this cannot be the whole story, and it gives one a rather uneasy feeling to observe that the most terrible and gripping scenes in this novel, the scenes of greatest pathos (surely it was here that Diderot wanted his readers to know he wept over his heroine's misfortunes),[19] those awful moments (pp. 132ff.) when the heroine, filthy, disheveled, despised, spat upon, her feet bleeding from the broken glass strewn in her path by the hateful nuns, her hands burned by the fiery poker they tricked her into picking up, trampled on by them as she lay on the corridor floor, groaning, almost suicidal, in suffering, shunned as if she were possessed by the devil ("Satan! éloignez-vous de moi," p. 163) – that all of this had been deliberately devised by Suzanne, even as it had been imagined by the author. We now have a fulfilment of the prediction of the mad nun, the one Suzanne saw as a mirror of herself in the first convent. Yet, ironically, the portrait was not merely an omen of the things cruel fate would bring, as we thought, it was also a declaration of the author's – and Suzanne's – own intentions.

But how curious, in a work supposedly denouncing the repressive evils of the convent, to discover that, by the heroine/author's own admission, many of the repressions and evil disorders turn out to be not really inherent in convents, but are the deliberate and gratuitous creation of the heroine/author who is allegedly combatting them! Suzanne was getting exactly what she had been asking for. This element of wilfulness on both their parts is enough to subvert the entire philosophical message of the work; it undermines everything the author is trying to say. And how typical of Diderot this sort of contradiction is. For, once again, the creative forces that brought into being this strangely powerful indictment of the cloister, also – through an equally strange reversed attraction of the contrary – brought into being an anti-indictment, in fact an antidote.[20] Of course, Diderot thought convents were unsocial, unnatural, and therefore evil; there can be no doubt about that. But at the same time – to simplify and codify matters that Diderot suggestively explored in terms of all the complexities of human experience – convents *are* a society, and those making them up are part of humanity too. This means that although in the convent all are victims,[21] since they are controlled, confined, and punished by that society's institutions, yet – to turn the coin over on the other side – all can also be viewed more actively and positively as forming the convent, creating its life, applying the rules, and hence, responsible for (guilty of) its punishments. Both these perspectives are very much present in the character of Suzanne; nor is Diderot willing to see the contradiction between them that – unless the two layers are kept unbelievably separate – could easily set off a mutual cancellation that would leave his polemic with a blank.

Given the gravity of Suzanne's physical sufferings and the intensity of her mental anguish, it would have been no surprise if she had perished from her cruel treatment. Yet, even though she falls extremely ill, Diderot does not let her perish from her malady. Rather it is her dearest and most faithful friend, Sainte Ursule, who, worn out from caring for her, catches her disease and dies in her stead.[22] This is another of the novel's most touching moments (pp. 198–201), and the nobility of this friend's selflessness, and Suzanne's moving appreciation of her generosity – all of this being set against the cruel callousness of the other nuns – creates scenes so heart-rending it never occurs to us to notice that Suzanne's love and affection are not exactly helpful to those females on whom they are bestowed. As the novel progresses we become uncomfortably aware that Suzanne's caresses are regularly becoming agents of death.

Philosophically the cruelty of these nuns is supposed to represent the quintessence of the evils of the cloister: this is how women behave when deprived of their natural freedom. Cloisters are like that. Nevertheless – another illogical contradiction – Suzanne's next convent doesn't display the same evil symptoms at all. In cloister number three (pp. 207ff.), the nuns actually seem happy; there is much bustle and gaiety among them. The lesbian Mother Superior, though completely erratic in behavior, is distinctly benign. At Suzanne's arrival, the nuns first crowd at the windows, and then come to meet her near the entrance, and Suzanne remarks that this is a sign of how different this convent is from the other one.

The lesbian Mother Superior is the center around which the life of the convent revolves, the key to everyone's well-being. Suzanne's romance with her comes as the culminating example of the refusal to take cognizance which we have already seen in both Suzanne and her author. But here their blindness becomes truly amazing.[23] Apparently Suzanne can absorb any amount of fondlings and embraces, even knee-rubbing from the Mother Superior, without ever taking into account the passionate nature of her/ their feelings. She can admit the Superior to her bed and be ready to let her press up against her without once saying to herself that this is love (instead she says she doesn't want the Superior to feel so cold). No doubt the author is completely aware of the Mother Superior's secret, but he is still hiding from himself the secrets of Suzanne. How revealing, in this connection, to compare Suzanne's almost grotesque description of the Mother Superior's odd behavior and irregular physical appearance at her arrival in the convent (pp. 207–10) with Suzanne's later portrait of the same Superior on the evening of the collation she gave for the nuns (pp. 244–5): all her oddities and irregularities have disappeared; in Suzanne's eyes at least, her oddities have become advantages; she looks positively lovely. Perhaps we should assume the changes are partly due to her affair with Suzanne: the author is imagining that the Superior's happiness has made her more beautiful. But at the same time, the differences are supposed to show us

Suzanne's own unspoken emotions. Suzanne's flattering portrait describes a woman transformed by someone who loves her.[24] But again, the author refuses to allow his character to register the meaning of her feelings, a meaning he has made quite obvious to us. In other words, at the very moment he brings her love into being on one fictional level, he is denying it on another, turning it into a secret from Suzanne, and also from himself (as her creator). Only the eye of the reader remains watchful.

Once Suzanne has begun her convent life, men play only occasional roles (they make infrequent visits to the convent), but of course their effect on the direction of the novel is crucial. For Suzanne, they often arouse passionate feelings. In the case of her devoted lawyer, this is not exactly recognized by her (though others see it), but in the case of her confessor Dom Morel, she finds in him a soulmate (pp. 266–8), someone who at last understands her, even as La Soeur de Moni had done, in her way. Most of the men in the novel, the Marquis de Croismare first among them (following Diderot, of course) represent forces of liberation: the visit of the wise prelate to the second convent brings Suzanne's persecutions to an end (p. 181). Her lawyer, though failing to get her vows rescinded, gets her out of the terrible convent, and into a better one, at least (p. 206). Her friendly confessor, Dom Morel, stimulates her will to be free. Another confessor, having understood the lesbian nature of the Mother Superior's advances, had earlier determined to sever the bond between the two women, and save Suzanne from the unspeakable sin of homosexuality. Suzanne, having once again turned into an automaton, dully maintains she cannot understand why her confessor is demanding she totally shun all physical contact with the Superior. Yet Diderot shows her as willing, even determined to obey. Her blindness is a source of "innocence." She will reject the Superior's advances, though without understanding why.

The novel now sets off once again on a downward course towards isolation, persecution, dishevelment, and even madness – the prediction of the nun in the mirror will be fulfilled once again – not in Suzanne, this time, but rather in the Mother Superior whom she will cause to replace her. And even as she casts the Superior in her own former role of victim and watches her painful descent, Suzanne herself will actually assume the part of the other Mother Superior, the cruel one with the heartless satellites. We remember how they had shunned Suzanne as if she were possessed by the devil; but now it is Suzanne who rejects the lesbian Superior with almost the exact same words once used against her: "Loin de moi, Satan" (p. 258).[25] Suzanne now looks on while the Superior lies in the corridor to be trampled on by the sisters (p. 266) – even as Suzanne had been; she is deprived of the sacraments – like Suzanne. In short, while her would-be lover turns into the mad woman in the mirror, Suzanne, through her rejection, causes the Superior to undergo all the torments she herself had endured. She brings these torments on the Superior just as wilfully as she had earlier brought them on herself.

The main difference between the two cases is that this Superior will be destroyed by her unhappiness and guilt, whereas Diderot had provided other female victims to die in Suzanne's stead (the lesbian being the last of them). And, to be sure, he had kept Suzanne supposedly blind, and therefore innocent,[26] of feelings that he is apparently calling "criminal," or at least unnatural – although Diderot vacillates on this issue: he first gives Suzanne the stern confessor who condemns the Mother Superior without any appeal as "indigne, libertine, mauvaise religieuse, femme pernicieuse, âme corrompue" (p. 254). This is, of course, the same confessor who commanded Suzanne to reject the lesbian. But then our author – who, after all, once penned a dialogue subtitled "sur l'inconvénient d'attacher des idées morales à certaines actions qui n'en comportent pas" – replaced this stern confessor with a milder one, who was not nearly so obsessed and upset by lesbianism, who in fact regarded it as the inevitable consequence of an evil institution, the cloister. Even though the new confessor didn't share the other confessor's theological views, or his views on convents, he let the other man's decisions concerning the Mother Superior stand as approved – to us, a weak and rather evasive compromise.

But it is time to look at one last passage which gives the essence of this contradictory work, as well as any single passage can. Suzanne is bringing Dom Morel, her new confessor, up to date concerning her behavior towards the lesbian:

[...] c'est le père le Moine qui m'a inspiré de l'éloignement pour ma supérieure. – Il a bien fait. – Et pourquoi? – Ma soeur, me répondit-il en prenant un air grave, tenez-vous en à ses conseils et tâchez d'ignorer la raison tant que vous vivrez [...] C'est votre innocence même qui en a imposé à votre supérieure; plus instruite, elle vous aurait moins respectée – [...] Où est donc le mal de s'aimer, de se le dire, de se le témoigner? Cela est si doux! – Il est vrai, dit dom Morel, en levant ses yeux sur moi qu'il avait toujours tenus baissés tandis que je parlais. – Et cela est-il donc si commun dans les maisons religieuses? Ma pauvre supérieure! dans quel état elle est tombée! – Il est facheux, et je crains bien qu'il n'empire; elle n'était pas faite pour son état, et voilà ce qui en arrive tôt ou tard. Quand on s'oppose au penchant général de la nature, cette contrainte la détourne à des affections déréglées qui sont d'autant plus violentes qu'elles sont moins fondées; c'est une espèce de folie. – Elle est folle! – Oui, elle l'est, et elle le deviendra davantage.   (pp. 270–1)[27]

But how can Suzanne exclaim "Elle est folle!" as if surprised, when she herself had been recording each step of the Superior's descent into madness, when she herself was responsible for it? Again we must assume that Suzanne's experience has erased itself. Though it happened, as Suzanne's memoirs attest, it now has not happened; she is restored to her famous "innocence." By the same token, she is now totally disengaged from the doomed Superior, in fact the foregoing passage bids her a fond farewell – another kiss of death, of course. But the sensual pleasure Suzanne has admitted to in this passage lives on after the Superior's disappearance, ready and waiting to be enjoyed by Dom Morel, whose eyes now for the first time seek Suzanne's own, hearing her mention the pleasures of loving. Perhaps the Marquis de Croismare's ears might be pricking up, too; at least Diderot pretended he thought they did, as we see in the ending he added in 1782 (p. 294).

Yet, no matter what the author himself was prepared to admit, this is, most assuredly, a novel about expiation, even as *Manon Lescaut* had been; in the last analysis, Suzanne's unspoken love for this Mother Superior – the culmination of all the passionate affections of the three convents – means love of the society of women, in fact it represents love of the cloister, and before Suzanne can get free and out of these walls, she will have to put behind her, and even kill off, *her own secret desires*. In the rich texture of Diderot's psychology, we find a woman battling not only against the constraints imposed on nature by society (here, the cloister), but battling too against her own impulses to find satisfactions, even sensual pleasures within these confines. I think this was why Diderot dreamed up Suzanne's unpardonable cruelty toward a woman (the last of three victims) whose only crime was in loving (Diderot's fantasy, too) his heroine too much.

As we know from his letters, Diderot in real life had been simply fascinated by lesbian love.[28] There is something vaguely disappointing – if inevitable – in this novel as we see his willingness to go along with such a conventional condemnation (a somewhat similar phenomenon occurs at the end of the *Rêve de d'Alembert* trilogy). At the same time, the experience of this novel suggests that Diderot could only give free rein to these unorthodox fantasies provided he and his heroine never took cognizance of them for what they were (at least, not while the fantasy was in progress), and that at the end they would all be sacrificed, done away with – however painfully and brutally – in favor of the normal heterosexual world, as Suzanne scales the wall to freedom. Ironically (and probably this tangled paradox was just why Diderot could not make parts of his final section comprehensible), this free world, which Suzanne had longed for so passionately, proves just as dangerous and cruel as the "hell" of confinement he and his heroine had left, destroyed, behind them.

9

A unique and forgotten opera libretto

During much of the French Enlightenment, regular tragedy and opera tragedy (*tragédie lyrique*) developed essentially as opposites.[1] Regular tragedy had always aimed above all at a concentrated experience, just as T. S. Eliot suggested and, narrowly circumscribed by the unities, it continued to require only a small cast with a single setting, and was dominated by a single serious mood. "Le merveilleux" and divine interventions were hardly ever employed, since they might have undermined the *vraisemblance* of the psychological motivations: miracles came from without, whereas the essence of tragedy came from within the characters and the situation; it was self-contained. Opera, by contrast, evoked a world of illusions based on almost totally different intentions: its aim, first of all, was to *divert*, and for this, variety was the key feature. It employed a large cast that included soloists and choruses, solo dancers and chorus dancers, all of them capable of producing a multitude of effects in sound, color, shapes, and movements. The stage settings were naturally diverse; the plot-line gloried in unpredictability and surprises, and the moods of opera were as various as the rainbow, going from humorous or merely happy, to bellicose, amorous, wistful, sad, or starkly tragic. "Le merveilleux" was counted on as a constant feature, the gods often pulling all the strings of the action. Opera was largely an external affair, and psychologically its characters often seem hollow: virtually any mood can be poured into them simply by changing the mood of the music, the plot situation, or the scenery. Opera called not for unity, but for a multifarious experience, for dispersal rather than concentration, and one marvels that two such opposite forms of theatre could have flowered simultaneously and been enjoyed so enthusiastically by exactly the same spectators.

Not that this opposition would remain forever. Indeed one of the ways to view the history of these two grand theatrical genres in the eighteenth century in France is to see them as gradually contaminating each other. Regular tragedy became somewhat more "operatic," as we see, for example, in the famous reforms of Voltaire, whose tragedies featured bolder use of choruses, of costumes and scenery, and even sound effects. As for opera itself it took longer to curb its extravagance, but even the Royal Academy of Music took on "classical" sobriety when Gluck's creations came to Paris. Furthermore, despite all the fundamental disparities we have noted, not absolutely everything was divergent in the two genres: at least both featured royal or divine destinies set in mythological, or antique, or distant, settings. Second, and more important for the present discussion, both opera librettos and the texts of regular tragedy employed a very small, "noble," vocabulary.

Curiously, the mannered vocabulary of opera was even tinier than that of non-musical tragedy: one might have thought that the greater variety of plot material in opera would have called for a more copious abundance of words, but just the opposite was the case.[2] It was as if the minuscule vocabulary of the libretto were somehow attempting to endow the almost voluptuous prodigality of the spectacle with a noble simplicity it would have lacked otherwise. But in any case, some sort of contrapuntal tension was inevitable, for in opera the vocabulary alone displayed the same tendencies one finds in regular tragedy, tendencies toward unity, simplicity, and concentration. Aesthetically this implies that the vocabulary, by its very nature, was pitted against everything else. Perhaps the discrepancy may have been less noticeable in the time of Lully, for then the paler harmonies of the music fitted better with the verses of the librettist. Thus, the conventional language of the poetry belonged with the musical expression at least. But as of Rameau's dazzlingly rich and colorful harmonies, and which featured not only the subtlest nuances but stark contrasts as well, this last congruence disappeared. Now the vocabulary of the poetry, virtually unchanged since Quinault's day, was out of kilter with absolutely everything else – which was probably one reason why the discerning Diderot so often made fun of it.[3]

Just once near the middle of the century there was an exception to this rule: a French opera in which the tiny vocabulary, instead of being set against the abundant variety of the spectacle, was allowed a story, setting, and characters entirely suited to it. The plot was tiny, also (almost nothing happens); the cast was as small as it had ever been in any serious opera, in fact the main characters number just two (briefly, three); there is a single setting, and the action takes place in a single act. Aesthetically it has all the concentrated unity of a regular stage play, and indeed it had been a stage play before it was turned into a libretto. Nor did the conversion result in the usual changes when a play became an opera – such as one finds when somber *Phèdre* turned into extravagant *Hippolyte et Aricie*, with humorous touches, a fire-belching monster onstage, a night scene in Aricie's lovely garden, and a happy ending. Here, for once, the essentials of the original plot remained intact; in fact it was actually simplified. The opera in question was *Deucalion et Pirrha*, the libretto being by Poullain de Saint-Foix,[4] the music by Giraud and Berton. It was staged on 30 September 1755 at the Royal Academy of Music, where it came and went with scarcely anyone bothering to notice it, and has rested in total obscurity ever since.

This neglect was probably due in part to the music which, although extremely competent, never shows the real talent of a Mouret, much less the genius of Rameau. (The score was never printed.) But the lack of success may also have been due to its not being at all what one expected to see at the Royal Academy. For, in this work, instead of external display, one found an inner psychological drama that gradually worked its way to a single moment of climax. To be sure, there is also a Prologue with a storm, the divine intervention of a goddess, and an evil allegorical personage trying to muddy the waters of the plot, and furthermore, at the end, a two-part ballet was tacked on – all of which was typical enough of operatic display. But in between, in the opera proper, there are just two personages singing onstage and the only "action" is the steadily increasing psychological tension between them.

Given the impossibly strict standards of decency at the Opéra, one might wonder how the librettist could have hoped to stage a legend that was already famous as a source of comic vulgarity, thanks to Piron's *Arlequin-Deucalion*.[5] Furthermore, the birth-motif of the main scene with the elderly couple[6] may have seemed slightly inappropriate for the traditional elevation of the Royal Academy of Music. Saint-Foix's solution to the dilemma was ingenious and it has a delicacy and discretion one likes to think of as typically French in this period. In place of the birth-giving stones, he substitutes a marble statue whose human form is indistinct – it might be either a man or a woman. Contrary to both Ovid and Piron, this author has made his hero and heroine young; nor have they ever seen each other before. And so, Deucalion and Pirrha, finding themselves alone on earth, receive instructions from the goddess to place a garland on the statue, which will then, they are told, come alive. Of course it was fated that Deucalion should love Pirrha, and so he does; but he is fearful that when the statue is endowed with life it will turn out to be a man, and thus a rival. Pirrha has similar fears that the statue will be a woman, for she, too, loves Deucalion. The drama of the opera lies entirely in the fears and hopes of the two characters as they prepare to make a gesture that risks sacrificing their love and losing one another to someone else. At last, despite his "pudeur," Deucalion confesses to Pirrha that he loves her, and, very discreetly, Pirrha lets it be known that her sentiments are not dissimilar. They sing a duet together, and, having agreed to flee the moment they do so, they place a garland on the statue. Now the stage brightens, and, as Deucalion and Pirrha start to run away, the statue reaches out and catches hold of them. Fearfully, they obey its command to look upon it, and discover that the statue is none other than the God of Love.

A unique and forgotten opera libretto

Few operas have ever displayed such a concentration of elements. For indeed the whole plot concerns the bringing into being of the sentiment the statue symbolizes, the sentiment of love. Hence the work of art, the statue, even – in another way – the opera itself comes alive as this meaning is manifest. We may note, too, that mythology functions here just as it does in a tragedy of Racine, forming an extension of the psychology of the characters. Thus everything serves to strengthen the unity of the piece. No other eighteenth-century French opera had been like this one;[7] in fact its plot structure is one of the most perfect ever conceived.

Alas, unless one were born breathing the air of the eighteenth century, one would never make the same claim for the mannered language of the libretto. "Que de charmes! . . . Grands dieux, puis-je / M'en garantir!"[8] sings Deucalion as he catches sight of Pirrha, and later, as she moves away from him, he sings: "Où portez-vous vos pas?"[9] (p. 6). When Pirrha confesses her feelings toward him, she uses so many subjunctives and conditionals the result rather resembles Proust's Tante Céline trying to thank Swann for the *vin d'Asti*. In response, Deucalion sends forth a whole cluster of clichés in the noble manner: "Quoi, Pirrha, vous m'aimez!" . . . "Quel discours enchanteur! . . . Quoi, Pirrha, vous daignez accepter mon hommage"[10] (p. 10). Whereupon Pirrha archly explains her reticence: "Je n'ai voulu qu'éprouver votre ardeur"[11] (p. 11).

The manuscript of the full musical score of the opera[12] has a number of surprises at this point and suggests how much one still needs to learn aesthetically before one can decipher a libretto such as this one with any degree of intelligence. To modern ears and minds, the passages just quoted seem like one of the climaxes of the work: at last, after all his struggles, Deucalion has confessed his love and discovers that, instead of being rejected for the promise of the statue, his feelings are reciprocated. Naturally he bursts out with "Quoi! Pirrha vous m'aimez!" If this had been the nineteenth century, to stress the feelings of passion and relief we might also have heard a crescendo from the full orchestra, perhaps even reinforced by a chorus. But this is the Age of Reason. All one hears is a dry *récitatif*, the only accompaniment to the solo voice being the "realized" bass line. Furthermore the manuscript indicates that this entire passage, containing both Deucalion's "Quoi!"'s and Pirrha's coy explanation, were actually cut out at the performance! Instead, the two singers went straight into an E major duo: "Ces bois reprennent leur verdure, / Cette onde par son doux murmure / Semble nous dire, aimez, soyez heureux . . . ,"[13] with music that is both lyric and suitably runny for the "onde" and "murmure." But the – to us – unaccountable omission of what we thought was the climax serves at least to put us on the alert that our modern senses of proportion are not at all the same as those of this era, and perhaps one of the reasons these opera librettos appear so unreadable to us today is that we have lost the keys to understanding them. Perhaps instead of thinking of them as banalities we should start to see them as mysteries.

But in any case, this particular libretto is a unique example of one kind of aristocratic art, a species in which extreme elevation of expression combines with virtually flawless employment of the unities. The opera version is far superior to the play version[14] in this regard. Indeed by comparison the play strikes one as chatty, almost verbose, with patches of pseudo-Marivaudage that are better suited to the drawing-room than to the universal deluge. In contrast, the opera, at its best, has the simplicity and strength of an eternal myth, and in this sense at least, the original performers of the opera were quite right to cut out the part containing Pirrha's coy rejoinder, which detracts momentarily from the purity of sentiment which is this opera's most appealing quality. Actually, the author was quite conscious of how unusual, in fact unique, it was to whittle the cast down to just two characters (three, counting the mostly silent "Amour"),[15] but he pointed out that this procedure simply brought to the fore the true essentials of life: what else could be needed besides a man, a woman, and love (p. 37)? Furthermore, if Parisian audiences had been slow to appreciate the play version, it had instantly been well received at Court,[16] where it obviously best belonged (p. 33).

The author also hints that this arch-aristocratic creation had, in its original play version, been conceived as an alternative to the earthy vulgarity and the social concerns found in Piron's *pièce en monologue*. In *Arlequin-Deucalion*, the myth of the flood had served to bring the human situation down to low comedy, a vantage point from which any sort of social pretension was shown up for what the author thought it was worth. Furthermore, his play's confinement to monologue was seen as a sort of challenge that the author would go to unbelievable lengths to overcome, and somehow succeeded: his play has such an astonishing variety of tones, moods, and plot situations, one constantly forgets it all comes from a single voice.

Saint-Foix's opera aims in precisely the opposite direction. For him the flood renders possible the noblest expression of human sentiment; it elevates. And indeed, since only two persons remain on earth, they are by definition sovereigns as well as subjects; they rule only over themselves. Thus social questions of any sort have been automatically eliminated by the dramatic situation. We note, too, that there is no mention in this libretto of eating, drinking, or sleeping. Saint-Foix's flood has deliberately abolished all concerns except the psychological, particularly the amorous. Nor was Saint-Foix unaware of the kind of social attitude he was rejecting, indeed he sneered scornfully at the social criticisms forming the climax of Piron's monologue.[17] Clearly his interests and style of expression were at the opposite pole from those of Piron. His drama was intentionally everything that Piron's was not.

As was usual in eighteenth-century terminology, this opera was called, on the title page, a "ballet," and to be sure, it was concluded by two sets of dances. Here, as the author admits, there was a slight problem, since Deucalion and Pirrha were supposed to be the sole survivors on earth and repopulation did not occur. How, then, could the author suddenly bring on other persons to dance in the ballet, since no one else yet existed? The problem, as he noted, was insoluble, so Saint-Foix simply ignored it and created a two-part ballet that had nothing to do with the rest.[18] The first *entrée* featured shepherds and shepherdesses dancing innocuously. But in the second *entrée* the plot veered suddenly off course. A monster appears and everyone is frightened. The author described the ensuing pantomime ballet with the monster as follows:

Un des Bergers l'attaque et le tue; tous les Bergers entourent leur défenseur, l'élèvent sur une espèce de Trône de verdure, et lui rendent hommage. La reconnaissance a fait le premier Roi.[19]

What an odd choice of *canevas*! Whereas the preceding part of the opera embodied a timeless truth and was set high above any vulgar reference to current issues, here with no warning or preparation, we suddenly have everyone's favorite topic in 1755: the origin in the state of nature of royal authority, and which Saint-Foix sees as homage to bravery and strength, in other words gratefulness for merit. According to this – admittedly brief – allegory, the first king was actually chosen by popular acclaim and rules with the consent of the governed. A door seems to be opening, almost before anyone notices it, onto the most controversial issue of the day. This is not to say that Saint-Foix was, in 1755, an incipient J.-J. Rousseau, or even a d'Alembert. Quite the contrary: he was the most aristocratic of aristocrats,[20] just as we infer from *Deucalion et Pirrha* proper. Perhaps the message of the ballet plot was only an optical illusion anyway, for the lines sung at the conclusion of the opera are royalist enough to have passed the test with Louis XIV, never mind his successor:

> Que le rang le plus glorieux
> De ce vainqueur consacre le courage;
> Que parmi nous il soit l'image
> Du souverain des Dieux:
> Celebrons sa victoire.
> Que son nom et sa gloire
> Volent jusques aux cieux.[21]

It is no wonder that this opera never became popular in the Age of Diderot.

As was mentioned earlier, the music of this opera, by Giraud and Berton,[22] is not exactly inspired, and there are several significant disappointments. The first is right at the beginning of the Prologue. The author's conception was as follows:

Le théâtre représente les suites du Déluge qui dure encore: on entend le bruit sourd et confus des vagues, des vents et du tonnere: on voit des arbres et différentes ruines qu'entraînent et qu'engloutissent les torrens: le nuage éclairé où Venus paroît avec les trois Graces, jette assez de lumière pour qu'on puisse appercevoir ces tristes objets à travers les ténèbres.[23]

Clearly the author intended that this strangely powerful scene of desolation and destruction be coming to an end as the opera opens. It lasts only for the moment which precedes the start of the action. Actually the rest of the myth will be essentially opposite to this scene, since the story concerns not disaster and destruction, but on the contrary, love and the renewal of life. In other words the Prologue is to give only a symbolical hint, a powerful one to be sure, of what the myth proper will be pulling against.

Unfortunately the composers of the music could not resist the chance to do a complete storm, from the hushed beginning with imitated raindrops (ascending D minor, G minor, D minor arpeggios played *piano* in the violins), lightning flashes (octuplets or sextuplets running up or down the scale), the whole overture ending with a great, loud cadence in D minor, which makes an effective backdrop for Venus' intervention: "Arrêtez!" (the rhythm going ♪ ♪ | o |) to be sure, but which also spoils the originality of the author's conception. For the rest, if one has in mind some of the great operatic storms that preceded this one, by Campra, Rameau, Colasse, or Marais, for example, these musical devices hardly startle one by their originality, in fact the whole thing suggests a cliché.

On the other hand, one has to forgive the composers for the trite music they gave to the allegorical figure of La Discorde and her accompanying Furies in this Prologue: the librettist's shopworn conception invited exactly the music he got. But at least some of the airs and *récitatifs* of the myth proper are rather appealing, occasionally sounding quite like Rameau's style, as in Pirrha's tenderly sad air in B minor,[24] sung when she believes Deucalion is hoping the statue will be a woman. Its opening, which perfectly weds the accents, and even the sense, of the words to the line of the melody, has a rhythm suggesting a "Gavotte tendre":

un doux es - poir — flat - te vo - tre â - me vous cro -

- yez dé - jà voir un ob - jet en - chan - teur

A unique and forgotten opera libretto

But quite aside from the quality of the airs, the music of the myth part of the opera deserves our attention in that its sole function is to reflect and express the various psychological moods of the two characters as they thread their way toward an understanding of one another. Of course there was nothing new in having music reflect psychology – music always did that in opera. But normally in the eighteenth century, opera music had a whole variety of additional functions: the personages marched to it, danced to it, were diverted, frightened, or made sad by it,[25] whereas here, for the first time at the Royal Academy, music is wholly and uniquely put to the service of inner sentiment, of the psychological experience. It has no other function. This was a milestone in the history of eighteenth-century French opera, and there is no mystery as to why it took place in this particular work: *Deucalion et Pirrha* was the only opera whose central part totally excluded the variety and *divertissements* that had always characterized such pieces. It was the only opera with a narrow, pure, single-minded plot, and the music simply reflected this situation.

But whatever the cause, this innovation brings one substantially nearer to what certain modern composers have felt to be the true function of opera music. Furthermore, in the immediate future it anticipated certain aspects of Rousseau's theatrical masterpiece, the "melodrama" *Pygmalion*.[26] One of course concedes that Saint-Foix's libretto is not nearly so moving as Rousseau's drama, nor was he so expressly concerned, as Rousseau was, with the nature of art and with identity. Yet both authors had imagined in their several ways that the sentiment of love should be consecrated, so to speak, as the marble statue, the work of art, comes alive, and they also believed that the purpose of music was to express the various shades of feeling that led to this manifestation. Finally, one notes that in *Pygmalion* Rousseau was so deeply absorbed by his theme that all social considerations had been left behind, forgotten in the intensity of the artistic experience. Here again, though on a very different scale of involvement, he exhibits an exclusionism that had been anticipated by Saint-Foix.

To say more than this would doubtless render the comparison odious. Rousseau's *Pygmalion* is an extraordinarily concentrated expression of the author's original genius, whereas one could never claim that Saint-Foix's opera had comparable artistic significance. We will be content to remember and admire it historically, and we do so not only because of the manner in which its music functions, but because the author, by setting himself against the sprawling diversity of traditional *tragédie lyrique* on the one hand, and against the sprawling vulgarity of the playwrights of the *foire* (such as Piron) on the other, achieved in this work an aristocratic unity and simplicity that had probably never been seen before, even in the age of Lully.

10

The rustic operas of Diderot's *Neveu de Rameau*

I

The first real moment of eloquence in Diderot's *Neveu de Rameau* delivers some unsettling surprises.[1] *Moi* has been building up steam, trying to convince *Lui*, and perhaps himself, too, that the personal defects of great geniuses and the incidental harm they do to those around them are negligible matters, compared to the major benefits they bestow on humanity in the long run. In keeping with the loftiness of his argument, *Moi* has been using a high style, full of edifying generalities. Time means nothing as *Moi* serenely invites the Nephew to consider the tears that will be shed over Racine a thousand years hence, in all the countries of the world (space doesn't mean much either). It is a breathtaking prospect, of course, and one that reduces the aggravations of everyday life to mere trifles. Given his exalted vantage point, one wonders whether such mundane necessities as eating and sleeping still exist for *Moi*. Naturally, he passes rather quickly over the temporary damage geniuses may do; yet he does concede he sometimes wishes they had better personal characters:

> Il serait à souhaiter que de Voltaire eût encore la douceur de Duclos, l'ingénuité de l'abbé Trublet, la droiture de l'abbé d'Olivet; mais puisque cela ne se put, regardons la chose du côté vraiment intéressant [. . .][2]

Having brushed aside this last inconvenience, *Moi* is ready to soar aloft, untrammeled, into a state so disinterested it resembles disembodiment:

> Oublions pour un moment le point que nous occupons dans l'espace et dans la durée et étendons notre vue sur les siècles à venir, les régions les plus eloignées et les peuples à naître. Songeons au bien de notre espece [. . .] (*ibid.*)[3]

Only at the very end of this *accès d'éloquence* does *Moi* come back down to earth with his marvelous insight, warning against throwing cold water on the head of Greuze for fear of extinguishing his talent along with his vanity, and against refashioning de Voltaire to be less sensitive to his critics, for fear he will no longer be able to descend into the soul of his greatest dramatic personages, as he had done so notably with Queen Mérope.

Read at face value this passage comes across as one of *Moi*'s most accomplished arguments; each phrase sustains his main purpose, combining eloquence with example in a most convincing way. One has to know the eighteenth century extremely well, as the late Jean Fabre did, to realize how one sentence, which looks entirely innocent and proper on the surface, can be completely out of kilter with everything else, setting up screeching dissonances against the general harmony of the whole. The sentence in question is the one in which *Moi* concedes he might wish de Voltaire had Duclos' "douceur," abbé Trublet's "ingénuité" and abbé d'Olivet's "droiture." We are led to assume that these men were all nice people, though intellectual mediocrities, in contrast to de Voltaire who was nasty, but a genius. Now it is true that these minor authors were mediocre enough to fit into the argument. The trouble is that they were all notoriously lacking in the redeeming qualities *Moi* attributes to them: "douceur" was the last thing one would have said of the social character of Duclos;[4] "ingénuité" hardly describes abbé Trublet, that quasi-perpetual candidate for the Académie Française who spent half his life fawning and flattering to get votes, and who for his own base ambitions betrayed his longstanding friend and benefactor, Helvétius;[5] and everyone in the Parisian philosophical camp at least agreed that abbé d'Olivet was a scoundrel and a hypocrite and boring, besides being a "pesant," as the Nephew will declare further on (p. 58). All the epithets are ironies, and scholars usually refer to "antiphrase" when discussing them – a term which does conveniently describe Diderot's procedure as rhetoric. But we still need to account for it aesthetically; and as for logic, what an odd, jarring note the coupling of these names to such unlikely attributes must have struck in the eighteenth century, especially in a conversation between two individuals who personally were acquainted with the three authors in question. *Moi* might as well have spoken of the "uprightness" of Tartuffe, or of the "candor" of Machiavelli.

The curious thing is that these ironies by "antiphrase" set up waves that go counter to *Moi*'s argument, breaking in with a bizarre jocular note at the critical moment, just before *Moi*'s flight of eloquence; they threaten the seriousness of the discussion and make one doubt whether *Moi* really means the words he is saying. Perhaps the oddity of Diderot's strategy will become clearer if we set alongside this passage the opening of the *Vision de Palissot*, a work which is usually attributed to Morellet but which sounds suspiciously like Grimm.[6] It dates from 1760, just the time when scholars think Diderot was composing parts of *Le Neveu de Rameau*, and it is possible that there is some sort of cross-relationship between the two texts. The beginning is as follows:

> Et le premier jour du mois de Janvier de l'an de grace 1760 j'étois dans une chambre, rue basse du Rempart, et je n'avois point d'argent.
> Et Madame de ** ne me payoit plus, parce que je ne lui étois plus bon à rien, et je ne pouvois plus vendre ***, parce que je l'avois déjà vendu plusieurs fois.

Et je me disois: oh, qui me donnera *l'éloquence de Chaumeix, la légèreté de Berthier et la profondeur de Fréron*, et je ferai une bonne Satyre contre quelqu'un de mes Bienfaiteurs, et je la vendrai 400 francs, et je me donnerai un habit neuf à Pâques. (Italics mine)[7]

This is the same unlikely coupling of names to attributes. However, they work perfectly with the author's intent to undermine and destroy Palissot's reputation by displaying for all the world to see not only his utter baseness, but his dreadful taste in literature, as proven by the three anti-philosophical hacks he looks to as models.

In contrast, Diderot's masterpiece is deliberately inconsistent. Nor would it have been difficult for Diderot to choose three examples that did fit his context: surely from all the centuries of literature he could have come up with three authors who were mediocre but nice, three names that would have helped rather than hindered. In my view this odd event in Diderot's text makes sense if *Moi*'s disparaging ironies are not construed so much as sideswipes against persons he doesn't like, but as nuggets of opposition *against his own argument*. These tiny reversals, upsets, come about paradoxically because *Moi* is making his point forcefully; it is as if in Diderot a strong positive could not exist without the potentially destructive challenge of a negative – within *Moi*'s discourse, as well as without it, in the counterargument of *Lui*. This would be a very special case in which one senses the attraction of contraries, a dialectic working creatively within the text.

Nor is this instance unique in the dialogue. Far from it, and it might be that if one knew enough about the text, and were on the lookout for them, inconsistencies such as these would crop up all over. In any event, I will point to one other example of this strange procedure of deliberately giving pieces that don't fit, and that work negatively against the main argument. The sentence in question has not caught the attention of scholars, but then it comes from one of the musical discussions in *Le Neveu de Rameau*, which have only begun to be explored.

This time, it is the Nephew's turn to be eloquent (pp. 79–81). The topic is French opera (i.e., *tragédie lyrique*), and its innumerable defects, in contrast to the divine music of the Italians. The "cher oncle" has been taking some rough handling as the Nephew dismisses Rameau's greatest operatic triumphs, along with the works of Campra, Mouret, and Lully, as tedious and boring. He claims no one goes to listen to them any more, except the Friday-evening "vieilles perruques" who wonder why they can't stop yawning. And he warns that since French audiences have been exposed to the eloquence and passion of the Italians the flat, tiresome musical style of French opera is done for. It's too late now, he says: they should have created laws against playing Italian music, even against Italian orchestral compositions, since one thing leads to another, and in the long run French opera was bound to be affected, too. And now, to reinforce his point, the Nephew launches into a series of four comparisons, or rather contrasts, that review – at length and with enthusiasm – the superior virtues of the Italians, and then curtly dismiss the French style with fewer words, plus a sneer at *les français* for thinking their music could survive the competition.

Naturally, the main quality for which he admires the Italians is their superiority in rendering the accents of passion; but he also praises them for their musical imitations of natural phenomena, and then scoffs at the French for thinking no one would notice how tiny and artificial the verbal mannerisms of their librettos are, with their eternal repetitions of words like "vol," "lance," "gloire," "triomphe," and "victoire." (Diderot had made a similar allusion in the prologue of *Le Neveu de Rameau*.) Next, he sets the flexibility and expressivity of the Italian language against the wooden monotony he attributes to French, and wonders at the French for believing no one would hear the difference. Finally, he waxes eloquent over the compelling dramas depicted in Italian operas, scenes that so affect the audience that they mingle their tears with those of the (onstage) mother grieving over the death of a son, or they shudder as the tyrant gives orders for a murder, and then he asks how the French thought they could hide the insipidity of their mythological *féerie*, the cloying sweetness of their music, the bankruptcy of their art. Surely the third of these four contrasts follows the same pattern:

Ils ont imaginé qu'ils pleureraient ou riraient à des scènes de tragédie ou de comédie musiquées, qu'on porteroit à leurs oreilles les accents de la fureur, de la haine, de la jalousie, les vraies plaintes de l'amour, les ironies, les plaisanteries du théâtre italien ou français, et qu'ils resteroient admirateurs de *Ragonde* ou de *Platée*. Je t'en réponds, tarare ponpon [. . .]

(p. 81)[8]

Naturally one assumes that *Ragonde* and the other opera mentioned here were examples of typical French artificiality, replete with all the mannered vocabulary, boring plot situations, and inexpressive, *féerie*-ridden mythology he has been attacking. Given the pattern of these contrasts and the nature of the Nephew's criticisms, it would almost be required that these operas exhibit the worst faults of the French style. But here we are brought up with a jolt, for actually they do not. In fact they are the only two operas produced at the Royal Academy of Music in the first half of the eighteenth century that don't fit this pattern; they are in the wrong company, as out of place as the word "droiture" next to the name abbé d'Olivet.

One of these operas, Rameau's *Platée*, is quite well known thanks to modern performances and recordings, but the other one, *Ragonde*, whose music is by Mouret and whose libretto is by Néricault-Destouches, has become very obscure, and unjustly so. It is time to investigate this forgotten work on its own terms.

*   *   *

Attraction of the contrary

Contrary to most of the expectations raised while reading *Le Neveu de Rameau*, *Ragonde* is not one of those mannered, high-style, mythologized French productions the Nephew has been attacking with his sarcasms.[9] *Ragonde* is at the opposite end of the scale: it is a rustic opera, a peasant opera, and it brought to the Académie Royale de Musique for the first time in the eighteenth century the rough humor and the sort of realism that crowds had been enjoying at the *théâtre de la foire*. This work struck a note of vulgarity that was unheard of at the Royal Academy: it is not merely middle-class; it is low-class. Furthermore, its three acts (originally called "intermèdes"), entitled "La Veillée," "Les Lutins," and "La Noce et le Charivari," distinctly suggest a folk-opera. It is true that its language is "stage-peasant" rather than authentic patois, and that very occasionally there are poetical hold-overs from conventional operatic pastorals (just enough to signal that they were in the author's mind). But this hardly affects the spirit of the whole, which is distinctly down-to-earth. *Ragonde* breaks with all tradition for comic opera at this time by using no speech at all, and, until the last number, no vaudevilles. Mouret's marvelous music sprinkles the opera with lively dances: bourrées, minuets, tambourins, gavottes, and so on. The graver dance forms are eschewed, but there is one quasi-serious air near the beginning of act II that is most effective, in addition to other airs of grace and charm. The choruses are delightful, and it ends with a superb finale, joyous, rollicking and punctuated by the echoing syllables "Charivari, charivari!" sung with alternating *soli* and *tutti*. The least one can say of the opera is that it is a distinct success. Viewed historically, it also appears as one of the most interesting and innovative operas of the first half of the century.

Its history is rather curious: originally it was produced in December 1714 for the *Grandes Nuits* of the Duchess of Sceaux, and it represented an effort by the Duchess to cut down on the extravagance of the preceding *Nuits*. Néricault-Destouches' libretto for the original production exists in a separate version (in fact, in two versions)[10] and presents some interesting variants – not only praises of the Duchess that were later cut out, but several passages that were also excised on account of their low tone. The Paris Opéra revived it, with various additions and deletions to make it more proper, in January 1742. (By this time the composer had been dead for four years, and the author of the libretto was in provincial retirement.) Five years after that, in 1748, Mme de Pompadour put it into performance in the petits appartements of Versailles after only three days of rehearsal. She herself took the role of the opera's "hero," Colin, which her voice teacher, the great "haute-contre" (i.e., high tenor) Jelyotte had sung in the Paris performances.[11] There were other Parisian revivals at the Opéra in 1743, 1752, 1769, and even as late as 1773; in other words, it was clearly a success.

The first "intermède" of *Ragonde* was called "La Veillée" or "la Soirée de village." At the 1714 Sceaux performances the scene looked like this:

Les Acteurs et les Actrices avec les Danseurs et les Danseuses, sont autour d'une table. Les femmes travaillent: les unes filent à la quenouille, les autres au rouet; et d'autres tricotent des bas.

(p. 255)[12]

The libretto of the Paris version speaks simply of a "choeur de filles du village, leur ouvrage à la main." But even if the Paris performance didn't use all of these trappings, the mere suggestion of something like spinning wheels and knitted stockings at the Royal Academy is extraordinary for its day. This is the kind of scenic innovation that socially conscious Sedaine would insist on twenty years later, at the Opéra Comique. It was unheard of at the Opéra. Nor is the plot anything like what one expected at the Royal Academy in this period: young Colin is in love with Colette, but Colette's ancient widowed mother, Ragonde, is determined Colin should marry her instead, despite her sixty years. Ragonde's motives are not exactly elevated:

> Oui, mon poupou; oui mon cher coeur.
> N'est-ce pas assez que trois mois de veuvage?
> Je ne puis plus supporter ces ennuis.
> Voici le temps des longues nuits.
> Et si bientôt je ne m'engage,
> Mon honneur à la fin pourra faire naufrage.
> Un plaisir légitime est tout ce que je veux [. . .]   (p. 260)[13]

Whereupon a trio chimes in, ironically, "Ragonde avec Colin, le charmant assemblage!"

For the sake of decency, the Paris Opéra cut out most of the foregoing, but this did not alter the fundamental vulgarity of the grotesque plot situation in which the determined old hag runs after the reluctant young swain – a situation which was actually part of the folkloric traditions of the topsy-turvy world, *le monde renversé*.[14]

The crudeness of the next incident in the plot was left intact in Paris: to amuse the women at their work, Ragonde calls for everyone to sing a song in turn, but specifies that they should be love songs, to remind her of her long-lost youth. When her turn comes, however, her song sounds more like a warning than a Romance. The message for Colin is all too clear:

> Un jeune berger de vingt ans
> Aimoit une bergère
> Mais il plaisoit fort à sa Mère,
> Qui vouloit l'éprouver en dépit de ses dents.
> La bonne femme étoit sorcière
> Pour punir le berger insensible à ses feux
> Elle en fit un matou, qui devint furieux,
> Et se précipita du haut d'une gouttière.   (pp. 266–7)[15]

Colin was not to be intimidated, nor was his song in rejoinder exactly respectful of the woman who had been asking him to wear her ribbon:

> Une vieille avoit quatre dents,
> Dont elle ne se servoit guere;
> Elle vouloit être encore mère
> En épousant par force un berger de vingt ans.
> Il méprisa cette mégère
> Elle voulut punir le berger dédaigneux
> Mais lui, pour empècher ses desseins dangereux
> L'envoya soupirer au fond de la rivière.   (p. 267)[16]

In the early version of the libretto, Ragonde then declares that rather than see Colin marry her daughter, she will strangle the two of them together!

But even the bowdlerized version gives a generous slice of peasant low life in the raw, and it may seem astonishing that such a bastion of courtly tradition as the Royal Academy in Paris could ever let it happen within its confines. Whereas courtly operas had plots in which all the pieces fitted together, this one had all the pieces out of joint on account of the disrupting presence of Ragonde, who both in Paris and in Versailles was played by a male. Nor was the raucous vulgarity limited to the first act. In act ii Colette (who really loves Lucas, but can only marry him if Ragonde marries Colin) pretends to give Colin an assignation in the woods at night, where, alone, he sings a rather sad air while waiting for her. (This would have been Mme de Pompadour's finest moment.) But instead of Colette come villagers disguised as goblins and demons, and who knock Colin about rather roughly (more roughly at Sceaux than at Paris). Singing to suitably spooky music ("Colin, Colin, Colin") they declare the sorceress Ragonde has sent them and threaten terrible punishments unless Colin does her will. Colin is so terrified he agrees to marry her. And so the last act features a double wedding procession (Colette will marry Lucas at the same time), led by peasant girls and boys in front and brought up in the rear by the two grooms in their finery, and Ragonde who in the Sceaux version is termed "ridicule" with a crown of flowers on her head and carrying an enormous bouquet of flowers before her. Choruses invite everyone to the wedding: "A la noce, A la noce, Allons, accourons-tous!," and there are lusty musical celebrations of Lucas and Colette for having found the secret of a happy marriage (their recipe is to treat one another as lover and mistress, rather than husband and wife). Colin tries to balk at the last moment, but he is soon brought to order when Ragonde threatens to summon her demons again. The opera ends happily, both pairs of lovers reconciled, and with the grotesque couple being mocked, just as folkloric traditions held they should be,[17] by a musical charivari.

*   *   *

As we have seen, various cuts were made in *Ragonde* to render it more palatable to audiences at the Royal Academy. There were also certain "adoucissements" added in the Paris revival to sweeten the brew. Here is one of them, Mathurine's air, sung at a strategic point, just before the finale:

> Bergers heureux,
> Suivez l'amour qui vous éclaire,
> Ici les ris, les jeux
> Tout sert à nos voeux:
> Le doux printems
> Commence et finit tous nos ans:
> L'Amour quitte sa mère,
> Pour voir nos champs.
> Chantons mille fois,
> Célébrons le Dieu qui fait nos choix;
> Il est moins à Cythère
> Que dans nos bois.[18]

These insipid verses are an arch-betrayal of the most interesting qualities of the original. Naturally the librettist, Néricault-Destouches, protested against such "fadeurs" and "petites maximes," added without his knowledge.[19] Particularly cruel was the use of mythology, because one of the signal merits and innovations of this opera was its doing without the usual God of Love and allusions to Cythère. It was situated in the here and now.

In contrast to the plain verses of the original, which are so lively with their zesty allusions to peasant realities, this quotation is quite precisely the convention-ridden opera poetry of the *pastorale héroïque*. And how weary it sounds. How could any self-respecting librettist in the 1740s still be writing of "doux printemps," "Bergers heureux," and "les ris, les jeux," after so many centuries of repetition? But of course respectable librettists *were* still writing in this tradition, and were rather proud of their productions. The genre was positively thriving with years of life before it. Perhaps one should take a look – briefly – at the literary side of its background.

The name *pastorale héroïque* implied that mythical divinities ("héros") would be mingling with "bergers," and especially "bergères," with results that could be either happy or tragic.[20] By the middle of the eighteenth century the language of the libretto had become so stylized as to preclude any poetical originality: one word or image inevitably brought on other words or images, which in turn implied the whole false universe inhabited by these mannered shepherds and shepherdesses dressed *à la* Boucher. Because of the demands of the *style noble*, the meters, the rhymes, and the given themes, librettists worked with resources that were rarefied, refined, and reduced to the point of paucity. This was a challenge: to produce acceptable poetry when the verbal possibilities were so severely limited.

The situation must have resembled the problems one faces when writing one of those tortuous musical counterpoint exercises, with all their strictures forbidding this or that interval, when one of the parts is already given. Likewise, at any moment in these pastorals the verbal possibilities might number just two or three at the most. For instance, as the shepherd chorus entered it was considered appropriate for them to sing something like –

Chantons, animons nos musettes [. . .]   (*Le Jugement de Paris*)

In fact, the idea of "chantons" almost *always* brought on "musettes," or at least "hautbois" or "chalumeaux," as we see from the next example, from another *ballet héroïque*:

Chantons, chantons cent et cent fois [. . .]
Que les Haut-bois, que les Musettes
Célèbrent le modèle [. . .]   (*Les Festes grecques et romaines*)

As we have already noted, Rameau's Nephew and Diderot, too, ironized about the overuse of certain words in operatic vocabulary – "lance," "gloire," "triomphe," "victoire," and so on. Indeed these words not only turn up in opera after opera, they usually all come together in the same spot because they belong to the same verbal ecology system. For example:

Règne toujours dans nos boccages
Amour, *lance* de nouveaux traits,
Et ne souffre dans nos forêts
D'insensibles, ni de volages.
Soutien tes droits, v[e]nge tes noeuds,
Triomphe, prend soin de ta *gloire*;
Mais use bien de ta *victoire* [. . .]   (*Le Jugement de Paris*)

As this passage reveals, the rustic action inevitably took place in a "forêt," or "boccages," or "bois" (in the plural). Sometimes "ormeaux" were specified. It was always a setting for love. One of the few choices available to the poet at this point allowed him to have either a brighter setting, or a more shaded one. Here is the brighter version:

Qu'à l'ombre des ormeaux
Les gazons reverdissent,
Que les troupeaux bondissent
Au son du chalumeau.
Que mille fleurs nouvelles,
Brillent dans les jardins,
Et vous Zéphires badins
Voltigez autour d'elles.   (*Les Plaisirs de la campagne*)

This was all purest cliché, of course; the words and combinations of words are so predictable, the passage might have written itself. However, most librettists favored a softer, more shaded setting, doubtless because it was more erotic. This was all cliché, too:

> Les doux Plaisirs habitent ce boccage [. . .]
> Le bruil des eaux, le Zéphire, et l'ombrage,
> Tout sert icy l'Amour et les Amants. (*Issé*)

As to what kind of love, there were again only two possibilities. Very occasionally fickle love was preferred:

> Changeons toujours dans nos amours,
> Heureux un coeur volage [. . .] (*Issé*)

But most often rustic love was given as constant, and its tranquil character set it apart from the "alarms" associated with love elsewhere:

> Dans ces lieux, loin des allarmes,
> Nous goûtons les charmes
> De la Paix [. . .] (*Le Jugement de Paris*)

Even though divinities regularly dallied with rustic mortals, there was never any social message in these pastorals (which would indeed have been Stendhal's pistol shot at the opera). They might constantly proclaim love in the woods to be superior, yet the advantages were left vague, and the text almost never specifies the alternative to which it is superior. The only quasi-exception to the rule that these operatic pastorals remain aloof from social messages of any sort is an *entrée* entitled *Les Saturnales* in a *ballet héroïque* by Fuzelier and Colin-de-Blamont (*Les Festes grecques et romaines*, Paris, 1723). The fiction of the *entrée* supposes that, as in the ancient Roman Saturnalia, the lower classes are allowed to say anything they wish. Since the potentialities of the Saturnalia as an art form are so exciting and important in this century,[21] perhaps one might hope that even in these operas could be detected some incipient social excitement, once the Bergers really have the field to themselves. But alas, as Montaigne used to say, "Nulles nouvelles." This is the best they can do:

> *Une Bergère*
> De nos Boccages
> Fuyez les Ombrages
> Vous qui ne connoissez que l'éclat de la Cour

> De nos Boccages
> Fuyez les Ombrages
> Nous n'offrons dans nos Bois, de l'encens qu'à l'Amour. (scene 3)[22]

The third line at least specifies that this easy and amorous life in the country is set against the brilliant life at court, and the last line is the closest these pastorals ever come to expressing any kind of egalitarian impulse – which is not very close at all; in fact, whatever urge there may have been to imagine a life in which homage was *not* paid to rank and wealth dissolves at the end into another gallant cliché about homage to the God of Love. Then, after a few more banalities stressing "feuillages" and "échos," everyone dances, thus consecrating the final fizzling out of social significance in the Royal Academy pastorals.

Seen in relation to this mannered tradition, the old hag Ragonde with her four useless teeth and her threats to turn Colin into a gutter cat must have felt like a minor revolution. And the music, lively, almost raucous at the end, spooky, graceful, creates a world vastly different from the delicate pastels we have been considering. There is some suggestion in the original text of *Ragonde* that this difference was intentional, and that *Ragonde* was deliberately designed as relief from the artificiality of court operas. In this connection we may note also that *Ragonde* was performed not at the *foire* or at the Comédie Italienne where one found audiences that mixed the classes of society and where playwrights intentionally appealed to the populace, but rather in places associated with distinctly aristocratic traditions: *Ragonde* at the Royal Academy or at Sceaux suggests an audience that is, if one may be forgiven a twentieth-century image, slumming, or at least eager to be amused by a way of life totally different from their own. (An attraction of contrary impulses is at work here, also.)

On the other hand, though *Ragonde* provided relief from the *pastorale héroïque*, it was not designed as parody. It virtually never satirizes operatic mannerisms. In fact the only element of parody in *Ragonde* is the burlesque of a rustic marriage one finds in the grotesque couple Ragonde–Colin that set up such a humorous contrast to the regular couple Lucas–Colette. This satire of rusticity implies that the opera contains no "social message" whatsoever: it does not attempt to glorify life in the country, for example (Ragonde's missing teeth take care of that), much less is it an indictment of civilization, or the court. Rousseau is still far, far away.

Nevertheless, the mannered clichés of the *pastorale héroïque* did indeed invite parody and comic authors were glad to produce them at the *foire* and the Comédie Italienne.[23] But the best of the parodies, the only one that could be termed "great," occurred right at the Académie Royale de Musique. This was the second opera mentioned by the Nephew as he sneered at the defects of French music: *Platée* by his uncle, the great Rameau.[24] Since this opera is so familiar to modern audiences through performances and recordings there is no reason to discuss its plot in any detail. But again, one marvels that the Royal Academy would have wanted to stage a work that actually presented a satire of itself, of its own noblest traditions, and that the infinitely irritable Rameau could ever have been persuaded to compose a mockery of his own musical style. *Platée* was a burlesque of the *pastorale héroïque* and this fact undoubtedly explains why, uniquely among Rameau's compositions, it won lasting approval from the whole Parisian philosophical camp: everyone was ready to laugh as they watched once-proud Jupiter

25. Charles-Antoine Coypel, "Portrait de l'acteur Jelyotte [dans le rôle de Platée]" (1745)

pretending to court a pretentious rustic naiad whose realm was a murky swamp peopled mainly by frogs. This "heroine," Platée, was played by a male singer (Jelyotte again), even as the role of Ragonde had been, and, as the plot works out, the mere sight of him/her beneath a wedding veil was enough to send angry Juno into musical gales of laughter, so that she forgave her faithless husband for all his pretended philandering.

Here everything is travesty. Rameau's music had always featured imitations of natural phenomena such as frightening musical storms, bird calls, musical breezes, and so on. But in *Platée* the musical imitations are all topsy-turvy parodies in which the musical values have been inverted:

instead of the usual sweet bird calls, one hears the croaking of frogs intermingled with cuckoo calls; the storm, instead of being frightening, is just what the moist dwellers of Platée's swamp had been hoping for. The heroine's joy at the prospect of marrying Jupiter, instead of being expressed as tender reticence, becomes a brisk chorus featuring the vaudeville refrain "Hé, bon bon bon!" Through the power of Rameau's music, the gayest of words become the saddest and most poignant of songs. Though the burlesque might apply quite generally to *tragédie lyrique*, the most obvious target of the spoof is the *pastorale héroïque* because, as we saw, this genre had always centered on the mingling of gods and rustics, which is precisely the main object of travesty and satire here. Certainly the quality of the music partly explains the unique popularity of *Platée* among so many of the *philosophes*. But this approval is also evidence that the time had come when these enlightened persons could enjoy the royal, courtly traditions of opera only if they were being made a mockery. Otherwise everyone went for the Italians.

And this, in a word, is why both *Ragonde* and *Platée* are such ill-fitting examples in the context of the Nephew of Rameau's main argument: *Ragonde* with its unmythological realism used a *monde renversé* motif to give relief from precisely the mannerisms which the Nephew found so undesirable; *Platée* supplied another kind of relief, through burlesque. It is as if the Nephew had perversely hit upon the only two operas that wouldn't work with his line of thought, that set up counter-vibrations, although not humorous ones, as the "douceur" of Duclos and the "droiture" of abbé d'Olivet had done. Now, it is true that if one inspects closely the particular part of the sentence in which the Nephew gives these examples, they become more plausible. The Nephew has turned the discussion, for the briefest moment, from *tragédie lyrique* to comedy, and he is contrasting unfavorably the ironic humor of *Ragonde* and *Platée* with the wit of the Italian comedies, or their French adaptations at the Comédie Italienne and the *théâtre de la foire*. The Nephew considered that Italian comedy put the French in the shade, and insofar as he argues in that narrow framework, his examples are not actually inconsistent. It is the larger dimensions of the topic that bring on the jarring note of impropriety, the rattles and squeaks produced by ironies that in Diderot are part of the heat of the creative process, life-sustaining elements of contradiction, whose frictions energize the whole movement of his eloquence. May we not imagine that the canny Nephew, also, with his exquisite musical taste, would have known, *au fond*, that these two operas were, in the long run, just the wrong examples?

II

Operatic depictions of rustic life were destined to have a lengthy and varied career in eighteenth-century French comic opera, and doubtless because comedy has always tended to derive its sustenance from contemporary goings-on, these operatic depictions did not fail to reflect the gathering social tensions of the times; indeed they added their own fuel to the flames: operatic depictions evolved into operatic *celebrations* of rusticity, and they acquired more and more of a cutting edge as they were taken up by librettists, such as Sedaine, who in fact had social axes to grind. In the final stage the rustic aesthetic was swept up by the tides of revolution, and became part of the action. The next part of the present chapter will suggest how this development took shape, by briefly considering four of the comic operas that led the way.

Neither *Platée* nor *Ragonde* put forth much propaganda in favor of life in the country: there was too much burlesque satire in both of them for that kind of message. But just a year after the 1742 Paris revival of *Ragonde*, there was a spin-off from that opera in which one notes a distinct improvement in attitudes towards rusticity and, given that this is now the generation of J.-J. Rousseau, we are observing an important trend in the making. The work in question is an *opéra comique* called *Le Coq de village*, the author being the noted impresario and playwright C. S. Favart, and his libretto enjoyed enormous popularity at the Foire St Germain where it was performed for the first time late in March 1743.[25] Since the Foire had been denied permission to use original music, Favart followed the usual practice and did his libretto partly in speech and partly with vaudevilles, that is, popular tunes the audience already knew, and to which he set new words appropriate for his plot. One of these familiar tunes was the "Charivari" from *Ragonde*.

The story is rather simple: Pierrot is being chased by all the girls in the village, from eleven-year-old Gogo, to two rich old widows, each of whom is determined to force her attentions on him – a double dose of the *monde renversé* plot of *Ragonde*. But Pierrot loves only Thérèse, who is very shy – almost as shy as the heroine of Rousseau's little rustic opera, *Le Devin du village*, was to be. Nevertheless, even though Thérèse is too bashful to admit it, Pierrot is sure she does love him, as he explains to his kindly uncle:

Je li fais des révérances [en] tournant mon chapeau; et ma politesse la rend toute honteuse. Alle badine d'une main avec le coin de son tablier, et de l'autre alle cache ses yeux, mais alle me regarde au travers des doigts, et je m'apperçois à son mouchoir de cou, que son petit estomac n'est pas plus tranquille que le mien.

(p. 7)[26]

Here, in the wake of *Ragonde*, we are finding a completely sympathetic depiction of love in the country, with not-too-objectionable "peasant" patois, and suitably "realistic" psychological details in which simple sentiments are combined with noticeable delicacy of feeling. *Ragonde*'s rough satire is still present in the rough behavior of the two lusty widows, but the effect of the whole has been mellowed with rustic charm. Nor is the delicacy confined to the girl: Pierrot is just as shy as Thérèse, and he needs much encouragement before he can bring himself to tell her he loves her. When finally he does get up the nerve to say "C'est que je vous aime bien" (p. 24) he instantly hides his face with his hat!

Being such a modest creature, Thérèse can hardly believe in Pierrot's affection, especially since he is being courted by ladies of wealth (i.e., the two old widows) beside whom she feels distressingly inferior. But Pierrot assures her she is the only one he wants to marry, her beauty and his love for her being more important than anything else. Meanwhile Pierrot's kindly uncle arranges a lottery (a detail which, like the title, was probably suggested by Dufresny's *Coquette de village*): each woman will buy a ticket, the winner getting Pierrot as a husband and the money paid for the tickets as a dowry. Fortunately the lottery has been rigged by the uncle so that Thérèse will win. But even when the cheat is discovered, Pierrot insists on keeping the girl he loves, even if it means giving up all the money (which actually it doesn't). The following song, to the tune of "L'autre jour, dessous un ormeau," sums up his feelings about Thérèse and forms the climax of the work:

> Je m'engage à toi pour jamais
> Sois-moi constante.
> De leurs biens et de leurs attraits,
> Rien ne me tente;
> Tu vas m'en dédommager,
> Sans vignes ni vergers
> J'aurons l'ame contente.
> Mes trésors et mon bonheur
> Sont au fond de ton coeur.[27]

All these motifs would be repeated in Rousseau's popular *Devin du village* (1752):[28] the shyness of the hero and heroine, their almost childish delicacy of feeling, the contrast between the corruptions of wealth and the purity of true love, which, it is felt, makes one richer than material goods ever can; the celebration of life in the country as a place where one finds simple people who are tenderer and more faithful; even Pierrot's song, "Je m'engage à toi pour jamais," has its counterpart in Rousseau's "A jamais, Colin, je t'engage . . ." Reappearances of such traits are far too numerous to be coincidental. Rousseau never admitted the whole extent of his debt, but he did dedicate the separate printing of the libretto of his opera to Favart at least,[29] and perhaps this gesture may be interpreted as confirmation of the filiation we are trying to establish.

Rousseau's social message is certainly clearer; indeed one of the strengths of his opera is the force of the social philosophy one senses behind the action. Naturally, its libretto is part of Rousseau's greater indictment of the corruptions of wealth and rank in the name of rustic simplicity. The tableau of village life shown in *Le Devin* has the aura of a covert manifesto, a revindication, a theme that is on the verge of turning seriously political.

A typically eighteenth-century twist of events is that with all its advanced social implications, *Le Devin du village* was put on, not at the *foire* or at the Comédie Italienne, but at the Royal Academy, and at the Court at Fontainebleau, thus roughly repeating the pattern of *Ragonde*. Furthermore, the language of its libretto is not nearly so earthy, or even so "authentic" as the language of *Ragonde* or *Le Coq de village*. There are moments when Rousseau even reverts to a kind of high style reminiscent of the *pastorale héroïque*.[30] In other words, paradoxically, Rousseau's little opera owes much to aristocratic traditions – one of the reasons it was so popular at court. A final peculiarity is that Rousseau's opera has a childlike quality in an intensity barely suggested by Favart. Rousseau's verses quite often resemble nursery rhymes, *comptines*, in which the meaning of the line barely makes its way through the heaviness of the rhythms and rhymes. Even Colette's opening song has something of this feature:

> J'ai perdu mon Serviteur
> J'ai perdu tout mon bonheur
> Colin me délaisse.[31]

The final vaudeville of the opera sets the artificiality of love in the city against love in the village – so much more natural, spontaneous, and also more childish:

> L'Amour ne sait guère
> Ce qu'il permet, ce qu'il défend;
> C'est un enfant, c'est un enfant.[32]

The simple, eminently singable, "catchy" tunes devised by Rousseau reinforce this quality for they, too, have something of the nursery rhyme about them. On the other hand, at the most important dramatic moment of the work, the celebrated Romance "Dans ma cabane obscure" stands as an exception to the rule: here, neither the verses nor the music are childlike at all; nor has Rousseau reverted to operatic high style. As Daniel Heartz has established in his authoritative and pioneering essay,[33] Rousseau in this piece was creating a new kind of Romance. But curiously (and here I am slightly departing from Professor Heartz's interpretation), this particular air did not entirely conform to the definitions he himself gave of the genre. According to Rousseau's article in the *Dictionnaire de musique*, a Romance was ordinarily an amorous air, often tragic; he also stressed the necessity that its melody be simple and naïve. "Dans ma cabane obscure" is indeed a simple love song, but of a special type whose intensity derives specifically from the poverty and hardship of the setting, a trait which Rousseau failed to mention. It sings of work in the fields in wind, sun, or cold, of the simple cottage in which they will be so happy together; in short, of love pitted against the travails of life, love with a social message. Today this may not seem extraordinary, but Rousseau's contemporaries felt in it something marvelously unique. Professor Heartz has revealed the ways in which it was remembered, treasured, and imitated by composers and librettists as no other Romance had ever been.

Already in the generation of C. S. Favart and Rousseau one sees that rustic themes were taking on a special excitement for the upper classes; rustic "realism" was starting to win out over the perennial court pastorals. Nor was this mode destined to pass away quickly, as fashions of the day typically did. On the contrary: judging by everything from china, tapestries, paintings and engravings, to architecture, garden-planning and the adulation shown to Benjamin Franklin, rusticity for the later eighteenth century was no longer a mode, it was a mania. And in this context, none of the arts of imitation is so revealing as the theatre, for, once planted, the seeds of these rustic themes were fated to be transmitted and transformed ceaselessly, almost without a break, and with ever-gathering force – negative, eventually revolutionary force – as 1789 approached.

The critical point in this development is *Annette et Lubin* (1762) by Madame Favart,[34] the notoriously-not-too-faithful wife of C. S. Favart, and who was herself an actress and playwright of some distinction. The plot of her one-act *opéra comique* comes from one of Marmontel's *Contes moraux*,[35] which in turn harks back to both Rousseau and Diderot. The original tale celebrates the pure, joyous, innocent love between two simple rustics, Annette and Lubin, who, having just reached puberty, are being accused of wrongdoing by the hateful *Bailli* – emissary of oppressive government and evil, sin-laden, civilized "morality" – who forbids them to make love and cohabit because they are cousins. Insofar as Marmontel's tale comes out for free love, stressing the innocent joys of sexuality, and in fact pregnancy, it sounds rather close to the Diderot tradition.[36] On the other hand, when it was slightly tidied up for the stage with ariettes and vaudevilles, the Rousseau side of the work came to the fore. How could one not think of Rousseau's Romance "Dans ma cabane obscure" in which Colin says how content he will be in his humble cottage because his beloved Colette is there, when one hears Lubin singing – in a lighter vein, to be sure –

> Avec Annette
> En ces lieux je me plais
> Ma maisonette
> Est un petit palais
> J'y trouverai toujours
> Les jours trop courts.　　　　　(scene 2)[37]

Elsewhere (scene 10) Mme Favart actually used the music from Rousseau's Romance, identified in the printed libretto as being the air to "Dans ma cabane obscure." Furthermore, the following lines, based on Marmontel's *Conte*, would seem, in both authors, to derive from Rousseau, and in effect they dramatize and clarify a social message that in Rousseau was more discreet. The result is astonishing, as Lubin sings:

> Les Grands ne sont heureux qu'en nous contrefaisant;
> Chez eux, la plus riche tenture
> Ne leur paroît un spectacle amusant
> Qu'autant qu'elle rend bien nos champs, notre verdure;
> Nos danses sous l'ormeau, nos travaux, nos loisirs,
> Ils appellent cela, je crois, un paysage.
>
> *Annette*
> Ah! Lubin, nous devons bien aimer nos plaisirs,
> Puisqu'il faut tant d'argent pour en avoir l'image.
>
> *Lubin*
> Pauvres gens! leur grandeur ne doit pas nous tenter.
> Ils peignent nos plaisirs, au lieu de les goûter.   (scene 3)[38]

With this *opéra comique* we are in the presence of one of those decisive moments of inversion that occur through the principle of contrariety. Traditional social values have been turned topsy-turvy: the rich are really the poor, the great are seen as the abject; wealth and artifice are being used to capture vain images of the simple rustic happiness they have lost precisely by being so wealthy and artificial. Indeed the "good" is being defined in terms of negativity: true happiness and true wealth are created by totally rejecting the life of those who have all the money, and who are surrounded by objects that are supposed to give pleasure. At the end of the opera the *Seigneur*, who has had designs on Annette, renounces his passion, recognizing that these simple folk have treasures he can never have:

> Du vrai bonheur voilà l'image.
> Ils jouissent de tout, en vivant simplement:
> Sous les humbles toits du village
> Règnent l'amour naïf et le pur sentiment.[39]

Needless to say, Rousseau agreed, and actually he had used the same assumptions and drawn the same social lines in his opera, although perhaps less noticeably. Indeed, the childlike atmosphere that prevailed in most of *Le Devin du village* rather beclouded the social message: the whole piece could be dismissed as charming child's play. Mme Favart is at least ever so slightly more adult; her rustics are supposed to have grown out of childhood (albeit only recently). And whereas Rousseau kept the high-born *Dame*, who had been dallying with Colin, offstage entirely, and only allowed the nobleman who was after Colette one brief appearance in a ballet–pantomime, Mme Favart's designing *Bailli* and the lusty Nobleman are two of the main characters. We cannot avoid facing the evils of rank and privilege.

Finally, there is another important and rather curious reversal in the quoted passage in the assumption that this opera setting *is* reality, real life – real enough to be imitated by the great in their paintings and tapestries. As the performance begins, art and life are assumed to have changed places.[40] This reversal is implied in Rousseau also, and it partly explains how this exemplary opponent of theatricality could have composed an opera: in Rousseau's mind this was no artifice, for artificiality implied aristocratic decadence, whereas his opera was a recreation of innocence and simplicity, life as it truly was, and as it ought to be.

We are now approaching the final stage in the development of the rustic aesthetic. This is a rather awesome historical moment in which we see a multitude of causes combining to force an idea into a reality, when the play literally crosses the boundary into life. Various interpretations might be essayed, but the most interesting way to view the theatrical developments that preceded this event is to consider them as an unlocking of the potentialities of the *pastorale héroïque*. For indeed those mannered, courtly creations, in which divinities descended to dally with shepherdesses and share their rustic pastimes, represent at least a momentary impulse to join in with simple people, perhaps even to change places with them. This urge never went anywhere, of course, except ultimately to confirm the courtly nobility of the framework in which it arose. The genre was totally self-contained. Nevertheless one can readily understand that these mannered operas would lead to parodies, such as *Platée*, and that they would inspire the wish to find earthy relief from their artificiality, as in *Ragonde*. This was perhaps inevitable. And then, given the social and sentimental trends of the Enlightenment, it seems predictable that the spin-off of *Ragonde* would try to soften the vulgarity and to add the kind of delicacy of sentiment one finds in Favart's *Coq de village*. *Tout était écrit là-haut.* Of course, when Rousseau took over the theme his celebration of shepherds and shepherdesses fitted into his philosophy of nature, as opposed to civilization, and his belief in the greatness of simple rustics, as opposed to pretentious and immoral aristocrats, though he formulated this more subtly than did Madame Favart in *Annette et Lubin* where one finds the kind of explicit social inversion I have been discussing. The prelude is ended; once and for all the lines have been definitively drawn.

Unbelievably, they were to become battle lines, for precisely this type of theatrical inversion was destined to form part of pre-Revolutionary consciousness in France. As early as 1769, the revolutionary playwright, L.-S. Mercier preached it as a key piece in his grandiose scheme for theatrical and social reform.[41] Of course Mercier's theories centered on his concept of *drame* as a powerful instrument by which to rid society of its ills, and his whole view of the history of the theatre was permeated with this kind of social concern.[42] He felt it was time for the theatre to address itself to the multitudes, to the *peuple* who had never been spoken to before (pp. 8–9); they could be brought into the action through "le cri de la nature" (p. 8) by which he means mainly the depiction of the sufferings and moral problems of simple people. By the same token, Classical tragedy is for Mercier a form from which he feels the deepest alienation: the pride Classical tragedy took in addressing only the few, the unreality and irrelevance of the royal destinies it depicted, its lack of concern for contemporary issues and for the lives being led by "le gros de la nation" (p. 8), all these traits were so many arguments condemning it. Mercier rewrites the history of the theatre to suit his theories, and he sometimes exhibits the blind intolerance towards the past that marks the true radical. Yet, if one views him as a state of pre-Revolutionary mind, Mercier is fascinating:

Chez les Grecs le but de la Tragédie était sensible. Elle devoit nourir le germe républicain, et rendre la Monarchie odieuse. J'entends fort bien Corneille; mais il faut l'avouer, il est devenu pour nous un Auteur presque étranger, et nous avons perdu jusqu'au droit de l'admirer [. . .] Corneille enfin devoit naître en Angleterre.

(p. 9)[43]

Historians would certainly *not* agree with Mercier's simplistic view that the aim of ancient Greek tragedy was merely to foster republicanism and render the monarchy hateful. Yet it does seem clear that these are Mercier's own aims for the theatre, and they reflect very well his sense of mission as a playwright. If he thinks one no longer has the right even to admire Corneille, the reason is certainly that Corneille supported and admired a government that to Mercier was tyranny. Naturally, in turning away from Corneille and his kind, Mercier also turns his back on Corneille's high-born audience. Proudly and eloquently he declares he will devote his art uniquely to the interests of those he terms his "semblables" (p. 9). And how much his term reveals in this anti-aristocratic context: lowering his own middle-class interests, Mercier is reaching out to embrace the masses in a movement of unification that comes from the bottom of society. The peculiar strength of his mission derives from the conviction that his concerns are those of vast multitudes, virtually the whole nation. Because they are his "semblables" he can imagine them joining with him to form a great unity, a whole new society, in which all share their joys, sorrows, and indignations.

Mercier's ideas tie together with a single-minded cohesion that allows virtually no room for nuances and hesitations. His is the compactness of the revolutionary, and it bespeaks a theatrical dynamism that was unknown to playwrights before him. No doubt his enlightened predecessors believed the theatre should take stands on political, moral, and social issues; in fact it was the accepted doctrine of the *philosophes* that the theatre was the equivalent of a church, and should preach the new gospel and spread reform. But Mercier went further, for he was calling for nothing less than a closing of the gap between playwriting and political action, and even between the theatre and life. A play was no longer to be thought of as an imitation; it was to convey reality, the play was a political gesture, *something like governance.* Mercier suggests how this new function might develop in an illustration that is perfect for the present context:

Il est donc singulier que parmi tant d'auteurs que leur goût portoit à la recherche et à la peinture des caractères, presque tous ayent dédaigné le commerce des habitans de la campagne, ou n'ayent vu en eux que leur grossièreté apparente. Quel trésor pour un Poëte moral, que la nature dans la simplicité! que de choses à peindre, à révéler à l'oreille des Princes! si je ne me trompe, vû nos progrès dans la Philosophie, ce seroit aujourd'hui au Monarque à descendre au rang des auditeurs, et ce seroit au Pâtre à monter sur la Scène. L'inverse du Théâtre deviendroit peut-être la forme la plus heureuse, comme la plus instructive. Le paysan du Danube paroît un instant au milieu du Sénat de Rome, et devient le plus éloquent des Orateurs. (pp. 9–10)[44]

In this decisive statement, Mercier has achieved a true inversion of values: a rustic, uneducated shepherd is now a veritable "treasure," worth more than monarchs, and also far more wise than they; true philosophy belongs to the peasant. By the same logic, it is the Prince who, with all his wealth and education, is found to be impoverished and ignorant. "Ce seroit au Pâtre à monter sur la Scène," Mercier declares, but "onstage" here doesn't mean at all presenting illusions, imitations, or idle entertainments, it means action, the truth of life, the focus of interest and importance for all humanity. Onstage is the equivalent of on the throne. Nor is the audience being thought of as real people who watch the staged illusion. On the contrary this audience consists of those who are out of the action, unworthy to speak the lines, pupils who are to listen to their masters. "L'inverse du Théâtre" Mercier calls the situation, and in fact the theatrical inversion whose course we have been observing reaches its logical conclusion here, when this revolutionary thinker pushes the prince off the scene and out of the action so that the shepherd can take over. The pastoral plot, so placidly anodyne in its original conception, has become not only inverted, but enlarged, energized, *electrified* (the metaphor is Mercier's),[45] transmitting irresistible lessons for the nation. Mercier is uncannily in tune with those mass forces – conscious and unconscious – that will coalesce into the Revolution; one almost expects this earnest and eloquent disciple of Diderot, as he prepares to give voice to the unspoken discontents of the multitude, to start writing of "le mugissement de la bête."

Naturally, real events are not always as bold as the theoretical statements that preceded them. But Mercier's scene of the wise, lesson-teaching *Pâtre* onstage while the Prince gives ear was destined to materialize in France in at least two, quite different, ways. Ironically, the first occurred in the artificial ambiance of Versailles, where Marie Antoinette revived, and performed in, a whole series of rustic plays and *opéras comiques*, most of them dating from the 1760s with librettos by the socially conscious Sedaine:[46] his *Le Roi et son fermier* came in August 1780; the rustic *opéra comique* by Philidor and Poinsinet, *Le Sorcier*, was followed by Sedaine's *Rose et Colas* and Rousseau's *Devin du village* in September of the same year. In March 1781 came another rustic *opéra comique*, *La Matinée et la veillée villageoise, ou le sabot perdu*; in 1783 there was Sedaine's *Blaise et Babet*. Not merely did rustic comic operas make their way to Versailles, they actually dominated court productions from 1780 until the famous performance of Beaumarchais' decidedly un-rustic *Barbier de Séville*, in August 1785, brought an end to the Trianon theatricals. This was the last chance these divinities of the court would have to change places and dally onstage with shepherds and shepherdesses. The King was indeed present, watching the performances, but obviously he did not give ear as Mercier thought he should; nor could these noble players be expected to perceive the urgent importance of the social message of the operas they were so expensively putting on. And yet, at the same time, the very fact that they felt the desire to stage them indicates they were, however unconsciously, obeying the grand forces of history and, to some degree at least, taking part in the great drama of their time, in fact they were making gestures towards the social forces that eventually would destroy them. No doubt there was a kind of titillation in playing at social revolution. One may surmise also that their play-acting represented some sort of wish to make these urgent social issues unreal, to tame them by having them absorbed into their own frivolous way of life. For ultimately these descents of the nobility to common fare functioned just as they always had in the *pastorale héroïque*: they confirmed the aristocratic framework in which they occurred. Given the falsely rustic players and the unseeing nature of the royal audience at Trianon, this was decidedly not yet the moment for Mercier's proposal regarding the "inverse du théâtre" to be taken seriously.

But there was a later instance, which did have an entirely serious context, and which makes Mercier's manifesto sound like a prophecy. For during the Revolution the whole French nation joined together to act out something quite suggestive of Mercier's inversion. This was the grandiose spectacle called the "Fête de la fédération" (1790), the first and most exciting of all the Revolutionary festivals.[47] In Paris there were not exactly shepherds involved, but a multitude of persons from various classes had joined together with shovels and wheelbarrows to ready the space for the vast parades and mingling throngs that collected on the Champs-de-Mars in 1790, and these included masses of non-aristocrats at least. They were all supposed to be symbolizing, and in fact establishing, a unification of the

26. Snuff-boxes showing Marie Antoinette's theatricals

27. Hubert Robert, "Fête de la Fédération"

nation on a basis that sounded like equality. And it was all staged for the
benefit and participation of the King, who was supposed to give ear, and
presumably to profit from the demonstration, just as Mercier had suggested, as well as to dignify, almost sanctify, it with his presence – an idea
that does not occur in Mercier's text. And this playing out by these masses
of a scenario at least somewhat suggestive of the one Mercier invented, as
they paraded their message of unity and liberty before the bored King, who
arrived late and lolled in uncomprehending distraction on his "throne"
during the endless ceremonies, all this produced a euphoria in the paraders,
the real actors, that was not to be felt again to this degree, though the
Revolutionaries would try again and again to reproduce it. There were
various reasons why this success was unique, but one of them was surely
that the two poles – King and simple citizens – of Mercier's reversal were
still intact and provided, through the dynamism of opposites, a dramatic
tension that somehow brought on feelings of patriotic bliss. The terrible,
almost desperate, emptiness of the Revolutionary *fêtes* would begin when
the citizens eliminated the King from the proceedings and staged the
demonstrations for themselves.

Though most of Mercier's *drames* are unreadable, he was, as even his own
age realized, a very great reporter in the modern sense, and his enormous
twelve-volume collection of vignettes called *Le Tableau de Paris* is an enthralling documentary on pre-Revolutionary Paris.[48] Mercier realized that
the Revolution was coming, and so this disciple of the era of the *Encyclopédie*
set about recording every aspect of the doomed civilization of Paris, in order
that the world would know exactly what it had been like, and also, seeing

the corruption that infected every part of it, would understand why it had perished. The great city comes alive in Mercier's pages as nowhere else: he lets us hear the creaking of shop signs swaying as the wind blows at night, along with the ghostly flicker of the lamplights (I, pp. 200–4). We see the army of water-carriers with their buckets down at the Seine each morning getting water for the houses (I, pp. 146–7), and the *décrotteurs* from Savoie standing on the street corners ready to scrape the mud off those who, in a city without sidewalks, got splattered by carriage wheels (VI, pp. 1–6). He takes particular pains to describe the infections of the scalp beneath the ornamental wigs people wore, since these were to him a symbol of the evils of the whole social system (II, pp. 182–5). And he tells of the sounds one hears in the streets at night, as the workmen and shopkeepers come home from their labors and go to bed, while the rich go forth in a rattle of carriages to the Comédie Française or the Opéra (VI, pp. 138–55). Indeed a whole civilization lives again in these volumes.

After the Terror, Mercier tried to do the same thing for what he termed *Le Nouveau Paris*[49] in order to tell what the city had been like during the Revolution. Again he uses the vignette form, giving sometimes brief descriptions of events, sometimes portraits of the makers of the Revolution, and often using poetic licence to scramble the order of the events. There are masterful pages in the collection describing the euphoria of the "Fête de la fédération" (I, pp. 76–85), the vote on the death of the King, the portraits of the terrorists, and so on.[50] Yet inevitably the whole is less successful: Mercier turned out to be a moderate, as the Revolution radicalized, and he found himself set against the leaders of the Terror, completely opposing their policies, and eventually he was imprisoned. He never lost his faith in the ideals of the Revolution, but at the same time *Le Nouveau Paris* reflects the fury and distress he felt at the treachery of those in power. Reading this varied collection of descriptions and anecdotes, one wonders what conclusion he will finally reach, how he can tie together so many diverse reactions and conflicting sentiments. Actually he never even attempts to sum up the whole experience. Even at the end of the sixth volume he is still adding vignettes and sending forth snarls at his various enemies – royalists, terrorists, priests, rich profiteers, or whatever. Yet throughout these hundreds of pages certain sentiments remain sacred and, above all, the feelings we know he associated with Rousseau: fruit-picking time in Belleville when the cherries (one recalls the famous ones in the *Confessions*) were "bright as rubies," or when the peasant girls picked currants or carried baskets of strawberries on their heads. Whole families, "transportées d'aise" (perhaps like Julie's mother in *La Nouvelle Héloïse*), went off for the day with their picnics to discover the glories of nature in the Près Saint Gervais, and then, came back in the twilight through the brightly lit *guinguettes* with their kitchen smells and the joyous cries of the dancers (VI, pp. 180–5).

In a similar vein, for the concluding pages of volume III, he gives a final vignette of a moment so affecting that, even after the Terror, the noblest spirit of the Revolution seems reborn as he recounts it. In tones heavy with nostalgia, he relates how the coffin bearing the remains of J.-J. Rousseau came to the Tuileries. It is the description of a (pre-) Romantic, and a poet. It begins:

Il n'y a pas un coeur sensible qui ne se rappelle avec délices cette belle soirée d'automne où les habitans d'Erménonville amenèrent à Paris le cercueil de l'auteur d'*Emile*, sous un berceau d'arbustes et de fleurs.

L'air étoit calme, le ciel pur: un long rideau de pourpre voiloit à l'horizon les rayons du soleil couchant. Un vent frais agitoit doucement les dernières feuilles.

(p. 246)[51]

Mercier goes on to describe the pious group that collected, the cortège and the music. They assembled at a *bassin* which had been decorated to look like the *Ile des peupliers*, whence the coffin had come, and they all wept, Mercier informs us, thinking of Julie, Sophie, and . . . Warens. He tells of the draped coffin, the torches, and the sad faces. And now, the end of the ceremony, and of Mercier's third volume, is at hand. The conclusion is that everyone sings a song together, a song they all know by heart, and which Mercier counts on his readers knowing as well, and which in fact we do, now that Professor Heartz has trained our ears to recognize the tune and our eyes to watch for the title:

On termina les obsèques par l'air "Dans ma cabane obscure"; et chacun en se retirant le chantoit encore avec attendrissement. (p. 248)[52]

For this ex-revolutionary journalist–playwright, Rousseau's Romance from his little operatic pastoral, *Le Devin du village*, represented, as well as any single piece ever could, both the essence of the man, Rousseau, and the essence of everyone's hopes for the Revolution they felt he had inspired. The nostalgia here is certainly due to the remembrance of a happier time of innocence before the nightmare of the Terror. But perhaps these euphoric emotions derived also from a recollection of the age when, for the Favarts, the Rousseaus, the Sedaines, and for Mercier himself, it had been so easy to know where true goodness lay because, with the evils of monarchy and social privilege all around, it was so simple to define quite precisely what goodness was *not*.

The spirit of Rousseau is present also in the passage quoted earlier in which Mercier imagines the Prince giving ear to the *Pâtre*. (Who else could have been behind "Quel trésor . . . que la nature dans sa simplicité!") But Mercier is drawing equally on Diderot when he writes, in the same sentence, of the "Poëte moral," and Diderot is probably present, too, in Mercier's reversal of the roles of those onstage and those in the audience.

28. Hubert Robert, "L'exposition des cendres de J.-J. Rousseau aux Tuileries la nuit du 10–11 Octobre 1794" (This is the ceremony described by Mercier.)

Diderot understood, better than anyone in his time, the importance of these reversals, that function in his own work as sustainers of life, elements, propagators of truths and anti-truths, generators, through a tension of contrariety, of salutary opposition. After so long a discussion it may seem a long way back to our point of departure, which was just such a textual reversal: an apparent mistake by Rameau's Nephew who gave two examples that, albeit appropriate enough for their one little *membre de phrase*, worked fundamentally against his main argument. We may certainly conclude, in the light of the previous discussion, that the Nephew's sneers at *Platée* and *Ragonde* are out of place, not only because these are both such memorable artistic achievements, but because they signify a development that eventually destroyed the aristocratic artificiality the Nephew thought so harmful in music. The examples were "wrong" on the Nephew's own terms. But perhaps we should note too that his deprecations of French music in the name of the Italians form only part of the picture, a moment in the dialogue. If one looks elsewhere in the text one finds him lavishly praising parts of French operas not only by Rameau, but also by Campra, and even Lully. This contradiction fits perfectly with the inequality of the Nephew's character, such as Diderot has created him. Furthermore, the sneers at *Platée* and *Ragonde* are partly sour grapes, a barely disguised cover-up for his envy of composers who succeeded where he has failed;

170

naturally he almost trips himself up by giving the wrong examples. But then, one can always see through the Nephew's pretenses ultimately, for Diderot has fashioned him to be essentially transparent – which is more than one can say of the great dialogue in which the Nephew lives, whose measure can never finally be taken because, like those archaic gods at the beginning of the world who somehow embodied good and evil in a single being, this dialogue eventually takes us beyond all distinctions.

The demise of classical tragedy in France

I

Thus far we have been concerned with the tensions and counter-points that grow out of the substance, the *matière propre* of eighteenth-century literature, and much less attention has been paid to the manner in which the substance is viewed. But of course "focus" was a topic of critical concern in the Enlightenment, and not merely because, thanks to recent discoveries in optics, people were learning new ways to talk about it, but because it was in the process of radical change, particularly in the theatre. No doubt it was a daring stroke of imagination (not unrelated to the experimental parodies of the *foire*) for Diderot to have the main character of his drama, *Le Fils naturel*, step out of the play and converse with the author in order to explain his conduct onstage, and the resulting dialogues, *Dorval et Moi*, are certainly some of the most suggestive theatrical criticism of the era.[1] We hardly pause to notice the relatively minor fact that in these dialogues the hero is being depicted as someone even an ordinary person might accost, a man dressed and behaving in some respects rather like you and me, and who may be inspected and queried at close range. But here Diderot was deliberately breaking one of the most sacred barriers of Classicism, and the effect is as daring, as revolutionary, as when in our own century (following Diderot's lead) the young Turks abolished the proscenium arch and made the audience part of the performance.

Classicism (the tradition Diderot was working against) depended literally for its life on distance, and although the theatre – where the audience is placed far away from the play itself – embodies this concept with particular clarity, one finds the impulse toward the remote expressed in all the arts, in the age of Classicism:[2] from garden-planning, where the eye travels outward through the geometrical forms to some precisely calculated point of rest in the distance, even to musical settings of Biblical texts, where a composer such as Couperin deliberately avoids vivid rendering of the literal meaning of the word.[3] Aesthetics are involved in such arrangements, of course, since it is always a question of how best to give pleasure to the audience; but it is also a matter of epistemology, for such placements tell us how the truths of a work of art were thought to be most perfectly perceived in that era, and hence most capable of producing the desired effect. In other words, these ample spaces were designed to fit with, and even to reflect as a kind of projection, the functioning of the mind and will. They diagram the movements of the "soul."

In French classical tragedy, the impulse that made authors choose remote subjects and place them on stages distant from the spectator is no doubt counterbalanced by the other factors pulling in the opposite direction: the rule that the action must last no longer than twenty-four hours, for example, actually draws the drama closer, since it establishes a more plausible relationship between the time enacted in the play and the audience's stay in the theatre. Even the unities of place and action may be bolstering the feeling of closeness by concentrating the experience of the play. And then, the idea of remoteness in the classical age had connotations quite different from those we feel in it today. For obviously in the seventeenth century, the way to depict passion most vividly was to have it expressed by some lofty personage from a distant country or time. To place things at a distance, far from blunting their impact, or rendering them obscure as it does for us, served to bring them more sharply into focus, and actually increased their power. Even to Descartes, truth was not to be found in the experiences closest and most immediate to us, i.e., in sense impressions. In fact, he thought one should be most wary of immediate reactions – the pain of the finger burned by the candle flame – since they were probably clouded over by confusion and error. It was only when we viewed these experiences more remotely by intellection that they came fully to life.[4]

Nor is it surprising that the language of classicism was so very much characterized by an absence of the concrete, for individual words too imply a focus of thought that either brings the material world close, or keeps it away – even as the spectacle itself does. And particularly if one has in mind the earthy language of Shakespeare or Webster, the absence of the concrete in the language of classical tragedy is a never-ending source of amazement. However did Corneille contrive again and again to compose five acts in which, except for an occasional cup containing poison, or symbols such as a crown or a sword, hardly any real *things* occur in the language at all? And again this clinging to the abstract or indirect was not merely a matter of aesthetics or even of good manners (although indeed material objects were considered base and unworthy of mention) but part of a general notion of the mental operations through which truth was perceived. D'Alembert, though writing much later, was actually expressing an eighteenth-century version of this same classical assumption when he observed that, on the one hand, we can never really know objects in themselves, and that, on the other, the more a concept is abstract, the greater is the degree of certitude it can possess.[5]

This is rather an extreme statement, as one might have expected from a geometer. With authors such as playwrights, who were thought to be dealing more directly with the complexities of human experience, one finds more moderation. In the theatre there is, rather, a mixture of tendencies pulling one way or the other, and it was this mixture that would be so profoundly disrupted in the century of Diderot. Since Enlightened playwrights were to go to such pains to dismantle the classical aesthetic in this regard, perhaps we may be forgiven for dotting the i's and crossing the t's concerning everyone's most familiar author in the eighteenth century, and one that haunted Diderot in particular: Racine.

Somewhat like that of Corneille, Racine's linguistic universe was largely devoid of those "accidents" that, before Descartes at least, were thought to give body and substance to the material world. However, Racine's abstractions function psychologically in a markedly different way, as critics have long been aware. In a play such as *Phèdre*, for example, where the structure is essentially a series of confrontations between characters, the high level of abstraction results in a sort of blanching-out of the language, as if the physical closeness of the characters onstage and the intensity of their feelings had to be compensated for by the remoteness of their expression. On those few occasions when the blanching-out fails to function, and material objects do appear, the result is disaster. Thus, to cite the most familiar example, the moment Phèdre takes verbal cognizance of Hippolyte's physical presence, she is lost. Even the labyrinth, which had started as a remote symbol, supposedly enabling her to avoid speaking directly of her passion, has, simply by mentioning it, confirmed its existence as a psychological reality from which she will never escape. To be sure, such moments are exceptions to the rule; for in *Phèdre* even the most intense emotions are usually conveyed at the level of intellection.

It is only in the last act of the play, during the "récit de Théramène," that the whole material universe suddenly erupts into the play, and the audience finds itself constrained to see, hear, and feel everything. The slow sway of the chariot gets the "récit" underway; we sense the silence of Hippolyte's guards around him; we see the idly dangling reins of the horses with their dull eyes, heads lowered (we are told) as if to share their master's own sad thoughts.

This is above all a tableau of introspection, and therefore what we see and hear conveys an odd kind of reversal of normal experience: the horses have eyes, yet here there is a suggestion that they do not see; their heads are not in a position to serve with useful efficiency; the tautness essential to the functioning rein has been lost and gone slack; clearly the driver no longer drives; even the boisterous noisiness always associated with guards on a journey now is absent. In fact each of the "objects" composing this tableau has been deprived of at least one essential quality that normally makes it what it is. The description, totally lacking in color, muted in sound – perhaps even silent, leaden in the heavy pensiveness of its movements –

creates a lulling, dreamlike effect. For an instant one wonders whether these floating reins, the dull-eyed horses, the silent guards and their sad hero are really located in the material world at all; they seem as if drifting, timeless, along the reaches of the imagination.

It is because the inward-turning qualities of this tableau are so intense that when we suddenly hear the great cry coming from the depths of the sea, and the groan from the bowels of the earth, we feel as if wrenched back into the real world again. Now the slow, silent tableau of the beginning will be replaced by noises that are deafening, enormous objects that frighten by their colossal size, unexpected bursts of color, movements that are swift and violent. All our unwilling senses will be strained to the limit of their capacities.

The eyes will fasten first upon the bristling manes of the horses, and then watch the mountain of water, boiling as it humps up from the flat plain of the sea. We smell the stench that "infects" the air, while the wave "vomits" the bellowing monster on the shore amid the streams of foam. We perceive not only its broad head with the dangerous horns, but its lower half too, the tail, with its disgusting twists and coils. When the monster, wounded by intrepid Hippolyte's javelin, belches fire upon the horses from its flaming mouth, they bolt across the rocks, reddening their bits with bloody foam, stampeded even more by his cries calling to them to stop. And now we hear the crack of the axle as it splits and the chariot flies to pieces around the hero and, by empathy at least, our sense of touch too is engaged as Hippolyte, caught in the horses' reins, is dragged along the ground, on and on, until finally, after the terrifyingly graphic phrase, his body: "one wound," the movement comes to an end. The last thing we see are the bloody rocks and dripping brambles. The last sounds we hear are those of Hippolyte's faint voice, before it breaks off, once and for all. Hippolyte is now spoken of as "défiguré," or again as "sans forme et sans couleur." There is nothing at all to identify him, even to Aricie. And so the "récit" ends as it had begun, with a mute tableau and an object that has been deprived of the essential qualities that once gave it form and life.

In the middle of the "récit," the monster is described as being covered with "écailles jaunissantes," a phrase that has provoked both embarrassment and mirth from critics, particularly because of the preceding rhyme with "cornes menaçantes."[6] But perhaps they have been overlooking its dramatic force: as has been pointed out, it includes the only color in the entire play whose value is purely pictorial,[7] that is to say, "jaunissantes" does not symbolize anything psychologically, the way the only other previous colors – white, red, and black – had done. Its function is simply to add to the horror of the scene by rendering it more vivid. Moreover the participial form of the adjective (probably suggesting the glinting of scales) adds an extra dimension of differentiation to our vision. In other words, this term brings us round the circle to the opposite pole of the usual language of the play. It emanates entirely from a world of matter and of the senses that of course proves totally destructive to the hero when he loses his equilibrium and falls among these "accidents" that literally tear him apart. It is Hippolyte's effort to save himself that proves his undoing, as if his gesture of throwing the dart to wound the monster signified his final acceptance, however coerced it might be, of a material world that he meets on its own terms. By striking so boldly and with such firm intent Hippolyte actually becomes an accomplice of the forces that will destroy him.

Curiously enough, the sudden explosion of sensual, material images into the language of the play, and the extraordinary violence of the action they so vividly describe, in no way upset the play's aesthetic equilibrium.[8] On the contrary, this "récit" brings the tragedy into final balance and rest. It is as if all the previous abstractions, the constant unwillingness to show objects in their sensual materiality, creates a sort of void in the audience, a cumulative desire, almost an expectation, that just once we will be allowed to indulge fully all our senses. The violent orgy of tangibility that erupts in this scene serves to appease once and for all our pent-up frustration. Nor does it upset the balance carefully established at the outset; for, even as the physical closeness of the characters confronting one another had been counterbalanced by the distant abstraction of the language, so here the explicitness of the language is balanced by the distance from us of the character. For Hippolyte is literally out of everyone's sight, on the most distant confines of the city as he meets his end.

II

It has long been clear that remoteness, or distance, whether in language, plot, or character, belongs specifically to an aristocratic perspective.[9] Even for Diderot whose attitudes toward Classicism in the theatre involve such a wide variety of feelings, what lies behind his criticism of the "false," artificial "coldness" of the theatrical style of his time was a strong reaction against the aristocratic associations of this tradition.[10] There is no need to dwell on the fact that the theatrical characters he himself created were literally closer to him, since they were drawn from everyday life and spoke what was supposed to pass for everyday – poetical – prose. And when Diderot speculated on the possibility of creating a sort of theatre in the round he was imagining a dramatic form in which the distance separating the characters and the audience would be closed also. Diderot's theories were the wave of the future, of course, and as, in the 1760s, middle-class aesthetics came more and more to replace aristocratic values – which in the theatre meant common people onstage in common situations, backed by common decors – inevitably there was a revolution in the epistemology of

29. Charles Le Brun, frontispiece for the original edition of Racine's *Phèdre et Hippolyte* (1677), engraved by Sébastien Le Clerc (The scene depicts the end of the "récit de Théramène".)

theatricality as well. The spaciousness of the Classical ways of perceiving, along with the assumption that distance was required if one were to understand the complex kind of structure that produced truly tragic emotions, gave way to a desire for a closer relationship between sense reactions and allegedly "tragic" responses. Thus, in the *drames* composed by the followers of Diderot, the mere depiction of poverty-stricken surroundings was supposed to awaken automatic feelings of sadness and pity. The mere sight of the helpless heroine brought on compassion. Gone were many of the intellectual strains required to take in the preliminary entanglements that crowded the expositions of classical tragedies. Authors could now rely on simple, ready-made dramatic clichés, gripping situations whose pathos the heart could sense in advance and absorb almost by intuition, with minimal movement on the part of the mental faculties: "melodrama," to use the modern term. For present purposes, the most important aspect of this epistemological revolution are the sociological implications. No longer was the average viewer forced to squint through telescopes at some remote object, projecting himself out of the present, and out of his own class, into a situation that had nothing to do with the experiences of his life, and where even the language was strange to him. At last the focal point fell within the range of objects he could see with his own eyes and feel with his own hands. Coming into perspective was a way of life that had almost never been taken cognizance of before, and that was acquiring a thrilling new dignity and dramatic interest. Now it was for the aristocrats to squint.

In this connection, one of the most curious eighteenth-century playwrights to observe is Voltaire. He had in a number of ways participated in the same bourgeois movement as Diderot, in fact the emotions depicted in certain of his plays have the same tonality as those we find in the *drame bourgeois*.[11] Yet, as is well known, he had not liked Diderot's *Père de famille* at all,[12] nor in his own tragedies was he willing to sacrifice the essential classical precepts: his plots were preferably situated in remote times and places; he continued to use *vers alexandrins* with rhymes; he prized the unities; his rhetoric derived mainly from Corneille and Racine. Towards the end of his life Voltaire was becoming if anything more conservative, an attitude we find revealed in one of the last things he completed before his death, a two-part address which was read before the Académie Française by Voltaire's younger friend d'Alembert.

The address in question is an attack upon Shakespeare,[13] whose works had recently been translated by Le Tourneur and sold in a handsome edition with royal patronage. Voltaire rightly saw the new publication as part of a trend that threatened the most cherished traditions of Classicism, and so, summoning all his wit, irony and eloquence, and using d'Alembert's voice, he determined to eliminate the danger once and for all.

It must have been a most entertaining occasion at the Académie Française: for, if Voltaire's French views were spoken for by d'Alembert, at the same time Shakespeare and the English were more than adequately represented in the presence of the awesome, the terrible Mrs Montagu, "Queen of the blue-stockings," and who afterwards claimed her side had won simply through the expression of disapproval she displayed, for all to see, on her visage throughout the reading. Judging by the portraits of her, the mere state of Mrs Montagu's face must have been, indeed, a powerful argument for the English. However, one may seriously doubt if even this were enough to counterbalance the masterful tactics of the Patriarch.

Voltaire freely admits in his address that, many years before, he had been one of Shakespeare's first champions in France; however, having now become older, and above all wiser, he finds he must have been too lenient. How can one forgive Shakespeare's gross ignorance of history; the shocking mixture of comedy and tragedy, and of prose and verse in the same play; the irregularities of the plots; the hopping about from one place to another; the jolting changes in time? But more than anything else, the vulgarity of Shakespeare's language constantly grates upon Voltaire's sensibilities: he shudders over the obscenities of the servants' scene from *Romeo and Juliet*, that, for the sake of decency, he quotes incompletely; and he deplores the fact that Shakespeare would subject our ears to the speech of cobblers, drunken porters, and grave-diggers; that even royalty would speak in a manner that was not always seemly. As a culminating example placed at the end of the first part of his address, Voltaire contrasts the noble line from Racine's *Iphigénie*: "Mais tout dort, et l'armée, et les vents, et Neptune . . ." with a phrase from a guard's speech in the opening scene of *Hamlet*: "Not a mouse stirring."

Je vous dirais, qu'il n'y a ni harmonie ni vérité intéressante dans ce quolibet d'un soldat: *Je n'ai pas entendu une souris trotter*. Que ce soldat ait vu ou n'ait pas vu passer de souris, cet événement est très-inutile à la tragédie d'*Hamlet*: ce n'est qu'un discours de *Gilles*, un proverbe bas, qui ne peut faire aucun effet.

(*Oeuvres complètes*, ed. Moland, xxx, p. 363)[14]

Speaking a little earlier of this same mouse, he had observed:

Oui, monsieur, un soldat peut répondre ainsi dans un corps de garde; mais non pas sur le théâtre, devant les premières personnes d'une nation, *qui s'expriment noblement*, et devant qui il faut s'exprimer de même.   (*ibid.*, italics mine)[15]

Voltaire has totally missed the point about Shakespeare, of course, and his blindness to the function of rodent images in *Hamlet* reveals all the one-sidedness of his bias. He had long since ceased to care about understanding Shakespeare: his unique concern was the aristocratic nature of tragedy, the purity and balance that he wisely realized would be fatally undermined if the verbal expression of base materiality were not strictly controlled – just as it had been in the time of Corneille and Racine.

There is something quite moving in the aged Voltaire's efforts to keep alive a past that was done for – his own – and if, in his discourse, the tone goes from irony to sarcasm to sneers of derision, no doubt it was because he sensed, however dimly, that the tides of events were running against him; time was running out. The least one can say is that history had abandoned the Patriarch and taken up with the enemy. History was with Shakespeare, of course, but above all it was with Shakespeare's admirers, playwrights like Diderot who had created the new dramatic tradition. Perhaps if Voltaire comes down so hard against the deceased author of *Hamlet* (newly translated, to be sure), it was partly because he couldn't speak out strongly against his own living and active ally, Diderot, or denounce the school he had inspired – a school that had brought to the stage the lower classes swarming in all their vulgarity.

But actually, viewing the matter from an ideal historical vantage point, the most logical target for Voltaire would have been, not Shakespeare, or even Diderot, but the author discussed in the previous chapter, Louis-Sébastien Mercier, the most controversial dramatic theorist of the late eighteenth century, who, as we have seen, turned Diderot's suggestive insights in the theatre into a dogmatic creed, in fact into a weapon with which to war against precisely the theatrical traditions Voltaire held most sacred.

Realizing that, in the theatre, Classicism and all its aristocratic tenets was the enemy,[16] Mercier determined that it should be destroyed, along with the evil political system that had given it life and sustained it for so long. For these destructive purposes, Mercier proposed to create a theatre that was literally an anti-body, formulated to provide negative replacements for all the aristocratic features of Classicism – everything Classicism had stood for. Here Mercier's motivations involve the "attraction of the contrary" in a far less subtle way than Diderot's. Since classical tragedies most often situated the action in ancient times, Mercier, as a general rule, simply abolished the past in the theatre, pointing out that the present was, for most people, easier to relate to; since Classicism featured exotic and/or foreign settings, Mercier suppressed these, too: the scene should shift to their own country, here and now.[17] Classical tragedy featured the highly born, the powerful, and the wealthy, therefore let the theatre feature the lowly born, the poor, and the downtrodden (p. 132). Classical plays were set in handsome palaces or in the houses of the rich, therefore Mercier sponsors the meanest of cottages, prisons, even solitary confinement cells (p. 136). The heroes and heroines of Classicism never worked for a living, therefore the theatre should create heroes and heroines that did always (p. 137); Classicism never said a word about the humble trades, therefore the new theatre should find ways to put these at the centre of the action (p. 108).

All these reforms implied that theatrical distance should be drastically reduced, in fact virtually abolished. Mercier had perceptively realized that in the classical theatre, distance ultimately bespoke the wrongful gap between the monarch (tyrant) and his people, and the equally wrongful gap between the privileged classes of society, the few, and the lowly born, the multitude. Thus, to write tragedies that featured kings and queens in their grand palaces amounted to celebrating royalty's ill-gotten and ill-used power. And also, because of the vast distance they placed between the simple person in the audience and the imaginary hero onstage, emanating from a time no one could remember and a country few knew or cared about, and having a social station so lofty as to be totally inaccessible, these plays confirmed the legitimacy of the most extreme social differences – to Mercier the worst feature of his society. The gaps must be closed; Classicism must go, and so must the kings and nobles it depended on.

There were a few exceptions, however, to his iron-clad rules. Aristocratic characters could appear in comedies on condition that their faults and ridiculous manners be laid bare and suitably chastized (p. 61). Comedy could become a form of punishment, in fact of torture, for aristocrats,[18] and Mercier fantasized that in these comedies of the future, the nobles would metaphorically be stripped naked onstage and beaten with sticks.[19] Similarly, antique personages could serve useful purposes, especially if they in no way suggested royalty. Thus he would allow certain classical heroes, chosen for their simplicity – mere peasants, really, as he tells it – to appear, one cooking vegetables, another mingling with his cattle, another seen with his nail-studded barrel (p. 49). Even the bad kings of history and legend might serve his purposes, provided their crimes were excoriated and they met the end they deserved (p. 39). Naturally, Mercier recommends Charles I of England as a particularly suitable subject, and one wonders if Mercier wanted the beheading to take place onstage. Nor is this question an idle one: Mercier was constantly brooding on the death of tyrants as he composed his treatise, and once he even went so far as to write down the whole scenario of the death of Nero, just as he wished some enterprising playwright might set it. Though printed as a long note, in some ways this passage is the emotional climax of Mercier's work:

Je voudrais voir l'empereur seul, livré aux tableaux effrayans que ses crimes lui retraceroient, ne sachant ni vivre ni mourir. Sa douleur seroit celle d'un impie, son repentir celui d'un lâche, son effroi celui d'une femmelette: il prendroit le fer d'une main tremblante, et l'essayant vingt fois il n'oseroit s'en frapper; il pleureroit, il porteroit de tous côtés des regards supplians, il imploreroit le bras du plus vil esclave: le sang de l'infame couleroit. Je voudrois le voir alors luttant contre la mort, tombant sur la terre, la grattant de ses mains, poussant des cris aigus en approchant du terme qui ramene tout à l'égalité. Je voudrois voir les mouvemens convulsifs des muscles de son visage, jadis insensibles aux tourmens de ses semblables, ses bras se roidir, sa poitrine s'enfler, tous ses nerfs se tendre sous l'effort de la destruction *prochaine et terrible; elle diroit à son ame épouvantée: viens, monstre, viens tomber dans l'abîme ténébreux où la mort va regner sur toi, où la justice que tu as méconnue va te saisir et te rendre tous les supplices que tu as infligés à tes pareils.* (p. 49)[20]

When it came to political allegories, Mercier was never famous for his light touch. But of course, regardless of its dubious potential as drama, this passage is endlessly fascinating as an imaginary rehearsal for the very real death of the Tyrant that, twenty years hence, would be staged in the same nation.[21] And theatrically, too, the text is endlessly rich. It is as anti-Classical as anything Mercier ever wrote. Particularly in the rather Villonesque dwelling on the most repulsive, physical aspects of death, it brings onstage for the eye of the spectator everything that Racine was most anxious to keep offstage, locked safely within the imagination. Yet paradoxically, one notes that Racine's description of Hippolyte's death is actually no less graphic than Mercier's death scene, in fact the physical details that crowd into the "récit de Théramène" are if anything more vivid and shocking than those in Mercier's leaden prose. Racine, too, was staging verbally his own Death of the Prince, and as – in our mind's eye at least – we watch his hero losing his lofty poise above the elements he used to control, falling down and being destroyed by his contact with them, it is as if this "récit" were a kind of emblem signifying the inherent danger of materiality and prefiguring its potential destructiveness to those highly born personages who, in order to exist, must remain free and detached from it. Mercier, for his part, was simply making capital from this same truth, as he opened wide the floodgates to the whole world of the concrete that Racine had so scrupulously locked, disembodied, into language. And as we watch Mercier's tyrant, who has come in from the wings and now lies before us in his death throes, scratching the earth, his face twitching, arms growing stiff, nerves distending in his agony, terror filling his soul, we are seeing an author deliberately killing off the classical tradition in the theatre and, at the same moment (and just as deliberately), putting an end to the monarchs who had nurtured it.

More than anything else, it was the abolition of distance that, in Mercier's hands, would prove so potentially lethal in art and society. For in this new perspective (or lack of perspective), monarchs (tyrants) now seen up close for the first time and scaled down to size, could be judged for what they truly were, and they turn out to be the most miserable of mortals, so criminal in their lives and so disgusting in their deaths that even the humblest (noblest) members of the audience will recoil from them in horror. Mercier knew that monarchs in particular could never survive in a world they couldn't rise above, a world swamped, *d'en bas*, by the commonest, basest accidents of matter, accidents that would bring down a whole society.

Ironically, Voltaire didn't even know of Mercier's treatise when composing his own Discourse to the Academy against Shakespeare. He wasn't aware of the extent to which the mice were stirring, and that lofty Classicism with all its Hippolytes had already been swept away, by Mercier's angry pen, for the creation of new and lower orders of theatre. The Revolution was still more than a decade off when Mercier wrote his treatise, but surely we are here again in the presence of a time bomb.

12

The Marriage of Figaro

a. GAMES

Beaumarchais' *Mariage de Figaro* is a mixture of ingredients so perfectly combined, it would be almost perverse to strain out any single element and call it the essence. The play is everything at once: situation comedy, farce, comic opera, *parade*, comedy of manners, erotic comedy, social satire, *drame bourgeois*, *comédie larmoyante*, revolutionary indictment of the system,[1] plea for unwed mothers and women's liberation, and so on. The action shifts focus constantly, and each time a new strand comes by the audience must catch on as best it can. If we look behind the play to its literary "sources" we find likewise a pleasantly heterogeneous jumble of overlapping fragments.[2] Behind the character of Figaro stands a virtually endless line of impudent theatrical valets stretching from the plays of Marivaux, Dancourt, Regnard, and Molière all the way back to the comedies of Terence and Plautus.[3] Count Almaviva, that jealous thwarter of young lovers, also falls heir to an abundant theatrical ancestry, going back at least to those hindering and slightly ridiculous fathers of ancient Roman times. Jacques Scherer reminds us that in the character of Suzanne we find something of the innumerable Dorines and Lisettes of Molière, Marivaux, and how many others in the eighteenth century.[4] Plays by Vadé and Rochon de Chabannes may have suggested, in germ, the scenes between Chérubin and the Countess; the trial scene may look back to the *Wasps* of Aristophanes, or to Rabelais, or to *Les Plaideurs* of Racine, among other possibilities. When Chérubin hides in the Countess' *cabinet*, is he not reenacting the same situation we find in Scarron's *La Précaution inutile* and in Sedaine's *La Gageure imprévue*? The scene in which the Count makes love to his own wife, believing her to be someone else, may be borrowed from Dufresny's *Le Double veuvage* (1702) or Vadé's *Trompeur trompé*.[5] As for the main plot of *Figaro*, W. D. Howarth has found records of no fewer than five plays antedating *Figaro*, all bearing the title "Le Droit du seigneur." One of them is by Voltaire.[6]

Certainly it is helpful to know about literary antecedents such as these. Yet, when one gets through reviewing the "sources" of *Figaro*, perhaps the most striking conclusion one reaches is how far short they fall of

Beaumarchais.[7] Voltaire's *Droit du seigneur* resembles the plot of *Figaro* only in the most general and mechanical way, with innumerable differences of detail. There may be other plays in which a young page or *écuyer* makes love to an older woman during the absence of her husband; yet, in their cheapness, they only make us appreciate still more the gracious subtlety and discretion we find in Beaumarchais.[8] Put all the valets of theatrical tradition together, even adding the Picaro progeny into the bargain, and how close are we to Figaro in his great monologue? Perhaps such a chasm between the "sources" and the emergent work is to be expected when one is dealing with a truly original author. Certainly the gap exists with Molière, as many scholars have observed.

We note, too, that for other plays by Beaumarchais literary sources are strikingly more important than they are for *Figaro*. *La Mère coupable* (1792), the last play of the Figaro trilogy, is literally dominated by Molière's *Tartuffe*, and Beaumarchais reminds us of this in the play's subtitle, *L'Autre Tartuffe*. *Le Barbier de Séville* (1775), the earliest of the Figaro trilogy, clearly looks back to the long line of comedies typified in Molière's *Ecole des femmes*. It is a conventional play in the best sense, bringing to a new perfection *données* that are quite traditional.[9] In short, whereas the two other plays of the Figaro cycle fall rather neatly into recognizable literary traditions, *Figaro* would appear rather as an exception.

We reach curiously similar conclusions if we compare *Figaro* and *Le Barbier* from the standpoint of the unities: whereas in *Le Barbier* the traditional unities of time, place and action are observed to perfection, forming an integral part of the play's structure and actually intensifying the comedy, in *Figaro* they really are not. Even though the play conforms to the letter of the rules, aesthetically *Figaro* never achieves unity, at least not in the way *Le Barbier* does. The locus of the play actually shifts, from the bedroom at the beginning, to increasingly larger rooms in the château, and finally into the *parc*, impelled as it were by the gathering energy and excitement of a plot that simply will not be contained within four walls. In a sense, the play is breaking out of the unity of place. The same is true of the action: though the theme of Figaro's marriage may provide a pivot around which most of the incidents revolve, aesthetically one is hardly aware of any unity. The plot unfolds as an endless series of surprises, adventures, novelties, and incredible happenings, worlds apart from the centered harmony one experiences in a play by Molière. And then, the character of Chérubin – unless one goes to desperate lengths to allegorize him as Eros – does not really belong anywhere in the main plot, though he is probably the author's most inspired creation and a frequent object of our concern and delight. The unity of time is also stretched beyond the point of credibility on this frantically crowded day. In short, whereas knowledge of both literary sources and structural conventions is quite helpful in enabling us to enjoy some of the finer and more original qualities of the two other plays in the trilogy, with *Figaro*, on the other hand, such knowledge really has little to do with the play's unique qualities, and sometimes it may actually hinder us from enjoying them: if one embarked on a determined search for the unities in *Figaro*,[10] in the same way one finds them in a play by Dancourt, one might be forced to conclude – quite wrongly – that Beaumarchais was a less successful author.

The truth is, rather, that we have not been looking in the right direction. For, despite Beaumarchais' worship of Diderot and Molière, *literary* traditions are not the key to this particular play. The unique comic spirit of *Figaro* is not literary; it is something far less learned and more spontaneous. What actually gives the play its special qualities, while at the same time underpinning much of its structure and provoking most of its laughter, is a whole series of children's games.[11] Of course, *Le Mariage de Figaro* observes the unity of place: it just moves from playroom at the beginning, to playground at the end. It observes the unity of action also, largely because, throughout the plot, the Count is "it."

The "game element" in *Figaro* makes it virtually unique not only in Beaumarchais' trilogy but in the tradition of the French theatre before him.[12] In this connection, it is useful to observe as a point of contrast that in an author such as Molière laughter is usually associated with some insight the audience has into character: the blind infatuation we see in Orgon, for example, gives a sense of rightness, almost of inevitability, to the absurd line "Le pauvre homme!"[13] Dorine's earthy directness, as against the vulnerable sensibilities of Mariane, is what makes "Vous serez, ma foi! tartuffiée" (II, iv) such a choice moment in the play. This is to say that Molière, in his great comedies, usually engages our maturity and our understanding while making us laugh: we are mirthful – in part at least – because we are wise about human character.

But let us now consider the first act of *Le Mariage de Figaro*, with Chérubin rushing to hide behind the chair as the Count comes in, and then the Count hiding behind the chair while Chérubin crouches on the seat underneath Suzanne's dress, and then the Count getting "caught" when he forgets to hide, and finally Chérubin getting "caught" too in the most droll and surprising way. Such terms as "comédie d'intrigue," or even "lazzi," are really quite inadequate to describe this situation, because the tension and laughter of this scene are the tension and laughter peculiar to a game of hide-and-seek: the suddenness of the movements, the daring and completely unexpected improvisations of hiding places, the complete seriousness of the players' efforts to escape the person who is "it," the near-discoveries, even the ironic feeling of inevitability connected with the catch at the end – all these things belong specifically to children's games.[14] In contrast to Molière, the identity of the players, or the individual qualities they may possess, are of relatively minor importance. Indeed, the same person can completely change character during the game, as the Count does when, having been the "seeker," he turns suddenly into a "hider" and crouches in a rather undignified manner behind the chair, just as Chérubin had done, and for once actually gains a measure of sympathy from the audience. Nor are we here in the traditions of the farce: the *coups de bâton*, in fact all the punishments that bring on laughter when performed by clowns, have little to do with the universe of hide-and-seek. What causes the laughter in this scene of *Figaro* is simply the suspense connected with being caught, and when, finally, Chérubin *is* caught, the tension is broken and a new round can begin. *Coups de bâton* are not really the point of the game.

For Chérubin the game of hide-and-seek goes on throughout the entire play; he seems to be endlessly turning up in new and unpredictable hiding places: fleeing into the Countess' *cabinet* (ii, xi), disappearing into the *pavillon* (v, vi), disguising himself as a girl (iv, v), or even jumping out the window when all else fails (ii, xv). Occasionally, he becomes a chaser himself, running after Suzanne to snatch the Countess' ribbon, or to make her give him a kiss (i, vi). No one else is a game player to this literal degree in the play, but then, no one else, except his partner Fanchette, is so young.

The games Figaro plays with the Count are more sophisticated and slightly more adult. They are mainly verbal, whereas Chérubin's are not. For example, in act ii, scene xxi, the Count backs Figaro into a corner with question after question concerning the incriminating officer's *brevet* that Chérubin had dropped while falling from the window. Figaro runs out of inventions and seems to be on the verge of revealing the truth, when, in the nick of time, whispered help is relayed from the other members of the team; Figaro learns the magic phrase "le cachet manque" and is made safe. Or again, in act iii, scene v, the Count attempts to find out whether Figaro knows of his designs on Suzanne. This time, not only do his thrusts fail to hit home, but, in a series of "turnabouts," they leave him wide open to half-disguised insults from Figaro. As critics have noted,[15] there is a verbal fencing match going on in such places and, indeed, Figaro parries the Count's thrusts skilfully: "Jouons serré," he says as the match begins, and then at the end: "Il a joué au fin avec moi; qu'a-t-il appris?" The Count, too, when he is alone, admits that a kind of match has taken place: "Le maraud m'embarrassait! en disputant, il prend son avantage, il vous serre, vous enveloppe . . . Ah! friponne et fripon! vous vous entendez pour me jouer?" (iii, viii).

These last words are interesting because they suggest that the Count in some way is supposed to know that Suzanne and Figaro are in league against him, just as he strongly suspects that Figaro did not really jump out the window.[16] But he is helpless to act on his knowledge. Whenever the situation is reduced to a sort of verbal guessing game, the symmetry of the game tends to make the players equal, and, just so long as Figaro is able to invent responses that literally satisfy convention, the Count has no choice but to accept them. In fact, merely by asking the question the Count has tacitly agreed to let Figaro go free if he can come up with an answer to his *devinette*. In the world of children's games both the hiders and the seekers obey the rules as law.

This is the reason the trial scene (III, xv) fits so perfectly into the general ambience of the play, although to critics looking for the conventional unities or for *vraisemblance* this part of the action has proved something of an embarrassment. It is true that the scene fits awkwardly into the main plot; moreover, it is entirely legitimate to wonder, as critics have done, why a person as familiar with real courts as Beaumarchais should deliberately create a "tribunal de fantaisie" quite unrelated to actual judicial procedure. The answer may be that, from the start, the audience never takes the trial seriously as a trial. Realistic details would only impede our enjoyment of such marvels as the legal wrangle over the copulative conjunction "et." It is a mock trial, of course, the merest *game* of "courts of law," with a pasteboard Brid'oison as judge, and everyone enjoying Figaro's inventiveness as he talks his way around the absurd evidence. There are occasional political overtones of a very serious nature in this scene, as there are in many other parts of the play; yet, precisely because they are held in suspension, diffused, so to speak, in the atmosphere of the games being played, they may deepen the tone, but they never become obtrusive. Johan Huizinga has pointed out that even real court procedures involve many "play elements," and in the trial scene of *Figaro*, play simply becomes the essence.[17]

Reading the book on children's games by Iona and Peter Opie, one is tempted to conclude that the tension between the seeker and the hiders, between the one who is "it" and the others who are not, has a good deal of the tension between the old and the young about it: what is being played out by children in these games may be the fundamental contest between the parent and the child. In hide-and-seek the game's playful tone and the deliberately limited scope of the action imply that there can be no true heroes, or villains, among the players – even though the hiders have all our sympathies, since they are the ones who are vulnerable to being caught, while there is something almost inherently distasteful about the role of "it."[18] Likewise, in *Figaro* there is no truly heroic character, nor does the Count qualify as a truly unpardonable villain, even though he is certainly unpopular enough: feared by Chérubin, taunted and jeered at by Figaro, mocked by Suzanne, and deceived even by the Countess. The audience enjoys all this because it disapproves of both the Count's determination to press an unfair advantage and the promiscuity of his marital infidelities. Yet this is surely not the whole explanation, for in his own way Chérubin is quite promiscuous also, and when we learn in *La Mère coupable* that eventually the Countess is supposed to have a child by Chérubin, we may revise our feelings somewhat about the Count's suspicions of him in the earlier play. Pomeau remarks that Figaro is not really so innocent either, and, given the ambiguous character traits he inherits from Beaumarchais himself, we may conjecture that were he in the Count's place he would not behave any better than the Count does (p. 189). However, we are willing to forgive Chérubin and Figaro for practically anything they do, partly because they are so young, partly because they have so little while the Count, the establishment personified, has so much, and – perhaps most of all – because as hiders they are vulnerable to being caught, and the Count is after them.

But then isn't the play in many ways a celebration of childhood – with gay songs to sing (II, xxii; IV, x), a march to walk in step to (IV, iv), a "tableau vivant" to pose in (II, iv), costumes to dress up in and disguises to wear (IV, iv), and even a kind of seesaw as Marceline and Suzanne curtsey back and forth to one another (I, v)? At the end, during almost the whole of act V, there is a grand game of blindman's buff, held just as it is getting dark – the time when the best hiding games are always played – with several players exchanging clothes to deceive the "blindman," the way real children do.

Actually, this last game is the most elaborate, and the entire cast takes part; even Marceline and Brid'oison get into the act somehow. There are three main rounds, with darkness serving as a blindfold: first Chérubin plays with the Countess, thinking he has caught Suzanne; then Figaro plays with Suzanne, thinking he has caught the Countess; finally, the Count plays with his own wife, thinking her to be a mistress. Thus, in rapid succession each of the three principal masculine characters has been "it," and has managed in a very short time to flirt with the wrong lady. Once there is even an extra layer of confusion as Figaro discovers that the person he took for the Countess is really Suzanne, and then turns the tables on her by feigning to have designs on the lady whose costume she wears. In the world of children's hiding games such "turnabouts" may occur with almost magical speed, and in *Figaro* swift surprises such as these account for a good deal of the hilarity of the play's dizzy pace which gets faster and faster as it approaches the end. But with blindman's buff, to watch the person who is "it" mixing everyone up is only half the fun; almost the best part comes when at last the light of torches brightens the stage and, one by one, the characters emerge from the dark *pavillons*. Then the Count learns how blindfolded he really has been, while we, the audience, just like the other players, have the pleasure of watching his dumbfounded amazement when he learns the true identity of those he has been trying to catch. Virtually everywhere in *Le Mariage de Figaro* we find the unifying spirit of child's play.

Even in the play's eroticism childhood, or adolescence – and Beaumarchais does not clearly distinguish between them – seems especially important: the Countess' feelings for Chérubin are aroused precisely because he is a child as well as a man. On a more comical level, we find a mixture, too, in Marceline as her desire for Figaro gives way to feelings that are mostly maternal, and she embraces him in as motherly a fashion as she can. If Figaro sheds his first tears, it is because, though a grown man, he finds himself like a lost child brought home to his mother. How often the characters in the play fall momentarily into a kind of reverie:[19] the Count (III, iv; III, viii) and the Countess (II, xxv) both experience this, the former for reasons of jealousy, the latter for reasons of love. Figaro's monologue is the most striking example, as we will see.

And yet, all this changes at the end, when the numerous pieces of the topsy-turvy plot return once and for all to their right places; the Count is beaten, the game is won, and the marriage really will take place. Meanwhile Chérubin, that timid little boy with his girlish complexion, has, almost miraculously, grown up and become a man. His game is ended too, and instead of running to hide, he now stands and faces the Count, even starting to draw his sword when he feels threatened by him. Seeing this gesture, one is tempted to infer that in the case of Chérubin, the beginning of manhood is symbolically a moment of revolution. One might say something similar about the character of Figaro and about the general spirit of this play, that in many senses ushers in a new age.[20]

Cervantes, writing with poignant irony of the great analogy between the theater and life, has observed that the end of a play, too, has its counterpart in our existences – in death itself (*Don Quixote*, II, chapter 21). Perhaps this explains the tinge of sadness one feels during the final vaudeville of *Figaro*: the falling curtain is bringing to an end the part of life, and the time in history, when one knew the joys of hide-and-seek. There are other reasons, too, as the second part of this chapter will suggest.

b. THE MONOLOGUE

Though the character of Figaro may be seen as deriving from a variety of stock theatrical types, the single one he relates to most obviously is the "impudent valet" in the classic "guardian and ward" plot – which is always the same:[21] a beautiful girl is being held under lock and key by a ridiculous old man, a dragon, bent on matrimony. Enter a handsome young hero, who is smitten with love at the mere sight of her, and who then uses the devices of his ingenious valet to out-fox the old guardian, and get the girl for himself. This kind of play, as ancient as the Greeks and Romans, had crystalized into a sort of perfection in the modern Classical period, in Molière's hilarious farce, *Les Fourberies de Scapin*. When we first meet Figaro, in

Beaumarchais' *Barbier de Séville*, he, too, is behaving rather like the wonderfully brash valet of Molière's comedy. Indeed, Beaumarchais' valet in the early play is so winningly clever he almost steals the first act of *Le Barbier* for himself. From then on, however, the Count comes more and more to dominate the action, and Figaro's function is reduced to the traditional one, that of conjuring away by his clever inventions the numerous impediments that keep the lovers apart. When Rosine's elderly guardian has been outsmarted, the play ends, naturally, in matrimony – an indispensable ingredient of the traditional plot. For in essence this play always celebrates the permanent triumph of love over the external hostilities that threatened it, even as youth wins out over old age. In one version of this ancient play, the impudent valet was actually a god in disguise.

If the valet's dominant trait was, typically, inventiveness, the lovers, by contrast, were at best characterized by near helplessness, and at worst by mental deficiency. The first pair of lovers in Molière's *Scapin* are a good example: their passion has apparently paralyzed their intellectual capacities, and their breeding has rendered them so exquisitely sensitive, so utterly lofty, that they can no longer cope with real life. This is why, in the classic situation, only a servant could help them, for by definition a servant is disengaged from true passion (a great help to his mental powers), and, theoretically at least, he has never done anything else in life but untangle its baser realities. The disparity between the elevation of the lovers and the dubious morality of the valet was translated also in the width of the social gap separating the two. Thus in *Scapin* the lowliness of the valet was counterbalanced by the wealthy bourgeois origins of his masters. In Beaumarchais' schema, such as we find it in *Le Barbier de Séville*, the gap was wider still, since the master was so pointedly a nobleman. And indeed, perhaps this plot, though it can exist in any period, was most at home in an aristocratic environment where the separation of functions, with feeling and nobility on one hand, and practicality and intelligence on the other, can be imagined most easily as reflecting the structure of society. No doubt this was why, having achieved such a lively perfection in the theatre of Molière and Beaumarchais, it became one of the temporary casualties of the French Revolution.

Le Mariage de Figaro is a far more complexly conceived play than *Le Barbier de Séville*; nevertheless it still features part of the classic plot: Figaro is still behaving very much like a traditional clever valet as he devises stratagems to bring off a marriage. Moreover, one of the results of his inventions is that, at the very end, the Count will be reunited in love with the Countess – no doubt a vestige of the classic situation. But of course the fact that the main matrimony Figaro is so busily improvising is his own completely upsets the original balance, leaving the traditional plot dangling in incompletion, in fact lacking the essential half that had always given it, morally, a sense of fulfilment: in the classic situation the audience gladly tolerated any amount of impudence, wiles and deceits on the part of Scapin, not merely because we all secretly envy someone who can so charmingly disregard the restrictive laws of society, but because his dubious activities at the same time are fully counterbalanced in the plot, indeed they actually help preserve the finer and more noble qualities we enjoy in the hero and heroine. Because he is so clever, they can remain pure. So it was absolutely inevitable that, despite all his *fourberies*, Scapin would finally be invited to join in the banquet at the end of Molière's play: everyone knew that it was only thanks to him and his dubious stratagems that virtue had won the day.

What we find in the first four acts of *Le Mariage de Figaro*, on the other hand, is a great deal of impudence and devious devices by the valet, tricks and games of all sorts, but morally there is no counterpoise: instead of a noble hero we are given a corrupt Count, almost a villain. And the *valet de chambre* we are left with in these early acts clearly does not yet fill the bill as hero. Though he is constantly measuring himself against the Count, and sometimes besting him in their verbal fencing matches, he is still, in essence, behaving according to type, as the impudent valet. Moreover, these skirmishes are minor affairs, the main one, over the Count's attempts to seduce Suzanne, still remaining unresolved. Even the revolutionary implications of these contests may not, so far as we can tell, go beyond those we find in the first act of *Le Barbier de Séville*: for all we know, they may eventually fizzle out, submerged in some larger dramatic situation, just as they had done in the earlier play. Meanwhile, as we watch the progress of the action, our interest wanders almost at random from the romance between Figaro and Suzanne, to Chérubin's getting caught, to the Countess' unhappiness over her husband's negligence, to Figaro's lawsuit and the Marceline subplot, and so on. The play doesn't have a dramatic centre, and in a sense the many scholars who have criticized it for not being unified were quite right. But then, one could hardly expect the action to have much focus so long as the play lacked such a key piece as its hero.

Le Mariage de Figaro gets a hero and finds its centre only in act v, during garo's great monologue – a unique moment in eighteenth-century theatre, if only for its extraordinary length. No other monologue in a "regular" comedy even approaches its size. To find monologues so gargantuan in proportions, monologues that contained such astonishingly diverse elements they are virtually whole plays in themselves, as this one is, one has to look back to the *pièces en monologue* of Piron's time, and these, to be sure, since they were the direct result of a rather peculiar sort of theatrical oppression, were devised to serve other purposes and had a very different cast to them.

Figaro's monologue is outlandish in a way all its own. In this connection, it may be useful to report that in actual Parisian performances, the monologue sometimes becomes not merely an incidental mishap, but a general catastrophe that does in once and for all the entire production. The play is already so long – again breaking all eighteenth-century records for comedy in France – that to bring the action to a dead halt so near to (although it actually turns out to be so far from) the end, just so that this valet can indulge himself in streams of consciousness, rambling thoughts about one thing and another, broken by all those pauses, musings and vague ideas that finally decide not to go anywhere after all, leaving us with *trois points de suspension* . . . this is a strategy fit to strain the patience of even the mildest gods of retribution. It may be an act of self-preservation to grope for the exit without waiting for the end.

Obviously the monologue demands the kind of superlatively great actor that Dazincourt might have been, someone whose skill can make an audience oblivious to the midnight hour and charm them into finding him alone to be just as enthralling as a whole stageful of characters, someone worth breaking the momentum of the action for. And since there is, dramatically, so much at stake in Figaro's monologue, one can easily understand why it can lead to total *déroute*, as well as – I presume – to exhilarating success. For in this enormous scene the play either creates, or fails to create, its hero. That is the possibility – or the problem. There don't seem to be any other Classical *comédies* constructed in quite this way, although certain tragedies, notably the famous ones by Corneille, also have monologues, moments of deep reflection like this one, in which the budding hero determines whether he will, or will not, achieve his essence. In these plays by Corneille he always does; and, in retrospect, the right decision was inevitable, because, even though he did indeed have free choice, it was a question of remaining true to a nobility that was a birthright, and hence an inherent part of his character. With Figaro, in contrast, it is a question of turning a servant – someone often associated with clowns in theatrical tradition as we have seen, almost a sort of puppet in the eyes of his master – into a hero, even a man.

Sagacious Diderot once remarked that, in effect, the notion of identity in an individual depends totally on knowledge of the past (or memory): if we had no idea of who we had been, we wouldn't have any idea of the kind of person we are. Perhaps Beaumarchais was thinking along these lines as he composed his monologue, for, as he reinvents Figaro, refashioning him to be a three-dimensional human being, he endows him with a long and diverting past, full of drama and incident, and this serves first of all to deepen our sense of his identity. He also gives him a many-faceted personality, displaying him as someone capable of expressing a wide range of emotions, from impudence and good-humored defiance to deepest melancholy; someone whose picaresque life – in and out of jails, knocking about from pillar to post – takes on new seriousness as we realize Figaro's keen sense of social injustice.

Now, Figaro is recreated here, not merely as some vague reflection of the author's own personality, as so many critics have maintained, but according to strict principle, and one that illustrates the attraction of the contrary to a kind of perfection. It is as if the intensity of this historic moment on the eve of the Revolution had imbued the familiar phenomenon of contrariness with all the potential force it had been accumulating in so many authors during the century. In this play the dynamism of opposition generates, momentarily, something like an explosion.

We have already been aware of the long theatrical tradition that represented noblemen and their valets as opposites – sometimes even to the advantage of the latter – but now Beaumarchais pushes this classic opposition to its extreme limits, so that it becomes a true antithesis. Figaro is triumphantly reconstructed to be an anti-nobleman: quite precisely everything that, according to the traditional stereotype, noblemen never are. Since noblemen by definition have noble lineage, Figaro has no family background at all – his wit replaces his genealogy; since they – as their noble particles imply – always come from a given place and are geographically fixed, Figaro comes from nowhere, constantly changes location, and is all the freer and more effective for not being tied down; they were never gainfully employed, therefore Figaro masters a dozen skills and occupations – clear proof of his superiority; they were pillars of the Church, therefore Figaro devotes himself to attacking religious abuses; they were hostile to freedom of the press and economic reform, therefore Figaro champions both, and becomes everyone's hero; they were soft and decadent, therefore Figaro is strong – vitality and youth personified.

This is no minor matter, for Figaro's energetic negations of nobility amount to a liberation: simply by coming into being as an antithesis he has denied the old order, deliberately cancelled out the *ancien régime*, and, in the freshness of his strength and intelligence, he embodies all that is most joyous in the Enlightenment's idea of life's possibilities. Since this emergent hero in his monologue has succeeded in imposing the values he represents, now in his triumph he threatens to take on all the aristocratic prerogatives of the character he has supplanted. The tables are turning decisively, the *renversement*, the Revolution is on its way to completion. In short, Beaumarchais' *Mariage de Figaro* doesn't *have* a hero, it *acquires* one, and with him the play gains not only the shape and dramatic focus, but the revolutionary significance it lacked before.

Hopefully this interpretation will seem plausible and consistent, for it certainly is part of the message the author is seeking to convey. And yet, staggering thought, it is by no means the whole story. For in addition to all the taunting defiance and impudent self-assertiveness, this monologue also contains one moment of self-doubt so problematic as to bring all the rest, everything that has been asserted, into question. The fact is that just a few lines before the end of the monologue, we see our newly formed hero, his plumes barely dry, on the verge of losing confidence completely. The famous anti-aristocratic principle that, even a moment before, had given such zest to the recounting of his life, now wears so thin it just spins in the air, barely able to sputter, while the tale of his adventures, as it reaches the present, ends in something very much like meaninglessness. Coming down in his narration to the here and now, he discovers that his existence has no more illusions, that everything is worn out. Instead of achieving a new identity through his negative outbursts, he realizes he does not even know who he is.

As the play is performed today, these are the merest hints, unexpected touches of seriousness that serve to heighten the dramatic tension, even as they contribute to the suspense surrounding the final scenes (will Figaro revive his sense of purpose in time for the happy ending?). And of course, even underplayed, they add most tellingly to the psychological richness of the character, supplying – more intensely here than elsewhere – a counter-poise to Figaro's customary brittleness. Originally, Beaumarchais had intended to give far more stress to this mood of depression and self-doubt. In an earlier version of the text, Figaro was to lose confidence to such an extent that he actually despaired of life, sinking in his depression into a symbolic kind of death. It was a question of his own identity and being, as well as of the meaning of life in general. Beaumarchais decided to cut out the following:

Vais-je enfin être un homme? Un homme? Il descend comme il est monté . . . se traînant où il a couru, . . . puis les dégoûts, les maladies, une vieille et débile poupée . . . une froide momie . . . un squelette ah et puis rien (*Il laisse tomber sa tête sur sa poitrine*) rien . . . (*Revenant à lui*) Brr! En quel abîme de rêveries suis-je tombé comme dans un puits sans fond. J'en suis glacé. J'ai froid. (*Il se lève*) Au diable l'animal. Suzon, Suzon [. . .][22]

Even in the original performances, where these lines were excised, Figaro apparently acted out this symbolic death:

[Figaro] *se laisse aller sur le banc, et demeure enséveli dans la plus profonde douleur.*[23]

But what an extraordinary glimpse this moment gives of the precarious-ness of the personality behind all the wisecracks (whether one sees this as Beaumarchais or Figaro), and of the precariousness, too, of this whole enormous dramatic enterprise that has so unpredictably, within sight of the end, jolted to a stop, the text turning out to be as hollow and vulnerable to cessation as the hero (or the author), the stage going silent, perhaps even the page going blank.

Ironically, particularly for the reader of the first version, nothing could be further from what actually transpires in the play than these fearful

surmises. On the contrary, this crisis of anguish and despair is what –
somehow, through some mysterious process of recreation – stores up and
then unleashes the extraordinary explosion of fun and laughter we experience in the final scenes. Not only is the riotous game of blindman's buff all
the more hilarious for being set against this somber point of contrast, but it
is as if Figaro's spiritual death were, paradoxically, just what brought the
end of the play to life. Indeed, in this instance the tension of opposition
against this "point mort" forms a generating force within the structure of
the play itself, the cessation of the action making the rebirth and con-
tinuance possible.

The scandalous circumstances under which the play was originally put
on, the incredible drama of Beaumarchais' efforts to get his comedy publicly
performed in spite of, or because of, the King's interdiction, the mere fact
that the great Revolution was only six years away, all this rightly politicizes
our view of this work, for Beaumarchais was quite aware of how combust-
ible the situation was in which he was so heedlessly striking sparks. Yet at
the same time the exhilarating, giddy timeliness of *Le Mariage de Figaro*
should not blind us to the strength of its ties to the past. This was the last
great pre-Revolutionary, the last great Classical, comedy anyone would
produce in France. And in the beautiful costumes so carefully indicated by
the author, in the flirtations in the Countess' apartment, in the clever
impudence of the valet, in all the things making up the lovely idleness that is
the very stuff of Beaumarchais' play, we are enjoying the aristocratic
pleasures of the social structure the author himself was helping to bring
down.

Deucalion's last eighteenth-century appearance

We have already noticed that in Piron's *Arlequin-Deucalion* the flood functions as an imaginary wiping clean of the social slate so that the play amounts to the imagining of a new start, a revolution, although ultimately a harmless, playful one (cranky, old La Harpe's later reproaches to the contrary, notwithstanding). But after the 1789 Revolution was over and the cynical immorality of the Directoire had begun, one anonymous poet composed a version of the same legend in which – though in a manner veiled

30. Jean-Baptiste Isabey, "Le petit Coblentz – Scène de moeurs sous le Directoire"

and obscure – the author seems to be quasi-seriously interpreting the flood in the manner Piron had foreseen and which La Harpe was to excoriate: the flood as Revolution (and also Terror). Only one printed copy of this work has come to light, in the Bibliothèque de l'Arsénal,[1] and on the title page it is attributed in manuscript to A. de T. Montalembert.[2] However, for many reasons the attribution would seem improbable.

The title is rather curious: DEUCALION ET PYRRHA, OU LE MONDE REPEUPLÉ, poëme très-court, moitié pour rire, moitié pour pleurer, à l'usage de tout le monde, et, entre autres choses, assez véridique [. . .], à Lanternopolis, chez maître Abraham Parchemin, l'an xxv de mes lunettes. (Elsewhere the year is identified as 1798.) The Latin motto on the title page suggests a serious purpose beneath the humor: *Ridendo dicere verum*. The same quirky personality is everywhere present in the work: "l'an xxv de mes lunettes," a spoof of the Revolutionary calendar, of course, also means that he has owned his present pair of glasses for twenty-five years, and at the end of the short *Préface* in prose that heads the poem proper, he explains that he has become so sleepy they are about to fall off his nose, and, since he doesn't want to break them after so long an ownership, he will bid his reader "Good night." In all this one can't help thinking of the whimsical fancies of Maître Alcofribas Nasier. But in addition to Rabelais, when one finds that in the poem proper the most deprecating self-mockery is joined to thoughts of death, Villon also comes to mind. These were unusual models for an author to look to, in this tail-end of the eighteenth century – not, to be sure, that this poet is in any sense their equal, for he totally lacks their verbal virtuosity, the sureness of their artistry; he seems shallow by comparison.

Yet this is a voice worth listening to, from the very beginning of the prose preface, allegedly composed (as the title page says), in "Lanternopolis," the city of lamps (the name comes from Lucian's *True History*).[3] And such an odd and strangely fascinating tale he tells of his encounter with the talking church-lamp, daughter of generations of church-lamps, who in her youth had known some of the greatest lamps of antiquity, and could repeat by heart the story of all the others: she spoke to him of her lamp "cousines" who with their odors had caused certain women to abort because they had once put her cousins out (Pliny), of her "tantes" who foretold wind and rain (Pliny and Virgil), of the festival of lamps at Saïs in Egypt, which she knew in detail (Plutarch), of her sister the inextinguishable lamp in the temple of Ammon, mentioned in Plutarch's "The oracles which have ceased." There were Biblical lamps, too:

Elle me fit rire aux larmes, en me racontant l'aventure des lampes que les vierges folles avaient laissé s'éteindre, n'ayant pas eu la précaution de se munir d'huile, lorsqu'elles allèrent au-devant de l'*époux* et qu'elles s'endormirent en l'attendant; elle loua grandement la sagesse des cinq autres lampes ses nièces, qui refusèrent de leur prêter un peu d'huile (Matthieu, évangile. chap. 25). Elle était si babillarde que je la pris long-temps pour une lampe de parloir de nones; elle me tira de cette erreur en m'apprenant comment elle avait été successivement lampe de moines et de chanoines. Depuis que les oracles avaient cessé, elle n'avait rien à faire, et son plaisir était de causer avec tous les étrangers qui venaient à Lanternopolis. Elle en avait tant vu, elle en savait tant sur le compte de ceux qu'elle avait éclairés de Mère en fille; elle m'en conta tant, que je m'endormis et qu'elle s'éteignit. Depuis cette conversation, je me rappelle toujours quelques-uns de ses contes toutes les fois que j'écris.

(pp. 4–5)[4]

As if to forestall anyone's imagining some hidden meaning behind the oddities of this passage, the author immediately declares that his only philosophy consists in living in a manner he terms "tranquille et douce" while waiting patiently for the end ("Ainsi soit-il"). The rest of the preface is trivia: his poem was composed "dans les premiers jours de frimaire an vii⁰"; he would like to chat further with his "cher lecteur" but sleepiness prevents him from saying more. So he bids us a good night – however we wish to spend it, promising to remain our obedient servant, nevertheless.

Thus the only real substance in the preface is the strange part about the lamps, whose meaning the author never really explains. He does suggest in one instance that lamps symbolize prying eyes, saying that young people, who seem more libertine than they had been in his day, will have to watch their step or they will be found out by their jealous, spiteful elders. Yet this is surely not the whole story. The classical allusions to lamps suggest that they could have innumerable different functions, even as the tales about them are potentially endless. Especially in view of the serious symbolism that occasionally rises to the surface in the ensuing poem, one wonders what other stories the author might have had his friend the church-lamp tell, if he had made her slightly more explicit, and himself less sleepy. What might she have said if she had spoken of events closer to her, before the lights went out, before (as she puts it) "the oracles had ceased"? – of the Revolution, which indeed had destroyed the oracles, when lamps in churches some-times looked down on frightening scenes of persecution and horror. Nor can we quite forget that this "city of lamps," of light, had also been the center of the movement everyone knew as "les lumières," a movement that in retrospect looked very empty and bleak, now that crass materialism and hypocritical morality were all that gave light. Perhaps one might recall that during the Revolution the "lanternes" of Lanternopolis had been given a ghastly new function, as enemies of the state were strung up on them: even at the time, people had ironized over the cruel pun according to which the "lumière" of Enlightenment sent its victims "à la lanterne."[5] On the other hand, perhaps this interpretation goes too far, for even though the key words in his preface had, simply through the march of history, become loaded with potential meanings, there is no way of knowing which ones the author might have intended. His worldly-wise church-lamp remains full of mystery, even as we ourselves remain in the dark. Just as with Villon, we suspect it is all (partly) a joke on us, the readers.

The same is certainly true of the poem that follows, which retells the Ovidian version of the Deucalion myth, with numerous commentaries and digressions by the author. The theme of non-sexual birth is openly given as an illusory compensation for the author's advanced age and sexual impotence: the poem is the author's joke on himself. As he recounts the story, there are surprising hints of pious morality (Deucalion and Pyrrha were *virtuous*; they had not abandoned the veneration of the Gods), his tale being a lesson for the dissolute, debauched youth of the day – a point that proceeds to fizzle out as he confesses that in his youth he had behaved exactly the same way and wishes he were still young enough to do so, thus leaving us wondering where he stands on the issue.

This same phenomenon recurs continually, in fact the poem is built upon contradictions that become so numerous as to induce bafflement: "prier Dieu" (p. 11) is mentioned as a worthy occupation early in the poem, while later the poet comes out for the materialism of Epicurus, "le Père des atomes" (p. 19). Bearing offerings to the holy priest is approved of in one spot, whereas later there is a diatribe against the priesthood and the poet resolves to live far from their disturbing presence. Males in general are condemned for their hardheartedness, and most especially because they are bringers of war; yet Napoleon's soldiers are celebrated for the "glory" of their conquests. Even Zeus' original intent to bring on the flood is expressed as a contradiction: "J'ai résolu de noyer mon image." Given this phenomenon, it is impossible to give a coherent interpretation of a poem which indeed was composed, as he says on the title page, "moitié pour rire, moitié pour pleurer." Finally, the confusion is further compounded by the author's contention that mankind is incorrigible, and hence behaves the same after the flood as it did before it. Thus chronological distinctions also become blurred.

In just one passage the veil of allegory wears thin enough for us to put a name on some of the meanings:

> L'homme, au contraire, apporta sur la terre
> La soif du sang, la discorde et la guerre.
> De ces cailloux il eut la dureté;
> Dans un coeur faux l'insensibilité;
> Il s'est masqué du fard de l'imposture,
> S'est fait tyran même de la nature;
> Il foule aux pieds le sang et l'amitié;
> Il assassine en parlant de pitié;
> Le mot *vertu* pare toujours sa bouche,
> Le crime habite en son ame farouche;
> Traître à l'honneur, à l'amour, à la foi.

Deucalion's last eighteenth-century appearance

Mes bons amis, vous savez mieux que moi,
En vous noyant, si l'on put vous refondre. [. . .][6]

Though the poet is speaking of mankind in general, in the aftermath of the Revolution these remarks would apply most appropriately to the promulgators of the Terror, in fact it had become classic to specify a combination of pretended virtue and infinite cruelty, when attacking the memory of Robespierre. Insofar as this poem can make sense, it centers around this overwhelming event, and indeed the most interesting way to interpret it is to see the poem as reflecting a kind of trauma, a forcible withdrawal from life which translates into sexual impotence, on the most explicit level, and also, on another, into an inability to cope with social or moral issues – another kind of impotence. Naturally such a statement teems with contradictions, short circuits, and jokes that leave everyone in the dark. Perhaps the poet was hinting at this as he speaks of the pleasures of nestling in the warm security of his private poetical creativity, while leaving all violence outside of his concern. His poem was built as a refuge, a modest one to be sure, using rather homely rhymes:

Au coin de feu j'entends siffler les vents,
Tomber la pluie et jurer les passans.
Là de mon luth les cordes mal tendues
Font résonner quelques rimes perdues.[7]

The end of the poem finds him waiting for death ("moment fatal"), and creating still one last joke about his age and impotence:

Je lis, j'écris, je bois, je ris, je chante,
Et si, beau sexe, arrivant à septante,
Je n'aime plus, n'entrez point en courroux;
J'en suis fâché plus pour moi que pour vous.[8]

Piron could have written that *boutade*. But more interesting than the precedents for this style is the way the poem is situated in regard to more contemporary matters. For in effect it embodies nothing less than the dissolution of the Classical way of writing poetry. To be sure, the poem, based on a Classical myth, is full of Classical allusions; they are as frequent as ever. Yet they are losing their traditional function as references to loci whose meaning is known and established. Instead, they are being used to form a rather bizarre private world whose meaning is strictly the property of the author – to the point that much of the time the public is actually excluded. Exactly the same can be said of the poem's relation to the traditions of the Enlightenment: it is full of political and religious allusions; yet the references seldom say anything, or at least anything that is not formally contradicted somewhere else. Ultimately the poem reflects a radical departure from the social consciousness of the age of Voltaire, a withdrawal from involvement with the world, as the poet turns within to the privacy of poetic creation, of self-amusement. Eroticism in the poem fits the same pattern: the attraction of women is crucial in the author's thinking; yet this is a poem about impotence, *un*creation, the only creation being the poem itself.

In short, the poem and its preface can be seen as foreshadowing a turning point in the history of literature, that will eventually lead toward the kind of alienation characterizing those who used to be called "les petits romantiques." We note too that this author's curiously elusive personality, his fantastic world of talking lamps, sputtering candles, and rainy nights sitting by the fire will all reappear in the marvelously accomplished prose-poems and verse of Aloysius Bertrand, Gautier, Nerval, and even of Baudelaire. Of course, poetically this humble versifier was nothing compared to such masters of art (who for the rest seem to have had no knowledge of him). Indeed, if suggestions of the future crop up in this poem, they do so by chance, without the author's awareness, for he belongs to the end of an era, not the beginning.

Taking this, admittedly minor, work as an indication, the eighteenth century would seem to be going out rather ingloriously. No doubt Napoleon is vaguely present in the poem, spoken of as being with his armies in Egypt, a campaign which the author duly salutes. But the poet's main point is that it is time now to bring the troops home. Just as in one of Rousseau's early opera librettos, he hopes that once the men see the beautiful women of France again, the soldiers will be tamed by love into laying down their arms, even as bellicose Mars was brought to submission by the charms of Venus – another legend that young Rousseau turned into opera and Marmontel into a *neuvaine*. The most compelling message of this poem is the yearning for peace, and perhaps it is in this framework that the phenomenon of contradiction becomes most interesting. Hitherto what I have termed the attraction of the contrary has usually functioned creatively: it was a way of imagining desirable and novel differences to cancel out undesirable familiarities. It enabled authors to give birth to ideas that were felt as daring, since they denied traditional values. Of course for some authors the Revolution was supposed to represent the most far-reaching embodiment of this effect, and when it went awry, so did the mechanism that produced it. It is this disillusion that is so clearly reflected in the present, modest poem. Vibrant enthusiasms for any cause are beyond this author; he cannot produce them. By the same token, the fair sex – to whom the poem is dedicated – is out of reach. There remain some vestigial efforts, of course, left-overs of a "philosophical" attitude, left-overs of the former lover; but now all the attraction of the contrary is capable of producing is a self-destructive cancellation, a dry clicking, short circuits, darkness – *faute de mieux*, art. Reading this retiring author as he closes the night shutters against the cold and rain, lights the candles, and takes his station by the fire, one would never dream that untamable, unstoppable, conquest-hungry Napoleon and a thousand thrills – not to mention the whole great tide of literary romantics – waited just around the corner.

Notes

Introduction

1. *La Crise de la conscience européenne*, 3 vols. (Paris: Boivin, 1935); new edn, 1967. Hazard has been chosen as the basis of this analysis partly because of the brilliance and originality of his synthesis which made history when it appeared, but mainly because his discussions point towards the problems of today. Since Hazard's time there have of course been a number of excellent general studies of the French Enlightenment (one thinks particularly of those by Peter Gay, Robert Niklaus, Lester Crocker, and S. Goyard-Fabre). On the other hand, the most recent attempt at a synthesis in English, Ira O. Wade's two-volume *Structure and Form of the French Enlightenment* (Princeton, 1977) is probably the least useful work this great scholar produced. I note also that currently the best general history of the literature of the Enlightenment in French is the work of a large team of specialists. (The same is true of all the "complete works" currently in progress.) For very good reasons, the scholarly team appears to be the wave of the future. On the problems of synthesis, see the concluding remarks of the article by John Lough, "Reflections on Enlightenment and Lumières," *British Journal for Eighteenth-Century Studies*, 8 (1985), 3–15. In the present context I am interested in Hazard's views only insofar as they concern the Enlightenment in France.
2. The classic identification of this problem in France and elsewhere remains George Boas, "In search of the Age of Reason," in Earl R. Wasserman, *Aspects of the Eighteenth Century* (Baltimore: The Johns Hopkins Press, 1965), pp. 1–19.
3. Jean Fabre, "Diderot et les théosophes," in Fabre, *Lumières et Romantisme* (Paris: Klincksieck, 2nd edn, 1980), pp. 67–83.
4. See Elizabeth B. Potulicki, *La Modernité de la pensée de Diderot dans les oeuvres philosophiques* (Paris: Nizet, 1980), and the brilliantly controversial study by Pierre Saint-Amand, *Diderot: Le Labyrinthe de la relation* (Paris: Vrin, 1984).
5. See below, chapter 4.
6. These problems became apparent to me while collaborating on Professor R. N. Schwab's *Inventory of Diderot's Encyclopédie*, 7 vols. (Geneva and Oxford: The Voltaire Foundation, 1971–84).
7. On Voltaire and atheism: Lester G. Crocker, *An Age of Crisis: Man and World in Eighteenth-Century French Thought* (Baltimore: The Johns Hopkins Press, 1959), pp. 78ff.; Jacques Roger, *Les Sciences de la vie dans la pensée française du XVIIIe siècle* (Paris: Armand Colin, 1963), pp. 732–48. On the tensions and dilemmas of Voltaire's rationalism: René Pomeau, *La Religion de Voltaire*, 2nd edn (Paris: Nizet, 1969), *passim*.
8. So far as I am aware, the first scholar to define and exploit the terms "latent

205

content" and "prolepsis" as tools for understanding pre-Revolutionary consciousness in France is Ronald Paulson, *Representations of Revolution (1789–1820)* (New Haven: Yale University Press, 1983), esp. pp. 28–36.

9. Among other French painters whose Roman sojourns partly coincided with his own were his friend Fragonard, Joseph Vernet (who arrived in 1754) and Boucher. See Maurice Andrieux, *Les Français à Rome* (Paris: Fayard, 1968), pp. 161–5.

10. Diderot, *Salons*, ed. Jean Seznec, 4 vols. (Oxford: The Clarendon Press, 1957–67), III, pp. 245–6.

> A large structure occupying the right, left, and background of the sketch. It is a palace, or rather it *was* one. The deterioration has gone so far that one can just barely make out the dwelling of one of those masters of the world, one of those wild beasts who devoured the kings who devour mankind. Under those arcades, which they built, and where a Verres once deposited the plunder of nations, now live herb sellers, horses, cows, oxen, and in the places no longer frequented by men, tigers, serpents, other robbers. Attached to this façade there is a hangar whose roof projects in a downward slope: the building resembles those dirty sheds that lean right up against the superb walls of the Louvre.

11.
> As for these lords of the earth who thought they were building for eternity, who constructed such superb edifices for themselves, and who in their madness thought all this would be handed down to an uninterrupted train of descendants who would inherit their names, their titles and their opulence, all that remains of their productions, their vast expenditures, their grand visions, are the remains that serve as shelter for the poorest, most miserable portion of humanity: more useful now as ruins than they ever were in their first splendor.

12. Roland Mortier, *Poétique des ruines en France: Ses origines, ses variations, de la Renaissance à Victor Hugo* (Geneva: Droz, 1974), p. 93.

13.
> Our gaze focuses on the remains of a triumphal arch, a portal, a pyramid, a temple, a palace, and we are brought to reflect upon ourselves. We anticipate the ravages of time, and our imagination scatters over the earth the very constructions we inhabit.

14. For chronology I have relied on Marie-Catherine Sahut, "Le thème de la galerie," in Sahut, *Le Louvre d'Hubert Robert* (Paris: Editions de la réunion des musées nationaux, 1979), pp. 21ff. See also *French Painting 1774–1830: The Age of Revolution* (Paris, Detroit, N.Y., 1975), pp. 589–93. Further discussions are in Hubert Burda, *Die Ruine in den Bildern Hubert Roberts* (Munich: Wilhelm Fink, 1967), esp. pp. 55ff. ("Das Galeriemotiv"), and, more imaginative and with far better documentation, André Corboz, *Peinture militante et architecture révolutionnaire: A propos du thème du tunnel chez Hubert Robert* (Basel and Stuttgart: Birkhäuser, 1978). On the persistence of certain themes in Robert's work there is the exemplary article by Jean Cailleux: "Introduction to the method of Hubert Robert," *Burlington Magazine*, 109 (Feb. 1967), supplement (at end of vol.), pp. i–iv.

15. Reproduced conveniently at the head of Jean Starobinski, *1789: Les Emblèmes de la raison* (Paris: Flammarion, 1977), p. 5.

16. Quotation in Louis Réau, "Hubert Robert, peintre de Paris," *Bulletin de la Société de l'histoire de l'art français*, 1927, pp. 216–17.

17. To be sure, this is not the whole story. One of Robert's most moving paintings of a ruin in the making shows the royal family celebrating Mass together during their imprisonment in the Tuileries. Such a touching scene surely indicates the moderation of Robert's Revolutionary views. Nevertheless, despite his sympathy for the plight of the royal family, it is clear that his loyalty to the ideals of 1789 remained alive even after his own incarceration during the Terror. See Louis Réau, "Hubert Robert, peintre de Paris," and the illustration given, below, in chapter 11.

18. My thinking on this point is very much in line with Kant's famous definition. See Frank E. Manuel, *The Changing of the Gods* (Hanover and London: University Press of New England, 1983), p. viii.

A number of texts from famous works by Voltaire and d'Alembert formulate this shift, but, as might be expected, the most imaginative description of it comes from Diderot:

> Aujourd'hui que la Philosophie s'avance à grands pas; qu'elle soûmet à son empire tous les objets de son ressort; que son ton est le ton dominant, et qu'on commence à secouer le joug de l'autorité et de l'exemple pour s'en tenir aux lois de la raison, il n'y a presque pas un ouvrage elementaire et dogmatique dont on soit entierement satisfait. On trouve ces productions calquées sur celles des hommes, et non sur la vérité de la nature. On ose proposer ses doutes à Aristote et à Platon; et le tems est arrivé, où des ouvrages qui joüissent encore de la plus haute réputation, en perdront une partie, ou même tomberont entierement dans l'oubli; certains genres de littérature, qui, faute d'une vie réelle et de moeurs subsistantes qui leur servent de modèles, ne peuvent avoir de poétique invariable et sensée, seront négligés; et d'autres qui resteront, et que leur valeur intrinseque soûtiendra, prendront une forme toute nouvelle. Tel est l'effet du progrès de la raison; progrès qui renversera tant de statues, et qui en relevera quelques-unes qui sont renversées. Ce sont celles des hommes rares, qui ont devancé leur siècle. Nous avons eu, s'il est permis de s'exprimer ainsi, des contemporains sous le siècle de Louis XIV. (Article "Encyclopédie" by Diderot in his *Encyclopédie* [. . .], v [1755], p. 636)

19. My interpretation is based on the version, edited by Suard, which appeared in print during Diderot's lifetime, in 1765. For the rest the implied *moralité* of the anecdote agrees with that of the *Code Denis* quoted below, note 23. A variant of the autograph manuscript suggests that Diderot had originally intended a double-edged *moralité* which lends itself less readily to the "revolutionary" extrapolation I am proposing. See the textual notes by Georges May for the piece he entitles "Sur Terence," in Diderot, *Oeuvres complètes* (Paris: Hermann), XIII (1980), pp. 451–2.

20. The procession started off quite late, towards noon; this was not because some people wanted to keep others waiting, the way despots did at their courtly entertainments. [Indeed] large numbers of people had gone early to the Barrier of the Throne; nor did they wait for the procession to get underway before starting the festivities. These began from the moment the people assembled and could enjoy the pleasure of being together. Nonetheless, the moment came when the procession had to begin [. . .]

On the site of the Bastille a sort of inauguration of the statue of liberty was enacted. We will omit the details and concentrate on the essentials of this popular festivity, the first of its kind, and one which, hopefully, may be repeated. The time that passed during the first halts of the procession gave the citizens who were ill-disposed [towards it] or credulous [concerning the harm it might do] a chance to reassure themselves somewhat and to move closer to the triumphal parade as it went by, favored, moreover, by the utter serenity of a spring day.

There was no display of finery; gold did not dazzle the eye and insult the modesty of means, or the honorable indigence, of the citizens. An arrogant soldiery, decked out in braid, did not, as it passed, send forth scornful glances, right and left, on the poorly clad onlookers. Here the actors and the observers often merged together, each forming the procession in turn. There was little order, but much concord; no sacrifices were made for the sake of vain and pompous behavior; no one tried to upstage the rest; boredom, which is born of uniformity, did not settle in among the different groups; at each step the scene changed; the chain of the procession broke many times, but the gaps were filled by the onlookers; everyone wanted to take part in the festival of liberty [. . .]

The procession completed half the circuit across Paris and could be seen making its way through an immense, unbroken crowd without encountering any obstacles. Gendarmes on foot and on horseback had no need to clear a path for it; two hedges of bayonets were not required to maintain a passage; the Minister of the Interior was in no way involved with the maintenance of public order; the department charged the municipality with the task, and the day prior to the ceremony there was a decree concerning the bearing of arms and the presence of vehicles, but it was the people themselves who took the responsibility for the implementation, and their conduct was a lesson for magistrates and an example for the National Guard. Four hundred thousand citizens were away from their homes for an entire half-day, and all converged on the same spot, without the least accident occurring. Words of peace were sufficient to contain this whole crowd: from the Bastille to the Champs-de-Mars, all stood aside, and lined up at the sight of a spike of wheat, which was their signal, in place of bayonets.

(From an anonymous article in *Révolutions de Paris*, quoted in Mona Ozouf, *La Fête révolutionnaire, 1789–1799* [Paris: Gallimard, 1976], p. 82, p. 84)

21. Précédés de leurs chaînes suspendues à des trophées et portées par de jeunes citoyennes vêtues de blanc, les quarante soldats Suisses du régiment de Chateau-Vieux [i.e., les anciens galériens] marchaient, confondus parmi plusieurs volontaires et des soldats de ligne. On ne distinguait nos quarante martyrs qu'à leurs épaulettes jaunes. [. . .]

(Quoted in Ozouf, *La Fête révolutionnaire, 1789–1799*, p. 83)

22. There is a curious parallel between the results of the negative inversion in this Revolutionary parade and the imaginary inversion created by Rabelais for his utopia, the Abbaye de Thélème. In very different ways, both attempted to represent a society of total freedom, in which no one rules and no one is governed. Furthermore, Thélème was characterized by the systematic rejection of accepted norms. As Rosalie L. Colie stated in *Paradoxia Epidemica: The Renaissance Tradition of Paradox* (Princeton, N.J., 1966), p. 50: "Technically topsy-turvy, the new Abbey [. . .] was reformed on lines precisely opposite to

those of existing institutions." Professor Colie then went on to demonstrate (pp. 50–1) how every aspect of Thélème was determined, negatively, by some objectionable feature of ordinary convents. Professor Colie saw the famous rule "Fais ce que vouldras" as being connected, positively, to Epicurean traditions. Of course it can also be interpreted, negatively, as an inversion of the conventual rule of obedience.

In connection with Rabelais, it turns out that Mikhail Bahktin's celebrated evocation of carnival in *Rabelais and his World* (1965) is only partially relevant to my approach in this study. Bahktin treated inversions as a specifically popular, low-class phenomenon, emanating from the underside of society. In the following chapters I see inversions as originating in the rejection of various social values, a phenomenon that may go in a variety of social directions. Thus, the inversion that produced Thélème had nothing to do with the world of carnival; other inversions, to be considered later on, actually reject vulgar modes of conduct to produce, in fantasy, upper-class situations; even the inversions of *Manon Lescaut*, which I interpret as producing an underworld, are only related to Bahktin's carnival underworld in effect, not in origin.

On the other hand, Bahktin's sense of the inherent subversiveness of the carnivalesque is indeed pertinent to other parts of this study, especially the discussions of the *théâtres de la foire* in chapter 3.

23. See *Le Code Denis* by Diderot:

> Dans ses états, à tout ce qui respire
> Un souverain prétend donner la loi;
>> C'est le contraire en mon empire:
>> Le sujet règne sur le roi.
>
> Diviser pour régner, la maxime est ancienne.
> Elle fut d'un tyran, ce n'est donc pas la mienne.
> Vous unir est mon voeu; j'aime la liberté;
>> Et si j'ai quelque volonté,
>> C'est que chacun fasse la sienne.
>>   [...]
> Qui veut d'un roi, qui cherche maître?
> Personne ici ne dira t'il: c'est moi?
> (Quoted in Grimm, *Correspondance littéraire*, VIII, pp. 442–3)

24. As Natalie Zemon Davis reminds us, writing of the sixteenth-century festivities that inverted the normal order of society: "Misrule always implies the Rule it parodies" (*Society and Culture in Early Modern France* [Stanford University Press, 1975], p. 100).

25. A useful summary of this topic and a copious bibliography will be found in the editor's introduction to Barbara A. Babcock, ed., *The Reversible World: Symbolic Inversion in Art and Society* (Ithaca and London: Cornell University Press, 1978), pp. 13–36; see also Julia Kristeva, *La Révolution du langage poétique* (Paris, 1974), pp. 101–50, and the fine article by Terry Castle, "The English masquerade, 1710–1790," *Eighteenth-Century Studies*, 18 (1983–4), 156–76. As will be seen at the conclusion of chapter 1, the phrase I will use to designate literary manifestations of this phenomenon is "the attraction of the contrary."

26. See Jean-Pierre Vidal, "L'infratexte, mode du génotexte ou fantasme de lecture," *La Nouvelle barre du jour*, 103 (May 1981), 21–54, esp. p. 46; also Philippe

Lacoue-Labarthe, "Diderot, le paradoxe et la mimésis," *Poétique*, II (1980), 267–81.

1 *Manon*'s hidden motives

1. "Ah! Be gone, lovely vision!"
2. The French text tells how powerless he is to resist the spell of her charms and declares that she is now the mistress of his heart.
3. *Pensées et fragments inédites* (Bordeaux, 1901), II, p. 61, quoted in F. Deloffre and R. Picard, eds., *Manon Lescaut* (Paris: Garnier, 1965), pp. clxiii–clxiv. The page numbers in the present chapter refer to the Pléiade edition, ed. Etiemble (Paris, 1960), in the anthology *Romanciers du XVIII siècle*, I, pp. 1219–371. Currently the *Oeuvres de Prévost* (Grenoble: Presses universitaires de Grenoble, 1977–), ed. Pierre Berthiaume, Jean Sgard, *et al.*, lacks the volume containing the commentary on *Manon*. The most recent edition is that of R. Mauzi (Paris: Imprimerie nationale, 1980). I am not aware of any other study which takes so radical a view of this novel as I do. However, amply corrective bibliographies will be found in the editions referred to above.
4. The French text says that to him she seemed so charming (the word implies something like a magic spell) that suddenly he found himself inflamed, even transported (by passion).
5. Sedaine caught the spirit of this perfectly in the Air No. 3 of his *opéra comique Le Diable à quatre* (music by Philidor, 1756):

> Je n'aimois pas le tabac beaucoup,
> J'en prenois peu, souvent point du tout;
> Mais mon mari me défend cela.
> Depuis ce moment là
> Je le trouve piquant,
> Quand
> J'en peux prendre à l'écart,
> Car
> Un plaisir vaut son pris,
> Pris
> En dépit des maris.

6. G. Genette, whose interpretation of *Manon* is in general totally different from my own, actually skirts this idea in *Palimpsestes* (Paris: du Seuil, 1982), p. 334: "le bon Tiberge, l'ami moralisateur mais généreux, toujours prêt à sermonner Des Grieux et à lui fournir les cinq cents pistoles nécessaires à l'entretien de sa mauvaise conduite."
7. On this point see Raymond Picard, "L'univers de *Manon Lescaut*," *Mercure de France*, 341 (1961), 608: "Selon l'image qu'Alcibiade avait trouvée pour Socrate, on serait tenté de comparer l'abbé Prévost à une torpille: délicieusement paralysé, le lecteur n'éprouve plus le besoin de juger; son monde moral se dissout et il s'abandonne à un agréable vertige."
8. The psychological basis for this kind of motivation has been analyzed by Freud in his 1925 essay entitled "Negation." See the *Collected Papers*, James Strachey, ed., 5 vols. (London: Hogarth Press, 1924–55), v, pp. 181–5.

2 Three literary approaches to the art of love

1. Jacques Proust, *L'Objet et le texte* (Geneva, 1980), pp. 108–10.
2. See the edition of *Le Sopha*, with an introduction by Albert-Marie Schmidt (Paris: Union générale d'édition, 1966), and the concluding "Réflexions" by Claude Labrosse in *Les Paradoxes du romancier: Les "Egarements" de Crébillon* (Presses universitaires de Grenoble, 1975), p. 185 (this volume also contains a useful bibliography). The most recent edition (Paris: Desjonquères, 1984) has a preface by Jean Sgard. The page numbers in my text refer to vol. v of the fourteen-volume 1777 edition of the *Oeuvres complètes*, allegedly printed in London.
3. A moment after I had found my spot, I beheld the entrance of the divine creature to whom I was to belong. She was the daughter of the omrah in whose home I was. In her face could be seen every imaginable charm and pleasing quality – youth, grace, beauty, and that mysterious something which must be present to bring out all these charms, which is more compelling and striking than any of them, but which somehow cannot be defined. The sight brought on such emotions in my soul, a thousand delicious sensations, feelings I didn't even know my soul was capable of.
4. See Werner Krauss, "Supplément II zum Dictionnaire philosophique (Die Metempsychose oder die Lehre der Transmigration der Seele in Frankreich während des 18 Jahrhunderts. Der Obszönitätenstreit in der Frühaufklärung)," *Lendemains*, 1:3 (Jan. 1976), 4–13; Henry L. Marchand, *The French Pornographers, Including a History of French Erotic Literature* (New York: Book Awards, 1965), p. 164.
5. I carefully selected the spot from which I could best observe Zeinis' charms, and I began to contemplate them with all the ardor of the most tenderhearted lover, with the admiration which even the most indifferent of men would be unable to refuse her. Great heavens! What a wealth of beauty greeted my eyes!
6. See Jean Ehrard, "Un romancier célèbre et méconnu: Crébillon, fils" in Ehrard, *Le XVIIIe siècle* (Paris: Arthaud, 1974), I, pp. 120–6.
7. *Histoire de Dom B. . . Portier des Chartreux, écrite par lui-même*. I use the text of the 1771 edition, reprinted with an excellent historical study by Pascal Pia (Paris: l'Or du temps, 1969). One of the most amusing sets of illustrations for this work has been reprinted in Antoine Borel, *Cent vignettes érotiques gravées par Elluin pour illustrer sept romans libertins du dix-huitième siècle* (Paris: Editions Borderie, 1978), pp. 51–75. My analysis in this chapter was conceived independently; however, it coincides on a number of points with Barry Ivker, *An Anthology and Analysis of 17th and 18th Century French Libertine Fiction* (Ann Arbor, Michigan, 1977). See also the brilliant article by Robert J. Ellrich, "Modes of discourse and the language of sexual reference in eighteenth-century French fiction," in R. P. Maccubbin, ed., *Unauthorized Sexual Behavior during the Enlightenment*, a special issue of *Eighteenth-Century Life* (9:3, May 1985), pp. 217–28.
8. Figurez-vous une femme d'une grandeur médiocre, poil brun, peau blanche, le visage laid en général, enluminé d'un rouge champenois, mais des yeux alertes, amoureux, & tétonnière autant que femme au monde. Ce fut d'abord la première bonne qualité que je lui remarquai: ç'a toujours été mon faible que ces deux boules-là. C'est aussi quelque chose de si joli,

quand vous tenez cela dans la main, quand vous . . . ah! chacun le sien, qu'on me passe celui-ci.

Sitôt que la Dame aperçut, elle jeta sur nous un regard de bonté, & sans changer de situation. Elle était couchée sur un Canapé, une jambe dessus & l'autre sur le parquet: elle n'avait qu'un simple jupon blanc assez court pour laisser voir un genou qui n'était pas assez couvert pour faire penser qu'il serait bien difficile de voir le reste: un petit corset de la même couleur & un pet-en-l'air de tafetas couleur de rose, bichonnée, d'un petit air négligé, & la main passée sous son jupon, jugez à quelle intention. Mon imagination fut au fait dans le moment & mon coeur la suivit de près [. . .]

9. Je l'examinais avec douleur, elle était dans le même habillement que la veille, elle n'avait rien sur la gorge, mais elle y avait suppléé d'une façon qui en rendait l'impression plus piquante, elle y avait mis son éventail qui suivait les mouvements du sein & se soulevait assez pour m'en laisser entrevoir la blancheur & la régularité. Pressé par mes désirs, je me sentais des envies de la réveiller, qui étaient sur le champ détruites par la crainte de l'indisposer & de faire évanouir, par mon impatience, un reste d'espoir dont son réveil me flattait encore. Je cédai cependant à la démangeaison de porter [. . .] une main tremblante sur un teton, tandis que je jettais les yeux sur le visage, prêt à finir au moindre signe qu'elle ferait: elle n'en fit pas; je continuai: à peine ma main osait-elle s'apesantir, elle ne faisait pour ainsi dire, que friser la superficie, comme une hirondelle qui rase l'eau, en y trempant de temps en temps ses ailes. Bientôt j'ôtai l'éventail, & bientôt je pris un baiser: rien ne la réveillait. Devenu plus hardi [. . .] je commençais à lever le jupon le plus doucement qu'il m'était possible: elle fit un mouvement, je la crus réveillée, je me retirai avec précipitation, & le coeur frappé d'un sentiment de frayeur tel que peut l'avoir un homme qui voit un précipice dont le hazard vient de le sauver. [. . .] Je reconnus avec plaisir que le mouvement qu'elle avait fait ne venait pas de son réveil, & je crus n'avoir à remercier que la fortune de l'heureuse situation dans laquelle elle venait de la mettre; ses jambes s'étaient décroisées, elle avait le genou droit élevé; & le jupon tombé par ce moyen sur son ventre, exposait à mes yeux & ses cuisses & ses jambes & sa motte & son Con. (pp. 137–40)

10. See the parallel passage from Chasles, *Les Illustres Françoises*, wittily suggested (among other delightful examples) in Erich Kohler, *"Belle Négligence,"* in Manfred Höfler, *et al.*, *Festschrift Kurt Baldinger* . . . (Tübingen: M. Niemeyer, 1979), II, pp. 407–28, esp. p. 409.

11. Je m'enyvrai de ce charmant spectacle: un bas proprement tiré, noué sur le genou avec une jarretière feu & argent, une jambe faite au tour, un petit pied mignon, une mule la plus jolie du monde, des cuisses, ah! des cuisses, dont la blancheur éblouissait, rondes, douces, fermes: un Con d'un rouge de carmin, entouré d'une haye de petits poils plus noirs que le jayet, & d'où sortait une odeur plus douce que celle des parfums les plus délicieux [. . .] (p. 140)

12. [. . .] elles n'épargnèrent rien pour y réussir: non seulement elles employèrent tous leurs charmes naturels, mais elles y joignirent encore ce que l'art le plus consommé peut suggérer à une Vieille Coquette Fouteuse, pour rappeler un jeune coeur entrainé par la vivacité de ses passions, tantôt se rangeant en cercle autour de moi, elles offraient à ma vue les tableaux les

plus lascifs, l'une mollement appuyée sur un lit, laissait voir négligemment la moitié de sa gorge, une petite jambe fait au tour, & des Cuisses plus blanches que l'albâtre, me promettaient le plus beau Con du monde; l'autre les genoux élevés, & dans l'attitude d'une femme qui se présente au combat, étendait les bras, soupirait, & marquait par la langueur & son agitation, l'ardeur qui la consumait; d'autres dans des postures toutes différentes, la gorge découverte, les jupes levées, se chatouillaient diversement le Con, en s'agitant avec fureur, & en exprimant par leurs soupirs & leurs exclamations le plaisir qu'elles ressentaient, marque assurée de celui qu'elles feraient ressentir; tantôt toutes se mettaient nues & me présentaient la volupté dans tous les points de vue qu'elles croyaient pouvoir me flatter, l'une le visage appuyé sur un Canapé, me montrait le revers de la Médaille, & passant sa main par dessous son ventre, elle écartait les Cuisses & se branlait, de manière qu'à chaque mouvement que faisait son doigt, je pouvais voir l'intérieur de cette partie, qui m'avait autrefois causé de si vives émotions; une autre sur un lit de Satin noir, couchée sur le dos, & les jambes pendantes & écartées, me présentait à l'endroit la même image que la précédente ne m'offrait qu'à l'envers. (pp. 257–9)

13. See the suggestion of R. Mortier, "Libertinage littéraire et tensions sociales dans la littérature de l'Ancien régime, de la 'picara' à la 'Fille de joie,' " *Revue de littérature comparée*, 56 (1972), 35–45, esp. note 3. Also Mortier, "Les voies obliques de la propagande 'philosophique,' " in R. J. Howells, A. Jason, *et al.*, eds., *Voltaire and his World: Studies Presented to W. H. Barber* (Oxford: Voltaire Foundation, 1985), pp. 382–3. On the essential conservatism of libertine fiction, along with a useful bibliography, see Jacques Rustin, "Définition et explication du roman libertin des Lumières," *Travaux de linguistique et de littérature* (Strasbourg, 1978), 16:2, 27–34.

14. This neglected work is now fortunately available in a scholarly edition, with notes, historical introduction and analysis of the text by James Maurice Kaplan in *SVEC*, 113 (1973). Text, pp. 73–143. See also Michael Cardy, *The Literary Doctrines of Jean-François Marmontel*, *SVEC*, 210 (1982), 63–74.

15. Kaplan edn., pp. 29–32.

16. See the article "Galerie" by Watelet, in Diderot's *Encyclopédie*, VII, pp. 443B–444A. Marmontel's poem represents a rather special sort of *ekphrasis*. On the classical background of this concept, see Emilie L. Bergmann, *Art Inscribed: Essays on Ekphrasis in Spanish Golden Age Poetry* (Cambridge, Mass.: Harvard University Press, 1979), pp. 1–14.

17. Beneath a clump of trees whose amorous leaves / Bent downward to mingle with the shade / Venus lay sleeping on a bed of fresh green grass. / The delicate coloring and the fresh bloom of youth, / The dazzling glow of health, / The graceful curves of an elegant bust / And the enticing shape of a beautiful bosom, / And those buttocks so white and so beautiful, / And a thousand other charms whose natural image it is not decent / To set before your eyes, / All these were displayed in this gorgeous body.

In her sleep a flattering dream / Charmed her, flitted upon her lips, / With a playful finger calling out to desire / And with a flutter of its wings awakening her to pleasure. / Venus sighed, and with a deeper hue of vermilion / Her complexion was suffused. / [. . .] She was nearing that moment when the soul is ready to take flight and leave its earthly bonds behind it / And is waiting only for a mouth into which its passion / Would gladly breathe forth its flame with a sigh.

A fiery young faun, lively and nimble, / The cock of the walk to the nymphs thereabouts, / Most eloquent in word and deed, / And, like a page, impudent where love's concerned, / Finds this heavenly beauty lying in this remote spot. / He stops, he admires, he approaches stealthily, / And drinks it all in with a shameless gaze. / "Ah! 'T'is Venus," says he. "I recognize her sash. / Love, you it is who have led me here. / Queen of our hearts, wonder of nature, / Venus, I am burning with desire and yet I fear to take you."

Then, as he lifts up the sash with one hand, / "There lies the throne of pleasure! / What a wealth of treasures! Ah! Let us dare to take our chance." / A novice might have been willing to content himself / With a kiss. The faun, less timid, / Goes straight to the heart of the matter, and the Queen of Gnidus, / Upon awakening, declares him her conqueror. (27–72)

18. A. P. de Mirimonde, "La Prétendue *Antiope* d'Antonio Allegri, dit 'Le Corrège' . . .," *Gazette des Beaux-Arts*, 95 (1980), 107–19.

19. Presumably, the wrong title ascribed to the painting by Correggio led to the misnaming of the Watteau. Actually the engraving that was made of Watteau's painting had been correctly identified by Heinecken as "Vénus avec un satyre"; however, the authors of the B. N. *Cabinet des estampes* catalogue rejected the identification in favor of "Antiope." See vol. IV, p. 140.

20. For the rest, Poussin is also in the background of this scene, possibly for his "Venus spied on by shepherds," reproduced in A. Blunt, *Poussin*, 2 vols. (New York: Bollingen, 1967), II, p. 35, and more probably for the "Satyre épiant une nymphe" (whose attribution is now questioned) reproduced in *Musée de Louvre: La Donation Kaufmann et Schlageter au Département des peintures* (Paris: Réunion des Musées nationaux, 1984), p. 86, and which closely resembles the version attributed to Fragonard.

On Venus' famous sash, see the article "Ceste" by Diderot in volume II of the *Encyclopédie*.

21. The arrow burns with desire to be shot in a piercing blow. / He holds it back, he adjusts it, he slips it in so gently . . .

22. The cool of the evening calmed the heat of the day. / The azure sky and its humid mists / Were heralding the return of dark night, / When the chariot whose reins are held by Venus / Parted the liquid plains of the serene air. / A thousand zephyrs flitted around her; / In the tresses of the Mother of Love / They frolicked and with fluttering wings / They spread them out on to two alabaster globes / Whose summits, pink as roses, are the golden throne of the sweet kiss. / This lovely body, which the great Praxiteles / Sculpted so well in his statue of Venus, / And which Paris saw unveiled / When he gave the apple to the greatest beauty, / This body was pressing beneath the softest satin / The swarthy muscles of the libertine faun. / And smiling, his divine conquest lay back, leaned her head towards him, / And urged him on with her movements and her eyes. / The cynical movement of both her arms / Stirred in him that responsive ardor / Which electrifies the dart of pleasure [. . .]

The faun was about to commit a great sin, / Had Venus' tender concern / Not presented to his blows the attitude / Of her lovely body leaning against the reins. / [...] Very demurely she suddenly receives / The fiery shaft he looses upon her, / And the sweet violence of the combat / Makes her drop the reins from her hand.

23. On this aspect of Boucher's art, see the perceptive remarks of Norman Bryson, *Word and Image: French Painting of the Ancien Régime* (Cambridge University Press), p. 95.

24. The "source" of this scene may have been Thomson's *Seasons*, lines 1027ff. (themselves an imitation of Spencer). See Virginia Foote Ireys, "Pastoral heroines in eighteenth-century English poetry," unpub. doctoral diss. (Berkeley, 1985), p. 103.

25. ... In my family, I want / Each one to love at liberty according to his choice. / Faun or mortal, god of the heavens or god of the woods, / It is all the same to me. A lover whose plea is heard, / If he is fortunate, has no doubt deserved it.

(429–32)

26. Kaplan edn, p. 41, wittily proposes the poem may celebrate Marmontel's ascension to a chair in the Académie Française.

27. It has long been clear that Boucher's Virgins often bear a physical resemblance to his Venus figures. Diderot came very close to mentioning this in his discussion of a nativity scene in the Salon of 1759: "Mais la Vierge est si belle, si amoureuse et si touchante. [...] Ce petit St. Jean couché sur le dos, qui tient un épi. Il me prend toujours envie d'imaginer une flèche à la place de cet épi." (Ed. Seznec and Adhémar [Oxford, 1957], pp. 68–9)

28. The art of destroying is no doubt a great art; / And so we speak of it with a shudder; / But I would rather create one single man, / Than to have conquered (let Folard take no offense) / All the heroes of Greece and Rome; / Let us gather myrtle boughs, and leave the laurel wreaths to others. / Let us sing of Love, which consoles the world / For all the ills brought upon it by warriors [...]
This opening was probably inspired by the opening of the *Amores* (I, i) by Ovid, who makes a similar disclaimer, while parodying Virgil.

29. The classic study of this topic is that of Adrienne Hytier, "Les philosophes et le problème de la guerre," *SVEC*, 127 (1974), 243–58. The origin of this theme is in Lucretius, *De rerum natura*, I, vv. 29–40. See Diderot, *Salons*, ed. Seznec, III (1983), p. 111.

30. The son of Alcmene and the God of War, / Ardent Pluto, impetuous Neptune, / Even Jupiter himself, when taking his pleasure, / Here is no more than a man with good luck / Gods and mortals, in the arena of love, / Are all equal, for all are fortunate. (1841–6)

31. Ronald Paulson, *Representations of Revolution* (New Haven: Yale University Press, 1983), pp. 21–2; pp. 28–35.

3 Inversions and subversions in the *théâtre de la foire*, or, the end of Piron's *Arlequin-Deucalion*

1. Diderot, *Le Neveu de Rameau*, ed. Jean Fabre (Geneva, 1950), p. 58.
2. The standard biographies remain those of P. Chaponnière: *Alexis Piron, sa vie et ses oeuvres* (Geneva, 1910) and *La Vie joyeuse de Piron* (Paris, 1935).
3. Fabre edn., p. 202, note 201.

4. Charles Collé, *Journal historique inédit pour les années 1761 et 1762*, ed. Ad. van Bever (Paris, 1911), p. 16, note 11.

5. Pierre Dufay, ed., *Oeuvres complètes illustrées de Alexis Piron*, 10 vols. (Paris, 1928–31), I, "Introduction," p. xxxi. (The source of this anecdote is Fréron's *Année littéraire*, 1773, II, pp. 101–2.) Epigrams against Voltaire are in vol. VIII, pp. 426–39 in this edition of Piron's *Oeuvres*.

6.   Un gros serpent mordit Aurelle,
                           Que croyez-vous qu'il arriva?
                           Qu'Aurelle en mourut . . . Bagatelle!
                           Ce fut le serpent qui creva.   (*Oeuvres complètes*, IX, p. 202)

7. Voltaire, *Oeuvres complètes*, ed. Moland.

8. Piron, *Oeuvres complètes*, I, p. clvii. Cf. Chasles, *Les Illustres Françoises*, the opening.

9. The most convenient bibliography of this topic is in the anthology by Jacques Truchet, *Théâtre du XVIIIᵉ siècle*, 2 vols. (Paris: Bibliothèque de la Pléiade, 1972), I, pp. lxiii–lxiv. A most readable and discerning study of the theatres of the *foire* is to be found in Frederick Brown, *Theatre and Revolution: The Culture of the French Stage* (New York: Viking, 1980), chapter 2, "The speechless tradition," esp. pp. 41–64, with numerous illustrations. The relationship between the fairs, the Comédie Italienne and the artistic life of the early part of the century (esp. Watteau) is explored in Thomas E. Crow, *Painters and Public Life in Eighteenth-Century Paris* (New Haven and London: Yale University Press, 1985), pp. 45ff.

10. Text in vol. III of the ten-volume *Théâtre de la foire ou l'Opéra-comique* (Paris, 1721–34). Résumés of this and the other works discussed in the present chapter will be found in J. A. J. Desboulmiers, *Histoire du théâtre de l'Opéra-comique*, 2 vols. (Paris, 1770; reprint AMS, 1978). A study of *Le monde renversé* has lately appeared: Pauline Baggio, "The ambiguity of social characterization in Lesage's *Théâtre de la foire*," *French Review*, 55 (1982), 622–3; however, points of agreement between it and the present chapter are entirely coincidental. Unfortunately, Robert M. Isherwood's *Farce and Fantasy: Popular Entertainment in Eighteenth-Century Paris* (New York and Oxford: Oxford University Press, 1986) appeared too late to be used in the present essays. However, many topics discussed in this chapter, and certain of those in chapter 10, may profitably be supplemented by the abundant bibliographies and background material his study affords. His discussion of *Le monde renversé* is on p. 79.

11. Helen F. Grant, *Images et gravures du monde à l'envers* . . . in Jean Lafond and Auguston Redondo, eds., *L'Image du monde renversé et ses représentations littéraires et para-littéraires* . . . (Paris: J. Vrin, 1979), pp. 17–33. David Kunzle, *World Upside Down: The Iconography of a European Broadsheet Type*, in Barbara A. Babcock, ed., *The Reversible World*, pp. 39–94. The most recent historical survey, sumptuously illustrated and with a useful bibliography, is Frédérick Tristan and Maurice Lever, *Le Monde à l'envers* (Paris: Hachette/Massin, 1980).

12. Babcock, *The Reversible World, passim*; Davis, *Society and Culture* . . ., pp. 100ff.

13. Kunzle, *World Upside Down*, p. 66. On the central importance of the topsy-turvy world in Bruegel's "Netherlandish Proverbs," see Alan Dundes and Claudia A. Stibbe, "The art of mixing metaphors: A folkloristic interpretation of the Netherlandish Proverbs by Pieter Bruegel, the Elder," (Helsinki: *Academia scientiarum Fennica*, 1981), pp. 28–9, no. 27; p. 67.

14. The traits of this never-never land are the classic ones of the traditional "pays de Cocagne." See François Delpech, "Aspects des pays de Cocagne – Programme

pour une recherche," in Lafond and Redondo, *L'Image du monde renversé*, pp. 35–48.

15.   . . . ce qui se joue et se re-présente sous des masques divers ce n'est pas un archétype; c'est une image variable dont une société a particulièrement besoin lorsque se manifeste en elle une crise profonde et lorsqu'elle ne peut penser cette crise que comme l'urgence d'un passage nécessaire, d'une transformation et d'une genèse. L'image d'un état, qui peut être aussi un lieu ou un temps, où la nature, avant de s'inverser en culture, produit spontanément la contrepartie anticipée des biens culturels qu'apportera la civilisation; état négatif et gratifiant qui est en même temps le gage et la préfiguration inversée du prochain avènement de ces biens.

(Delpech, "Aspects," p. 46)

16.   Complete references to all these *opéras comiques* will be found in C. D. Brenner, *A Bibliographical List of Plays in the French Language, 1700–1789* (Berkeley, 1947; reprint AMS, n.d.).

17.   The essentials of this plot had been used by La Fontaine (*Fables*, book XII, no. 1, for which Oudry made one of his most delightful illustrations). There are also a host of classical, Renaissance, and seventeenth-century sources possibly in its background, including *Circe* by Gelli. See the Grands Ecrivains de la France edition of La Fontaine, *Oeuvres* (ed. Ad. Reginer), III, pp. 178–80; pp. 389–92.

18.   This plot had topical overtones, see René Le Forestier, *Maçonnerie féminine et loges académiques* (Milan: Arché, 1979).

19.   *Le Diable à quatre, ou la double métamorphose*, the music consisting of both vaudevilles and ariettes (by Philidor), was first produced at the Foire St Laurent in August 1756 and then, in February 1757, at the Foire St Germain, in which year it was also published. The plot derives from Patu's translation, published in 1756, of *The Devil to Pay or the Wives Metamorphosed*, by Charles Coffey (1731), which itself was an adaptation of Thomas Jevons' "The Devil of a wife, or, a comical Transformation" (1686). The English play, at least as it comes through in Patu's translation, centers on the main character as an eccentric and makes most of the comedy out of her eccentricity. For Sedaine, on the other hand, the play becomes more of a vehicle for a social statement, the main character representing, to a greater degree than she does in the English version, a lady who abuses her social privilege. This work has not received the attention from scholars that it deserves. (For Patu's translation, see his *Choix de petites pièces du Théâtre anglois, Traduites des Originaux*, 2 vols. (London and Paris, 1756), pp. 147–218. (cf. Isherwood, *Farce and Fantasy*, p. 116).)

20.   C. D. Brenner, *Plays in the French Language*, lists the titles of some three hundred plays that begin with the world "Arlequin." On the historical background of this character, see Allardyce Nicoll, *The World of Harlequin: A Critical Study of the "Commedia dell'Arte"* (Cambridge University Press, 1963).

21.   Arlequin German baron, English tailor, cabaret owner and actor, merchant's boy, pastry maker, astrologer, paralyzed barber, hermit, Freemason, sorcerer without knowing it, [. . .] invisible, silent, dead, swallowed by the whale, at the witches' sabbath, in the Elysian Fields, officer, colonel, deserter, recruiter, prisoner, assassin, happy gardener, *honnête homme* and good father of the family, gentleman in spite of himself, prime minister, king of the Chinamen, king of the ogres [. . .], eunuch, virgin in spite of

himself. [Finally, a single play:] Arlequin child, statue, parrot, chimney sweep, astrologer, Catalonian grenadier, skeleton, and Arabian notary.

22. Opera parodies remain to be studied as they deserve. There are a few useful indications in Robert Fajon, *L'Opéra à Paris, du Roi Soleil à Louis le bien-aimé* (Paris–Geneva: Slatkine, 1984), pp. 375–84.

23. G. Lanson, "La Parodie dramatique au XVIIe siècle," *Homme et livres* (Paris, 1895), pp. 261ff.

24. On this and all other matters relating to parody, the standard source remains Valleria Belt Grannis, *Dramatic Parody in Eighteenth-Century France* (New York, 1931).

25. I myself have located some twenty-three parodies of, or sequels to, *Le Mariage de Figaro*. Professor Donald Spinelli has apparently located eighty-five!

26. Reproduced in N. Decugis and S. Reymond, *Le Décor de théâtre en France* (Paris, 1953), p. 23.

27. Bidault de Montigny, *Sémiramis* (Amsterdam, 1749). See Grannis, *Dramatic Parody*, pp. 329ff.

28. *Intérêt*: One ought to make it a bit briefer when one is expiring, Madame.

29. Text in Pierre Dufay, ed., *Oeuvres complètes de Alexis Piron*, 10 vols. (Paris, 1928–31), VII, pp. 70–119. The parody dates from 1725.

30. The basic source of information about these inventions remains P. Parfaict, *Mémoires pour servir à l'histoire des spectacles de la foire*, 2 vols. (Paris, 1743). See also the fine article by Robert W. Isherwood, "Entertainments in the Parisian Fairs," *Journal of Modern History*, 53 (1981), 24–48.

31. On the "pièces à écriteaux," see Ardelle Striker, "A curious form of protest theatre: The *pièce à écriteaux*," *Theatre Survey*, 14 (1973), 55–71.

32. Maurice Albert, *Les Théâtres de la foire (1660–1789)* (Paris, 1900; reprint New York: Burt Franklin, 1970). Roselyn Laplace, "Des Théâtres d'enfants au XVIIIe siècle," *Revue d'histoire du théâtre*, 32 (1980), 21–31. F. W. Lindsay, *Dramatic Parody by Marionettes in Eighteenth Century Paris* (New York, 1946).

33. Piron, *Oeuvres complètes*, VI, pp. 106–25.

34. Strictly speaking, the genial parody to which I refer, *Le Roué vertueux, poëme en prose, En quatre Chants, Propre à faire, en cas de besoin, un Drame à jouer deux fois par semaine. Orné de Gravures* (Lausanne, 1770) does not belong with the others, since its witty author, Coqueley de Chaussepierre, far from being connected with the persecuted *forains*, was legal counsel for the Comédie Française. However, for the purposes of argument, I am assuming he might have been partly inspired by the inventions of the *forains*. On Coqueley's career, see Anne-Marie Chouillet, *et al.*, *Supplément IV* to Jean Sgard, *et al.*, *Dictionnaire des journalistes (1600–1789)* (Grenoble: Centre de Recherches, 1985), pp. 45–52.

35. Text in Truchet, ed., *Théâtre du XVIIIe siècle*, I, pp. 491–516. See Pierre Gobin, "L'Arlequin-Deucalion de Piron: pertinance de l'impertinance," *SVEC*, 192 (1980), 1468–86.

36. The music for this storm was, according to one source, composed by Rameau. There is a rather piquant parallel between Piron's situation in real life – half-blind from birth, he was truly down and out, with no resources – and the play, for this monologue was Piron's barrel which would float him to money, food, and safety. (Actually, there is some indication that Piron himself was aware of the parallel. See *Oeuvres d'Alexis Piron*, 3 vols. [Paris, 1758], III, "Préface," pp. 227–9.)

37. By heaven, nothing less would do! This flood was just the wash we needed for scrubbing the earth and cleaning up the human race. Things do come clean when the sea has gone over them. And so my rascal friends are all drowned; if that doesn't cure them, I don't know what will . . .

38. [Melpomene] glides majestically about the stage, taking no notice of Deucalion, her face assuming fervent looks, while she utters *ah!, alas!, ye gods!, What's that I hear?*, and grandly gesticulates with her arms.

Obviously the comedy here derives from skimming off the paroxysms of tragedy (so to speak), detaching them from any plot substance that might make them meaningful. One may compare this to the anecdote related by the author of *La Littérature renversée, ou L'art de faire des pièces de théâtre sans paroles, Ouvrage utile aux Poètes Dramatiques de nos jours* . . . (Berne and Paris, 1775) (attributed to Jean-Baptiste Nougaret), p. 57: "Vous dites donc que le Geste n'est rien sans la parole? Vous n'avez sans doute jamais su ce vieux conte qu'on fait d'un Prédicateur: se trouvant court en chaire, il s'avisa de prononcer des *si*, des *mais*, des *car*, et d'autres monosyllabes pareils, qu'il accompagnait de mouvemens des pieds et des mains, comme s'il avait débité à son Auditoire les meilleures choses du monde. Après avoir ainsi fixé l'attention pendant plus d'une heure, il se retira, laissant tous les Auditeurs très-émerveillés de son éloquence."

39. My brothers and I, just a moment ago, were set up on the surface of the earth like chess pieces on a chessboard. Kings, queens, knights, bishops, and pawns of every stripe were in their places. The gods were playing with us; we came and went, willy-nilly, according to their whim. A bad sport among them – I don't know which one – was checkmated and lost the game. It was his own fault, of course, but he insisted on blaming the pieces, and, like losers at cards who tear them apart in a frenzy, in his rage he gathered up everything in a jumble and threw it all, head over heels, into this box here (pointing to himself), pawns, knights, queens, kings, and bishops. I am the little box that contains so many fine things. Let the rabble and the potentates issue forth from me! Take the key and open the lid again for that wretched multitude. Let us marry . . .

40. [God] created humans in His own likeness, / Only to degrade them more; / He gave us sinful / Hearts, only for the right to punish us; / He made us love pleasure, the better to torment / Us with frightful woes . . .
Blind in His blessings, blind in His wrath, / No sooner had He brought us into the world, / Than He caused us all to perish. / He commanded the sea to submerge the earth.

For the complete French text, ed. Ira O. Wade, see *PMLA*, 47 (1932), 1066–112.

41. When I had unwound the entire ball of string attached to the kite on which I had placed you – while taking to the water myself – I realized I had lost sight of you up in the air, so I decided the only thing to do was quickly to tie the remainder of the string around my neck and go on swimming, while you went on flying in the strong wind there was. You served as my sail, while the gale that was blowing you from astern had me slicing through the waves to beat the devil. After traveling in this fashion all morning long, each of us supporting the other – you the motor force and I the point of application – I heard, below my chest, noon striking in the bells of the steeple on whose weather cock I found myself perched. I had gone without

eating and was a bit weary. Well, lo and behold, was that not a barrel I spied rolling in the waves nearby? The sight of such an interesting object made me strain every muscle to reach it. But the current was taking it off to the left, while the blasted wind kept flying you off to the right, and my instinct was pulling me towards the barrel. I saw in a flash that you were about to disgrace yourself by the murder of your dear husband: you were strangling me. To save you from parricide, I took out some scissors from my pocket and, snip, I restored my comfort, while recommending you to the gods . . .

This kind of fantastic improvisation was one of the stock possibilities of the Arlequin character. David Garrick's *Harlequin's Invasion* (1759) likewise soars aloft into amiable idiocy:

Clown Simon (to Harlequin): Pray, friend Whirligig, what profession are you of?

Harlequin: A fly catcher – I was formerly altogether among the stars – I plied as ticket-porter in the milky way, and carried the Howdyes from one planet to another; but finding that too fatiguing I got into the service of the Rainbow, and now I wear his livery. Don't you think I fib now, Friend Simon? (i, iii).

Quoted in George Winchester Stone, Jr, "David Garrick and the eighteenth-century stage: Notes toward a new biography," *In Search of Restoration and Eighteenth-Century Theatrical Biography* (Los Angeles: William Andrews Clark Memorial Library, 1976), p. 20. See, too, Arlequin's description of his ascent to the moon in Anon., *Arlequin empereur dans la lune*, the 1684 version in *Le Théâtre italien de Gherardi* . . ., i (Amsterdam: Braakman, 1701), pp. 143–4.

42. [. . .] que penseront-ils [sc. nos neveux] d'une génération de la même espèce qui se sera coupée, et dont le demi-quart d'une aura dit au reste: "Retirez-vous, insectes, vous ne nous ressemblez point; vous et nous, sommes deux"? Cela les fera rire. Ils béniront le brouillement des cartes. Ma suprématie aura soin de les égaliser: les cadets seront frères de leur aînés; et, l'inégalité détruite, je réponds du bon ordre et de la félicité universelle. [. . .] (pp. 509–10)

La Harpe, who had lived through the Revolution and the Terror, and spent the rest of his life writing against the Revolutionaries and their works, went right off his rocker as he read this passage:

Ecoutez, écoutez *Arlequin-Deucalion*, en 1722, faisant des hommes à coups de pierre, comme on a fait depuis des *citoyens* à coups de canon. [. . .] "*L'inégalité détruite je réponds du bon ordre et de la félicité universelle.*" *Je réponds!* N'est-il pas sûr de son fait comme un *philosophe*? Des malveillans [sic!] diront qu'il eût été peut-être un peu embarrassé s'il avait vu, comme nous, cette *félicité universelle* après *l'inégalité détruite.* Point du tout, il eût fait comme ses successeurs; il aurait toujours *répondu* de tout *pour la génération suivante*; il aurait, comme eux, *répondu* de tout, de semaine en semaine, de mois en mois, d'année en année [. . .] jusqu'à la fin du monde.

(*Lycée ou Cours de littérature ancienne et moderne*, 18 vols. [Paris, 1823–4], xiv, pp. 140–1)

43. See the commentary of J. Truchet on this passage, edn (as note 35), p. 1388.

44. My lordship, do show a little modesty. Your sole talent will consist in knowing how to kill.

45. I see you there with your deceitful, lusting glances, your sensuous nose ready for dainty morsels, your hands ready to claw money.

46. The fifth son wears a large skullcap on his head, a jaunty wig [*à la cavalière en bourse*], a long friar's beard, a little collar, a coat of colored cloth; a sword at one side; there is a packet of quills in his hand; one white stocking, one black stocking, breeches red on one side, black on the other, etc., etc., etc.

Piron writes of this costume as if the one white stocking, one black stocking, one red breech, one black breech should be instantly recognizable. Actually, I have discovered only one stock character whose costume is "pied" laterally in an even vaguely similar way: the fool, or "folly," as this figure appears, for example, in Watteau's famous depiction of the Italian Comedians, in the National Gallery in Washington, D.C.

47. What strange species have we here? It looks as if there are only four females, and that male there has no better half. Ah, I've got it. He doesn't have to worry about multiplying; the race will be all too numerous without marriage coming into it. Like Prometheus, my Grandfather, they will perpetuate their kind without ever having wives in childbed at home. I knew people like that by the thousands before the flood. Some threatened us on behalf of the offended gods; others prattled about the innocence of mankind's beginnings, and all of them heaped up crimes and swelled the storm. They were swallowed up just like the others.

48. *Oeuvres complètes*, VII, p. 276.

49. The character of Scaramouche always wore such a "petit collet," and Hallays-Dabot relates (*Histoire de la censure théâtrale en France* [Paris, 1862], p. 44) that in Piron's parody of *Télégone* by Pellegrin, the actor playing the part mimicked a priest.

50. I have discussed these images in greater detail in *Essays on Pierre Bayle and Religious Controversy* (The Hague: Nijhoff, 1965).

51. In the Preface and Dedicatory Epistle of the tragedy Piron had clearly suggested his hostility toward rank and privilege, and he openly confessed his intent, while composing the tragedy, to topple this tyrant from the pedestal on which tradition had placed him. Piron was deliberately putting forth this contest between rampant, menacing Power on the one hand, and pure tranquil Heroism on the other, as an edifying lesson for Nations, and especially, he declared, for Kings (he prudently excepted Louis XV, of course). His emotional praises of the virtues of Sparta, which he contrasts with the corruptions of Alexander's tyranny, ring with a fervor that actually anticipates J.-J. Rousseau. Apparently his contemporaries paid no attention to the kind of serious concerns Piron displayed in the following passage:

Quel objet plus brillant et plus intéressant pouvois-je présenter sur la Scène héroïque et sous les yeux des Nations? Quel plus grand exemple et quoi de plus instructif, pour tant de Rois qui n'auront pas le bonheur de ressembler à celui dont il plaît au Ciel de nous gratifier dans sa bienveillance!

A ce farouche orgueil enflé du poison de la flaterie et du torrent des prospérités, j'ai cru ne pouvoir aussi rien opposer de plus frapant, que la pleine franchise d'un Homme sage et d'une Femme forte; du Philosophe Callisthène et de sa Soeur Léonide; les deux seuls Personnages qui se trouvoient libres et indépendans au milieu d'une Cour de Flateurs et d'Esclaves; tous deux, Citoyens de la seule Ville de Grèce qui avoit refusé de concourir au Projet du Destructeur de l'Asie; tous deux, l'honneur de leur Patrie, de Sparte, de la ville unique et fameuse, où l'un et l'autre Sexe suçaient avec le lait et conservoient jusqu'au tombeau, les sentimens de la vertu la plus âpre; le mépris des richesses, des rangs, de la Tyrannie, de la mort, et même des tourmens. Seul Peuple que, sans l'amour de la gloire et la peur de la honte, on auroit pû dire au-dessus de toutes les misères humaines.

La Puissance éffrénée et menaçante d'un côté, le pur et tranquille Héroïsme de l'autre: quel plus beau contraste! Hé quoi, si comme il est vrai, les grandes images nous enflent le coeur, et nous recréent l'ame en l'elevant; l'intime satisfaction de voir le Vice armé du plein pouvoir, gémir de son impuissance devant la Vérité nuë et paisible; cette satisfaction, dis-je, ne devroit-elle pas être pour le moins aussi délicieuse au Spectateur, qu'une espèce d'horreur ou qu'une vaine commisération excitée par les traits odieux de la Vengeance, ou par les honteuses foiblesses de l'Amour? [. . .] (*Oeuvres d'Alexis Piron*, 3 vols. [Paris, 1758], 1, pp. 247–9)

Some information on the performance of this tragedy may be found in Gunnar von Proschwitz, ed., *Alexis Piron Epistolier* (Göteborg, Sweden, 1982).

52. See above note 42.

4 Crispin's inventions

1. The play is in one act (twenty-six scenes). On its sources, historical background and social import, see the edition by Jacques Truchet in the Pléiade anthology, *Théâtre du XVIIIe siècle* (Paris, 1972), 1, pp. 1346–9, and the separate edition by T. E. Lawrenson (University of London Press, 1961). A full-length study has been written about the original, seventeenth-century Crispin: A. Ross Curtis, *Crispin Ier, la vie et l'oeuvre de Raymond Poisson . . .* (Toronto and Buffalo: University of Toronto Press, 1972). The only other eighteenth-century play featuring Crispin that modern readers may know is Palissot's *Les Philosophes* (1760), in which Crispin played a mock Jean-Jacques Rousseau.

2. René Bray, *Formation de la doctrine classique* (Paris, 1963), pp. 191–214; H. T. Barnwell, *The Tragic Drama of Corneille and Racine: An Old Parallel Revisited* (Oxford: The Clarendon Press, 1982), pp. 71–92; Jacques Truchet, *La Tragédie classique en France* (Paris, 1975), pp. 34–8; Gérard Genette, *Figures II* (Paris, 1976), pp. 71–99. *Vraisemblance* is one of the central issues of the recent study by Marian Hobson, *The Object of Art: The Theory of Illusion in Eighteenth-Century France* (Cambridge University Press, 1982), *passim*.

3. Pierre-Jean Baptiste Nougaret defined this perfectly: "La vraisemblance théâtrale, est un rapport si parfait des choses les unes aux autres, qu'il paraît impossible qu'elles se soient passées différemment qu'on les représente" (*De l'Art du théâtre, où il est parlé des différens genres de spectacles et De la Musique Adaptée au Théâtre*, 2 vols. [Paris, 1769], 1, pp. 278–9). Nougaret goes on to distinguish "vraisemblance théâtrale" from "vraisemblance dans le monde" and eventually concludes (p. 282) that "Le vrai ne compose presque jamais une action théâtrale."

Piron had used a similar distinction between the art of the theatre and life (his terms were "vraisemblable idéale" and "vraisemblable simple") to defend his tragedy *Gustave Wasa* against the criticism that its plot was unlikely. (See the *Préface* to *Gustave Wasa* in *Oeuvres d'Alexis Piron*, 3 vols. [Paris, 1758], I, p. 67.)

Le Comte de Lauragais pushed the idea of consistency to its ultimate limit in his discussion of perfection in tragedy. Curiously, his enemy Diderot might have agreed with him, on this point at least: "Le comble de la perfection dans une Tragédie, seroit que chacune des scenes qui la composent eût tellement le caractère de l'action totale, qu'une de ces scenes quelconque pût faire retrouver l'ensemble de l'action dans laquelle elle est comprise, à un Poète dramatique: comme l'attitude, la force, ou la mollesse d'un seul doigt de la main, auroit peut-être fait retrouver à Bouchardon la proportion de la figure entière, dont il n'avoit qu'une si petite partie" (*Dissertation sur les Oedipes, de Sophocle, de Corneille, de Voltaire, de la Mote, et sur Jocaste* [n.p., n.d.], p. 35). This undated text can have been published no earlier than 1770.

On the problem of *vraisemblance* considered more generally, see *Communications*, 11 (1968), edited by Todorov.

4. Text in Pierre Dufay, ed., *Oeuvres complètes . . . de Alexis Piron*, 10 vols. (Paris, 1928–31), II, pp. 219–311. On its success, see edn, I, pp. lxxiii–lxxv.
5. As early as the start of Voltaire's career as a tragedian, one unkindly anonymous critic had listed almost one hundred lines from *Oedipe* along with the lines from classical plays, usually by Corneille or Racine, which Voltaire was "imitating." See *Lettre à M. de Voltaire sur la nouvelle Tragédie d'Oedipe* (Paris, 1719), pp. 24–35. See also the opening line of the third act of *Mérope*:

O douleur! ô regrets! ô vieillesse pesante!

6. See Truchet, *Théâtre du XVIIIᵉ siècle*, above, note 1, p. 1347.

5 On Voltaire's *Mérope*

1. I use the text in Jacques Truchet, ed., *Théâtre du XVIIIᵉ siècle*, 1, pp. 813–69, which also provides information on the play's sources (pp. 1433–7) and a bibliography of important studies on Voltaire's tragedies (p. 1374, note 1). The old Louis Moland edition of Voltaire, *Oeuvres complètes*, 52 vols. (Paris, 1877–85), IV, pp. 171–97, furnishes other useful documentation.
2. On the relation of this plot to its classical source the most extensive discussion is in G. E. Lessing, *Hamburg Dramaturgy* (nos. 36–53), trans. Helen Zimmern (New York: Dover, 1962) pp. 102–60.
3. A copious bibliography of this topic will be found in Warren Roberts, *Morality and Social Class in Eighteenth-Century French Literature and Painting* (Toronto, 1974), pp. 165–80.
4. My heart never ceased to see the son I longed for;
   Dismay at his peril gave life to my tender feelings for him:
   My righteous concern grew stronger as time passed.
5. See the Moland edition, IV, pp. 171–97. The text of Maffei's *La Merope* is most easily accessible in G. Gasparini, ed., *La tragedia classica* (Turin, 1963), pp. 659–78.
6. See the Moland edition, IV, p. 180.
7. The empire belongs to my son . . .
8. Turning again towards me his dying eye [literally, eyelid]
9. Cresphont pressed me in his arms as he expired.

10. *Appel à toutes les nations*, in *Oeuvres complètes*, ed. Moland, xxiv, p. 20.

11. Barbarian! He is my son.

12. Much of this *récit* was inspired by that of Maffei (see his v, vi, 277–345), which is even more flamboyantly gory than Voltaire's. However, because the language of the Italian play is generally quite earthy and concrete, while the language of the *Mérope française* is generally very elevated and abstract, Voltaire's *récit* is even more dramatically set off by contrast.

13. Come let us go mount the throne, where I will place my mother.

14. See the Moland edition, iv, pp. 177–8. Voltaire had made the same claim for an early version of *Oedipe*. (See José-Michel Moreaux, *L'Oedipe de Voltaire: Introduction à une psycholecture* [Paris: Lettres Modernes, 1973], pp. 23ff.) This is part of a significant pattern of thought, as will be discussed below.

15. See lines 245 and 786, as opposed to Mérope's description in i, i.

16. See lines 17, 81, 256, 621, 1245.

17. Edn, p. 660, note 18.

18. I guided him, for sixteen years, from one safe refuge to another.

19. *Lettre écrite en 1719 qui contient la critique d'Oedipe de Sophocle, de celui de Corneille, et celui de l'auteur*, in *Oeuvres complètes*, edn, p. 33; *Commentaires sur Corneille*, "Remarques sur Oedipe, Tragédie représentée en 1659," in *Oeuvres complètes*, edn, pp. 167–70. In his own *Oedipe* Voltaire reduced the number to four.

20. This fact was brought to my attention by an article by J. D. Hubert, "L'Anti-Oedipe de Corneille," *XVIIᵉ Siècle*, 37 (1985), 53.

21. On this psychology, see above, chapter 1, note 7.

6 On the background of Rousseau's First Discourse

1. Text reprinted in Rousseau, *Oeuvres complètes*, ed. Bernard Gragnebin, *et al.*, 4 vols. (Paris: Pléiade, 1959–69) (henceforth O.C.), ii, pp. 810–41.

2. O.C., i, p. 294.

3. I am also omitting the subplot of the opera, encountered in the opening scenes, because it bears only indirectly on the subject at hand.

4. Unfortunate Chieftain / Your exploits have come to nought, your reign is finished; / This day puts your power in other hands. / Your peoples, enslaved under a hateful yoke / Will lose forever the dearest gifts of the Gods, / Their liberty, their innocence.

5. Proud children of the Sun, you triumph over us / Your arts give you the Victory over our Virtues.

6. Let us triumph, let us triumph on land and on wave, / Let us give Laws to the Universe. / Through our daring we have, this day, discovered a new world. / It is made to bear our shackles.

7. Lose liberty; but bear without complaint / A yoke still more precious.

8. What purpose will our valor and arms serve? / Now it is our turn to be enchained.

9. Let us spread throughout the universe / Our treasure and our bounty. / Let us unite through our Alliance / Two worlds separated by the abyss of the seas.

10. The "argument" of Rousseau's opera runs exactly parallel to Molinier's argument in favor of absolute monarchy, as he formulated it against Voltaire: "la liberté avec toute son étendüe est une belle idée dont les hommes ne peuvent

joüir raisonnablement. Les fers sont durs à porter, mais heureusement, c'est une expression poëtique qu'on emploïe ordinairement en amour, comme en politique, et dont on ne doit pas être plus effraïé dans ce pays, que les amans le sont à Cithère." (Jean-Baptiste Molinier, *Lettres servant de réponse aux Lettres Philosophiques de M. de V-*, n.p., n.d.). This text probably dates from 1735.

11. See Georges May, *Rousseau par lui-même* (Paris: Seuil, 1961), pp. 13–20; Mario Einaudi, *The Early Rousseau* (Ithaca, New York: Cornell University Press, 1967), pp. 61–73; Lester G. Crocker, *Jean-Jacques Rousseau*, 2 vols. (1958; New York: Macmillan, 1973), I, pp. 126–36; Jean Guéhenno, *Jean-Jacques Rousseau*, 2 vols. (London and New York: Grasset and Gallimard, 1966), I, pp. 108–11; Pierre-Maurice Masson, *La Religion de Jean-Jacques Rousseau*, 3 vols. (1916; reprint, Paris: Hachette, 1970), I, pp. 67–82. Jean Starobinski, "Tout le mal vient de l'inégalité," *Europe*, 39 (1961), 142–3.

12. Text in O.C., II, pp. 1136–44.

13. I learned to respect an illustrious Nobility / Which can add luster even to virtue.

14. Part of the autobiographical poem *Le Verger de Mme. de Warens* (O.C., II, pp. 1123–9) tells a similar story.

15. Text in O.C., II, pp. 1130–3.

16. Happy city, ornament of France, / Treasure of the Universe, source of abundance, / Lyon, charming sojourn of the children of Plutus, / Within your tranquil walls, all the arts are made welcome . . .

17. See Masson, *La Religion*, I, pp. 67–82.

18. O.C., I, p. 122.

19. *Fragment d'une Epître à M.B.[ordes]* in O.C., II, pp. 1144–5. Cf. Masson, *La Religion*, I, pp. 135–6.

20. O.C., I, pp. 200–1.

21. Cf. Rousseau's discussion of his military enthusiasm for France in the *Confessions*, O.C., I, pp. 182–4, and Frédéric's eulogy in *Les Prisonniers de la guerre* (O.C., II, p. 870).

22. The most extraordinary manifestation of this anti-Genevan principle is the famous incident when Rousseau contrived to put into the hands of the *avocat* Coccelli a *mémoire* that revealed the defects in the fortifications of his native city (O.C., I, p. 218). Rousseau does not doubt that the *mémoire* found its way to the court of Geneva's "greatest enemy," the King of Sardinia, but Rousseau remained totally blind to the psychological implications of his gesture. And in fact Rousseau seemed determined never to face the element of hostility implicit in his conduct during this period. He constantly, almost compulsively, disguises such emotions, passing his actions off as mere boyish foolishness and vanity (as in the above instance), or as his natural desire not to give offense to some kindly benefactor (such as the curé de Confignon), or by pretending that cruel destiny alone accounted for his behavior. This is too complex a topic to be dealt with adequately in the present chapter, but it seems clear that behind Rousseau's anger at Geneva we find his anger at his proud Genevan father, and if he cannot look squarely at his feelings in this regard, it is certainly because he could not face the degree to which his father's neglect had wounded him. Oddly, Dr Pierre-Paul Clément's psychoanalytic study, *Jean-Jacques Rousseau: de l'éros coupable à l'éros glorieux*, though most illuminating about other aspects of Rousseau's relationship with his father, misses this point entirely.

23. See Perry Miller, *The New England Mind* (1939; reprint, Cambridge, Mass.: Harvard University Press, 1954), pp. 25–33, 280–91. (The Puritan version of this doctrine is in all essentials identical with that of the Swiss Calvinists.) Masson's study does not bring out this connection (*La Religion*, I, pp. 165–8).

24. Kenneth Clark, *The Romantic Rebellion* (New York: Harper and Row, 1973), pp. 151.

25. Can it be that you are governed by Rhetoricians and speech makers? Was it merely to enable Architects, Painters, Sculptors and miserable Comedians to live in opulence that Greece and Asia were watered with your blood? Are the spoils of Carthage to be squandered by a flute-player? Romans, do not delay: tear down these amphitheaters, smash these marble statues, burn these paintings, drive out these slaves who have become your masters and whose deadly arts are leading to your corruption.

26. When Cineas took our Senate for an assembly of kings, he was not dazzled by vain pomp or affected elegance . . . But what, then, did he see that had such majesty? O citizens! He beheld a spectacle that all your arts and wealth can never procure, the fairest spectacle that ever was beneath the heavens: the Assembly of two hundred virtuous men.

27. The Sciences, Letters and the Arts, less despotic but perhaps more powerful, spread garlands of flowers over the chains that men bear, stifling the sentiment of that original liberty which seemed their natural birthright, making them love their enslavement.

28. Jean Starobinski, "La Prosopopée de Fabricius," *Revue des sciences humaines*, 41 (1976), 83–96.

29. Text in O.C., I, pp. 1135–6.

30. Cf. Masson, *La Religion*, I, pp. 165–6; Jacques Roger, "Introduction" to Rousseau, *Discours sur les sciences et les arts* . . . (Paris: Garnier-Flammarion, 1971), pp. 15–16.

31. One of the most successful attempts at fitting the arguments of the First Discourse into a system of thought is that of Victor Gourevitch, "Rousseau on the Arts and Sciences," *The Journal of Philosophy*, 19 (1972), 737–54.

32. As Rousseau himself asserts: "Cependent cet ouvrage, plein de chaleur et de force, manque absolument de logique et d'ordre . . ." (O.C., I, p. 352).

33. Powers of the Earth, well may you cherish talents and protect those who cultivate them. Subject peoples, well may you cultivate them, too: Happy slaves, you owe to them that fine and delicate taste you are so proud of; that gentleness of character and urbanity of manner which makes commerce among you so engaging and easy; in a word, the outward appearance of all the virtues without the substance of any.

34. This interpretation seems to be borne out by the description of his social life at Chambéry, in the *Confessions*: "me voilà tout à coup jeté parmi le beau monde, admis, recherché dans les meilleures maisons; par tout en accueil gracieux, caressant, un air de fête: d'aimables Demoiselles bien parées m'attendent, me reçoivent avec empressement; je ne vois que des objets charmans, je ne sens que la rose et la fleur d'orange. . . . Voilà presque l'unique fois qu'en n'écoutant que mes penchans, je n'ai pas vu tromper mon attente. L'accueil aisé, l'esprit *liant*, l'humeur *facile* des habitans du pays me rendit le commerce du monde aimable, et le goût que j'y pris alors m'a bien prouvé que si je n'aime pas à vivre parmi les hommes, c'est moins ma faute que la leur" (O.C., I, p. 188, emphasis mine; see

also p. 362). Cf. Basil Muntéano, *Solitude et contradictions de Jean-Jacques Rousseau* (Paris: Nizet, 1975), p. 41.

35. When one reflects on current mores, one cannot help but take pleasure in recalling the simplicity of the earliest times. The image is of a beautiful shore embellished only by the hands of nature, toward which one turns one's eyes again and again, and from which one draws away with a feeling of regret. When men were innocent and virtuous, they liked together in the same huts, and they liked having the gods as witnesses of their actions; but soon becoming mean-hearted, they grew tired of those inconvenient spectators and removed them into magnificent temples. Eventually they drove them out of these and installed themselves within, or at all events the temples of the gods could no longer be distinguished from the houses of the citizens. It was then that the depravity was complete; and never were the vices carried further than when one saw them, as it were, supported on marble columns at the entrance of the palaces of the great, and graven on Corinthian capitals.

36. See my monograph, *Essays on Pierre Bayle and Religious Controversy*, pp. 3–25.

37. These contradictions continue to preoccupy scholars. A useful résumé of traditional approaches to the problem will be found in Basil Muntéano, *Solitude et contradictions de Jean-Jacques Rousseau*, pp. 9ff.; further bibliography will be found in David Bensoussan, *L'Unité chez Jean-Jacques Rousseau: Une quête de l'impossible* (Paris: Nizet, 1977), to which one may add R. Mortier, "Solitude et sociabilité chez. J.-J. Rousseau," *Le Flambeau*, 46 (1963), 400–26, R. Trousson, "Jean-Jacques et les biographes," in R. Mortier and H. Hasquin, eds., *Etudes sur le XVIIIᵉ siècle* (Université de Bruxelles, 1974), pp. 57–8, and Felicity Baker, "La Route contraire," in Simon Harvey *et al.*, eds., *Reappraisals of Rousseau: Studies in Honour of R. A. Leigh* (Manchester University Press, 1980), pp. 132–62.

38. O.C., I, pp. 363, 1015.

39. O.C., I, pp. 391–2.

40. Cf. Pierre-Paul Clément, *Jean-Jacques Rousseau*, p. 52.

41. Cf. the negative evaluation of the Discourse by Robert Wokler, "The *Discours sur les sciences et les arts* and its offspring: Rousseau in reply to his critics," in Harvey *et al.*, eds., *Reappraisals of Rousseau*, esp. pp. 250–1.

7. On the figure of music in the frontispiece of Diderot's *Encyclopédie*

1. The frontispiece, since it was designed by Charles-Nicolas Cochin, *fils*, in 1764, did not accompany volume I when it appeared in 1751, but was published in 1772, the year of the distribution of the final volumes of plates. For the historical background of the frontispiece, and a more detailed discussion of certain of its figures, see Georges May, "Observations on an allegory: the frontispiece of the *Encyclopédie*," *Diderot Studies*, 16 (1973), 159–74.

2. Cf. Ovid, *Metamorphoses*, book II, lines 13–14:
   ... Facies non omnibus una
   Non diversa tamen, qualem decet esse sororum.

3. See May, "Observations on an allegory," pp. 170–2. For the identification of the musical accoutrements in the following discussion I am indebted to Professor J. Le Corbeiller of the New School for Social Research, New York.

4. Jacques Chouillet, *La Formation des idées esthétiques de Diderot, 1745–1763* (Paris, 1973), p. 241.
5. *Encyclopédie*, I (1751), p. xii.
6. Although by now somewhat out of date the standard study of this topic remains A. R. Oliver, *The Encyclopedists as Critics of Music* (New York, 1947). See also Jean Mongrédien, "La Théorie de l'imitation en musique au début du romantisme," *Romantisme*, 8 (1974), 86–91.
7. D'Alembert, *De la Liberté de la musique*, reprinted in Denise Launay, ed., *La Querelle des bouffons*, 3 vols. (Geneva: Minkoff, 1973), III, p. 2275. This text is assumed to date from 1754. According to Daniel Heartz, the *boutade* attributed to Fontanelle was quoted by Algarotti in the *Saggio* of 1751. It was also repeated by Beccaria (see Jansen, *Jean-Jacques Rousseau als Musiker*, Berlin, 1884 [reprinted 1971], p. 29). See Hobson, *The Object of Art . . .* (ref. above, chapter 4, note 2), p. 53.
8. *Encyclopédie*, I (1751), p. xii.
9. Professor Heartz informs me that this musical effect occurs in Campra, *Idoménée*, act II, scene I. Later the same device was used by Rameau; see *Les Indes galantes*, in the *Première Entrée* of the *Prologue* ("Choeur des matelots").
10. *Réflexions sur la musique françoise en particulier* (1754), reprinted in Launay, *La Querelle des Bouffons*, III, pp. 1648–50. The following is a free English translation of the passage:

    [Musical] sounds can paint anything that itself is capable of producing noise: thunder, wind, the roaring of the sea, the clash of arms, the melodious warbling of birds, the falling cascade of water, the soft murmur of a brook, and so on. . . . But these ideas are often linked to other ideas in our minds, and which are automatically aroused, the moment we identify the first ideas. Thus if a musician manages to imitate the roaring of the sea, thunderclaps, the whistling of the north winds, the terrible cracking noise of a ship as it breaks up upon the rocks, if he lets us hear the cries of the frantic sailors, there is no one in whom the idea of a shipwreck will not be awakened, and who will not think he sees waves, rocks, and the unfortunate people lost in the fury of the waters. [Likewise] the links one idea has with another will make us think we see a pleasant secluded spot in the country when we hear the [musical] imitation of bird songs, the murmuring of a brook, a light wind, the rustle of branches: we think we've been transported to a meadow brightened with flowers. Add a bagpipe and we see a shepherd courting his shepherdess while their mingling herds gambol on the grass, or perhaps one imagines a smiling slope with a gushing fountain watering a thousand flowers as it flows down to the valley. . . .

11. *Ibid.*, p. 1653. In English:

    I have never heard the overture to [Rameau's opera] Pygmalion played, without imagining myself in Le Moine's studio. [In my mind] I would see this clever artist, chisel in hand, chipping away at a block of marble. Out of it would come a Venus.

12. Certain of these ideas have received considerable critical attention because they are discussed in Rousseau's *Essai sur l'origine des langues*, a text that for a time was of prime importance to semioticists. See Jacques Derrida, *De la grammatologie* (Paris, 1976), pp. 279–309, and Paul de Man, *Blindness and Insight: Essays in the Rhetoric of Contemporary Criticism* (New York, 1971), pp. 123–31. For further

bibliography of the literature on Rousseau's *Essai*, see Charles Porset, 'L'Inquiétante étrangeté de l'*Essai sur l'origine des langues*. . . .," *SVEC*, 154 (1976), 1729–49.

13. *Encyclopédie*, xv (1765), pp. 348A–B.

14. On the extraordinary qualities of her voice, see A. Pougin, *Pierre Jélyotte . . .* (Paris, 1905), pp. 54–64.

15. Jean Starobinski, *Jean-Jacques Rousseau, la transparence et l'obstacle*, 2nd edn (Paris, 1972), pp. 1–316.

16. On the life and experiments of le père Castel, see Anne-Marie Chouillet-Roche, "Le Clavecin oculaire du père Castel," *XVIIIe Siècle*, viii (1976), 141–66. On Diderot's interest in him, see Diderot, *Oeuvres philosophiques*, ed. Vernière (Paris: Garnier, 1964), p. 311.

17. Diderot, *ibid.*, pp. 271–4; pp. 367–8. Cf. J. Proust, "Variations sur un thème de l'*Entretien avec d'Alembert*," *Revue des sciences humaines*, fasc. 112 (1963), 253–70.

18. The Fabre edition, pp. 27–8.

19. Edn, p. 26.

20. Pages 82–6.

21. Pages 81–5.

> What did he not do, as I watched him? He wept, he laughed, he sighed; his look grew pitying, tranquil, or furious; he was a woman fainting with pain and grief, he was a miserable wretch in all the convulsions of despair; a temple which ascends; birds falling silent in the setting sun; waters murmuring in some cool, secluded spot, or which descend in torrents from the mountain tops; a storm, a tempest, the wail of those about to perish mixed with the whistling of the wind, the clap of thunder; he was night with its darkness; he was shadow and silence; for even silence is painted by sound. He had quite lost his head.

Insofar as this passage is *comedy*, it can be related to Piron's *pièce en monologue*. See above, chapter 3, note 38.

22. See above, note 9. I wish to thank Mary Cyr for letting me read her unpublished paper "The storm in eighteenth-century French opera" (1975).

23. Reproductions may be seen in J. Starobinski, *The Invention of Liberty* (Geneva, 1964), p. 170, and in the catalogue of the Vernet exposition entitled *Claude-Joseph Vernet (1714–1789)* held under the auspices of the Iveagh Bequest, Kenwood, and published by the Greater London Council in 1976.

24. Rousseau satirized two of these machines in *La Nouvelle Héloïse* (1761):

> . . . La mer agitée est composée de longues lanternes angulaires de toile ou de carton bleu, qu'on enfile à des broches parallèles, et qu'on fait tourner par des poliçons. Le tonnere est une lourde charrette qu'on promène sur le ceintre, et qui n'est pas le moins touchant instrument de cette agréable musique . . .   (Rousseau, O.C., ii, p. 283).

25. The important texts have been collected in Diderot, *Oeuvres esthétiques*, ed. P. Vernière (Paris: Garnier, 1968), pp. 562–84 (esp. pp. 562–3).

26. The only example I have found is in an *opéra comique* by Le Sage, *Le Temple de Mémoire* performed in 1725 at the Foire St Laurent and in the Théâtre du Palais Royal. See *Théâtre de la Foire*, iv (Paris, 1731), p. 29. *La Folie* casts a magic spell with her *marotte*: "Aussi-tôt le Temple de Mémoire s'élève sur la pointe du Mont escarpé. C'est un petit Dôme bleu et or."

27. See the edition by Paul Hugo Meyer in *Diderot Studies*, 7 (1965), 101–3. On the curious problem of the identity of the correspondent, see P. H. Meyer, review of L. L. Bongie, *Diderot's Femme Savante*, in *The French Review*, 51 (1978), 609–10.

28. A list of the paintings by Vernet bearing the title "Nuit" will be found in Chouillet, *La Formation*, p. 554.

29. Edn, p. 102.

> For the rest, music has greater need to find in us favorably disposed organs than either painting or poetry. Music's hieroglyphic – i.e., poetical meaning – is so slight, so fleeting, it is so easy to lose it or misinterpret it, that the finest piece of orchestral music would have no great effect, if the sudden and irresistible pleasure of sensation, pure and simple, was not infinitely stronger than the pleasure of something that is often expressed ambiguously. Painting shows the object itself, poetry describes it, music awakens scarcely any idea of it at all. Music's only resource is in the intervals between sounds, and their duration: what sort of analogy is there between painting materials such as these and springtime, darkness, solitude, and other such objects of imitation? How can it be, then, that of the three arts that imitate nature, music, the one whose expression is most arbitrary, and the least precise, speaks most strongly to the soul? Might it be that in showing objects less, it gives freer rein to our imaginations, or that, since we need to be shaken up in order to be moved, music is more proper than painting and poetry to produce in us this tumultuous effect?

30. For a different interpretation of this passage, see Yvon Belaval, *L'Esthétique sans paradoxe de Diderot* (Paris, 1954), p. 97.

31. In philology examples of this phenomenon have become quite familiar. To choose just the best-known ones: in Latin, "Altus" (high) also has a mirror image meaning "deep" (cf. "high seas"). "Fast," the most rapid of movements, also signifies an immobile denial of movement ("stay" or "cling fast"); "cleave" either means to "sunder apart" or it indicates a refusal of all sundering ("cleave to a belief"). French is particularly prone to such contrarieties ("plus," "personne," etc.).

> Freud was especially interested in this linguistic phenomenon of contrariety because he saw it as connected to the language of dreams. In "The Antithetical Sense of Primal Words" (1910), he summarized the investigations of the philologist Karl Abel who had found such contradictions to be basic to the language of ancient Egypt. Indeed, noted Abel, the Egyptians communicated mainly through a vocabulary whose words had two contradictory meanings, or in which the meaning of one syllable directly contradicted the meaning of the next. Noting, too, that this civilization was among the most enlightened in antiquity, Abel concluded that this phenomenon in no sense indicated stupidity or lack of intellectual rigor on the part of the Egyptians. It derived instead from the fact that "Our conceptions arise through comparison," which is to say (in Abel's words):

>> Were it always light we should not distinguish between light and dark, and accordingly could not have either the conception of, nor the word for, light.
>> ... It is clear that everything on this planet is relative and has independent existence only insofar as it is distinguished in its relations to and from other things. ... Since every conception is thus the twin of its opposite, how could it be thought of first, how could it be communicated to others who tried to

think it, except by being measured against its opposite? . . . Since any conception of strength was impossible except in contrast with weakness, the word which denoted "strong" contained a simultaneous reminder of "weak," as of that by which it first came into existence. In reality this word indicated neither "strong" nor "weak," but the relation between the two, and also the difference between them which created both in equal proportion. . . . Man has not been able to acquire even his oldest and simplest conceptions otherwise than in contrast with their opposite; he only gradually learnt to separate the two sides of the antithesis and think of the one without conscious comparison with the other.

(Freud, *Collected Papers*, Strachey edn, IV, p. 187)

Abel found that the phenomenon extended also to other ancient tongues, notably the Semitic and Indo-European, and he noted that, in Egyptian, words could reverse their sound as well as their sense, another phenomenon already observed in Diderot.

It is intriguing to speculate on how much of his own thought patterns Diderot might have recognized in the "logic" of antagonisms developed by Stéphane Lupasco. See especially Lupasco's *Logique et contradiction* (Paris: Presses Universitaires, 1947) and *Le Principe d'antagonisme et la logique de l'énergie* (Paris: Hermann, 1951).

8 Secrets from Suzanne: the tangled motives of *La Religieuse*

1. Of the Fabre edition (Geneva: Droz, 1963).
2. On this phenomenon see my article "Two scenes from *Le Neveu de Rameau*," *Diderot Studies*, 20 (1981).
3. As already noted, in a different context, by Raymond Joly, "Entre *Le Père de famille* et *Le Neveu de Rameau*, conscience morale et réalisme romanesque dans *La Religieuse*," *SVEC*, 88 (1972), 845–57. Page numbers in my text refer to the edition of *La Religieuse* annotated by Georges May in Diderot, *Oeuvres complètes* (Paris: Hermann, 1975–, XI, pp. 1–294. (The *Préface-Annexe* will generally be excluded from present considerations.) For recent bibliography on *La Religieuse*, see Jacques Rustin, "*La Religieuse* de Diderot: Mémoires ou journal intime?" in V. del Litto, ed., *Le Journal intime et ses formes littéraires* (Geneva: Droz, 1978), pp. 27–47. Though independently conceived, the present study agrees with a number of points stressed by Roger Lewinter in *Diderot, ou les mots de l'absence: Essai sur la forme de l'oeuvre* (Paris: Editions Champ Libre, 1976), pp. 65–97.
4. Fortunately, present purposes do not require delving into the thorny problems of the genre(s) to which this work ultimately belongs (as debated by Jean Parrish, Georges May, E. Lizé, and Jacques Rustin, among others). See Rustin's article, referred to in the previous note.
5. See Roger Kempf, *Diderot et le Roman* (Paris, 1964), pp. 36–7.
6. *La Religieuse*, p. 127, note 45. Jean Catrysse, *Diderot et la mystification* (Paris: Nizet, 1970), pp. 224ff.
7. The classic study of this topic is Robert Ellrich, "The rhetoric of *La Religieuse* and eighteenth century forensic rhetoric," *Diderot Studies*, 3 (1961), 129–54.
8. Maria Teresa Biason has taken a semiotic approach to this topic in "Rivela-

zione et occultamenti nella *Religieuse* di Diderot," *Strumenti critici*, 11 (1977), 349–83.

9. See Raymond Joly, "Entre *Le Père de famille* et *Le Neveu de Rameau*" (above, note 3), p. 857, who notes this phenomenon and explains it as a "dénégation . . . de la part de l'auteur, qui accepte de se laisser duper par sa créature." This blindness may suggest something of what Freudians call "Ichspaltung" (*clivage du moi*). See J. Laplanche and J.-B. Pontalis, *Vocabulaire de la psychanalyse* [Paris: Presses universitaires, 1973], pp. 67–70).

10. The next night, when everyone was asleep and the convent had grown silent, she got up. After wandering for a while in the corridors, she came to my cell; I'm a light sleeper, I thought I recognized her. She stopped; leaning her forehead, apparently, against my door she made enough noise to have awakened me if I had been asleep. I remained silent. I thought I heard a voice moaning, someone sighing; at first I gave a slight shiver, then I decided to say *Ave*; instead of answering, the person went softly away. The person came back some time later; the moaning and sighs began again; again I said *Ave* and the person went away for the second time. Reassured, I went to sleep. While I slept, the person entered and sat beside my bed, my curtains were slightly parted, the person held a little candle whose light shone on my face, and the woman who held the candle watched me as I slept – at least so I surmised from her attitude when I opened my eyes; and that person was the Superior. At once I sat up; she saw my fright, and said to me, "Suzanne, don't be afraid, it's I . . ." I put my head back on the pillow and said to her, "Dear Mother, what are you doing here at this hour? Whatever brought you here? Why are you not asleep?"

11. I saw her. This was the moment of my good fortune, or my misery, depending, Sir, on how you will treat me. I have never seen anything so hideous. She was dishevelled, with almost no clothes on; she was dragging iron chains; her eyes were wild, she pulled out her hair, beat her breast with her fists. She ran, she shrieked, she tried to find a window, to hurl herself out. Fright seized me. I trembled in every limb. I saw my own destiny in this unfortunate creature, and straightway made a vow in my heart that I would die a thousand deaths rather than undergo such a fate.

12. My interpretation of both of these passages agrees with that of Roger Lewinter, *Diderot, ou les mots de l'absence*, pp. 77–8; see also, Jack Undank, *Diderot: Inside, Outside, and In-Between* (Madison, Wisconsin: Coda Press, 1979), p. 119.

13. It seemed as though the spirit of God inspired her. Her thoughts, her expressions, her images penetrated to the depths of the heart; first one listened, then little by little one began to be swayed; you united with her; your soul thrilled; you shared her transports. Her design was not to seduce, but assuredly that was what she did. One left her with a heart aflame, and ecstasy glowing on one's face. And the tears one shed were so sweet!

14. My soul takes fire easily, becomes exalted, ecstatic, and that good Superior told me a hundred times while embracing me, that no one could have loved God as I did, that I had a heart of flesh, while the others had hearts of stone. It is sure that I found it extremely easy to share her ecstasy, and during the prayers she spoke out loud, sometimes it happened that I myself began to speak, to follow the thread of her thought, and as if by inspiration, to

happen upon a part of what she would have said herself. The others listened
to her in silence or followed after her, whereas I would interrupt or go before
her, or speak along with her; the experience would remain with me for a
long time after, and apparently I must have given back to her something of
what I had received, for, if one could always discern in the others that they
had been speaking with her, one could always discern in her that she had
been speaking with me.

15. Lewinter, *Diderot, ou les mots de l'absence*, pp. 81–2.
16. See Georges May, *Diderot et la Religieuse* (New Haven and Paris, 1954), p. 191.
17. Cf. Henri Coulet, *Le Roman jusqu'à la Révolution* (Paris, 1967), p. 501; p. 502. Lewinter, *Diderot, ou les mots de l'absence*, p. 70. Raymond Joly, "Entre *Le Père de famille* et *Le Neveu de Rameau*," p. 855.
18.   I omitted nothing that could make me feared, hated, and ruin me; I succeeded.
19. Herbert Dieckmann, "The Préface-Annexe of *La Religieuse*," *Diderot Studies*, 2 (1952), 28–9.
20. See the perceptive interpretation by Raymond Joly, "Entre *Le Père de famille* et *Le Neveu de Rameau*," p. 857.
21. Georges May, *Diderot et la Religieuse*, p. 192.
22. Cf. Lewinter, *Diderot ou les mots de l'absence*, p. 84.
23. Roger Kempf, *Diderot et le Roman*, p. 192.
24. Diderot himself wrote of this kind of subjective transformation in his review of Watelet's poem on the art of painting: "L'auteur fait ici une supposition très bien choisie et qu'il suit avec goût. C'est une jeune fille innocente et naïve, vuë par un indifférent, vuë par son père, et vuë par son amant: il montre l'intérêt et la grace s'accroître dans cette figure, selon les spectateurs auxquels il la présente." (Grimm, *Corresp. litt.* [1 January–15 June 1760], edn, p. 53).
25. Lewinter, *Diderot, ou les mots de l'absence*, pp. 85–6.
26. Cf. J. Proust, *L'objet et le texte*, pp. 155–6.
27.   It was Father Le Moine who inspired my withdrawal from my Superior – He did well. – Why was that? – My sister, he replied assuming a grave air, cleave to his counsel, but try to ignore the reason why, so long as you shall live. [. . .] Actually it was your innocence which compelled respect from your Superior; had you known more, she would have respected you less – [. . .] What is the harm in loving one another, in saying so, and showing it to one another? It is so pleasant! – That is true, said Dom Morel, raising upon me his eyes which, until I spoke, he had kept lowered. – And is that, then, so common in convents? My poor Superior. What sad state she had fallen into! – It is indeed distressing, and I fear it will get worse: she was not suited for her calling, and this is what always happens sooner or later. When one thwarts the general inclination of nature, the constraint inevitably perverts the affections, which become all the more violent, because they have no true foundation; it is a kind of madness. – She is mad? – Yes, she is, and she will become more so.
28. Georges May, *Diderot et la Religieuse*, pp. 98ff.

9 A unique and forgotten opera libretto

1. One of the most discerning eighteenth-century critics of opera libretto, J. F. de la Harpe, stresses this opposition as he mocks those who, in the wake of Gluck, would have refashioned opera after the model of regular tragedy: "Quelle erreur! Quoi! un spectacle où l'on va chercher tous les plaisirs des sens pourrait avoir les mêmes effets que celui qui ne promet absolument d'autres plaisirs que ceux d'âme et de l'esprit! un spectacle où tous les objets du désir, tous les tableaux de la volupté, sont étalés sans cesse aux yeux et à l'imagination, pourrait être le même que celui qui ne connaît d'autres moyens d'émotion que la terreur et la pitié! . . . Mais qui ne voit, du premier coup d'oeil, que cette illusion soutenue, qui est vraiment l'effet de la tragédie régulière bien jouée, cette illusion qui est le plaisir qu'on y va prendre, ne peut jamais se trouver à l'Opéra, où les accessoires, qui ne sont que l'assemblage de toutes les séductions des sens, font à tout moment oublier le drame et même la musique? Si vous voulez avoir là du vrai tragique, commencez donc par supprimer vos danses voluptueuses . . ." (*Lycée*, edn, XIV, pp. 58–9). Probably the most stimulating discussion of the general characteristics of eighteenth-century opera remains that of Paul-Marie Masson, *L'Opéra de Rameau* (Paris, 1930), pp. 5–38. A more thorough investigation of the matters under discussion will be found in Cuthbert Girdlestone, *La Tragédie en musique 1673–1710 considérée comme genre littéraire* (Geneva, 1972), pp. 3–54.

2. For librettists the small number of permitted words had become a sort of torture, as was wittily attested to by a professional, Montdorge: ". . . quand on est obligé de suivre la liste des mots enregistrés au théâtre lyrique, et d'observer les longues et les brèves sur la note, on veille des nuits entières sans pouvoir fixer dans un rigaudon *les Zéphirs dont les désirs font naître les plaisirs*, et le lendemain on est bien heureux si on a pu mettre en mesure *ces langueurs sans alarmes, ces rigueurs et ces larmes, ces fadeurs et ces charmes* dont le ridicule est si bien connu' (*Réflexions d'un peintre sur l'opéra* [Paris, 1743], pp. 27–8, quoted in Masson, *L'Opéra de Rameau*, pp. 103–4).

3. Not only in *Le Neveu de Rameau* (twice), but also in *Dorval et Moi*. See the Jean Fabre edition of *Le Neveu de Rameau* (Geneva, 1950), p. 6; p. 81; p. 120, note 18.

4. The text of the libretto was printed separately: *Deucalion et Pirrha Ballet représenté pour la première fois par l'Académie Royale de Musique le Mardi 30 Septembre 1755 Aux Dépens de l'Académie* (Paris, 1755), which edition reveals that Pirrha was played by Mlle Fel, and Deucalion was M. Godard. The reprinting in Saint-Foix, *Oeuvres complètes*, 6 vols. (Paris, 1778), I, pp. 64ff., is valuable mainly on account of a short "Avant-propos," p. 65, not in the original edition, and which seems to imply that Saint-Foix was the sole author of the libretto. The *Titelkatalogue I*, p. 313, of the Stieger *Opernlexicon* lists a collaborator, P. Morand.

5. See above, chapter 3.

6. See Ovid, *Metamorphoses*, I, pp. 318ff.

7. I do not except even Rameau's exquisite *Pigmalion* (1748, libretto by Houdard de la Motte) which is the opera that comes closest to *Deucalion et Pirrha*, and was probably one of its main "sources." But even though *Pigmalion* begins in the purest simplicity, with the sculptor immersed in the private world of his love for the statue, once the statue comes alive, the private emotions give way to public display. Other characters enter: not only "Amour," but "les Jeux, les Ris et les

Grâces" who teach the Statue to dance, and this is followed by a whole series of *divertissements*, the stage being at moments crowded with singers and dancers. The result aesthetically is that the moving simplicity of the beginning is counterbalanced by the amusing profusion of the rest, thus giving a more complex texture to the whole.

In contrast, the simplicity of Saint-Foix's libretto remains constant throughout his myth, which is self-contained; the ballets at the end, as will be seen, are unrelated to it.

8. "What charms! . . . Ye Gods, how may I resist them!"

9. "Where are you turning your steps?"

10. "What! Pyrrha, you love me! . . . What enchanting speech! . . ." "What! Pyrrha, you deign to accept my homage."

11. "I only wanted to put your ardor to the test."

12. Bibliothèque de l'Opéra (Paris), ms A 194 (unnumbered folios).

13. The woods become green again, / The sweet murmur of the brook / Seems to say "Love, be happy . . ."

14. *Deucalion et Pyrrha, comédie en un acte. Représentée pour la première fois Sur le Théâtre de la Comédie françoise le 20 Fevrier 1741*, in *Oeuvres*, I, pp. 40ff.

As for the superior qualities of the opera libretto, my own twentieth-century opinion is in almost total disagreement with the only surviving judgment of the opera dating from the time of its first performance, that of the crochety Marquis d'Argenson: "Ce n'est pas le fort de M. de *St-Foix* de faire des vers, surtout des vers lyriques. A peine y a-t-il quelques *arriètes* supportables, le reste est très prosaïque. Le sujet est *factice* et de l'invention de l'autheur, il est trop abondant pour un seul acte. Cependant l'*autheur* excelle dans les *allégories*, et véritablement celle-cy exprime beaucoup. Pour la *musique* elle a le malheur de se ressentir de la mode *italienne*, *musique* basse, guaye si l'on veut, et à contresens. On a joué cet acte avec l'*Europe galante*, et la nouveauté a donné quelque argent de plus aux *entrepreneurs* de l'*Opéra*" (Le Marquis d'Argenson, *Notices sur les Oeuvres de théâtre*, ed. H. Lagrave, 2 vols. [Geneva: Institut et Musée Voltaire, 1966], II, pp. 482–3).

When the play version was revived on 11 January 1777, Le Vacher de Charnois noticed the inappropriateness of epigrams in the gallant style for the dramatic situation, but decided that this "defect" actually gave the work "du piquant" and hence should be forgiven. He said he preferred the play, with all its verbal mannerisms, to the "vers assez médiocres" of the opera, which he had read, but probably never saw (Le Vacher de Charnois, *Journal des théâtres, ou le nouveau spectateur*, I [1777], pp. 71–2).

15. The author, speaking through a fictitious "Chevalier" also explained: "J'ai cru, je vous l'avoue que son action simple et réduite à elle-même, plairoit par son unité, et que soutenue par une expression de sentiment qui m'a paru noble, vraie, naturelle, on devoit absolument en bannir l'art et la parure empruntée, pour n'y conserver que des nuances simples et peu colorées" (*Oeuvres*, I, pp. 37–8).

16. The performance at Fontainebleau took place on 30 October 1764, at which time the text was reprinted (see B. N. Réserve Yf 4477) with a short *Préface* that apparently did not appear in the original printed version of 1742. On the same program was *Ariane* by Thomas Corneille. Curiously, this was the only contemporary work performed during the 1764 fall season at court which showed

markedly aristocratic tendencies. Among the other works performed at that time, Chamfort's one-act verse play, *La Jeune indienne* (11 October 1764), includes a violent diatribe against the evils of civilization. *Le Peintre amoureux de son modèle*, with music by Duni, is middle-class comedy, and of course was part of the Italian reform that caused such excitement at the Opéra. It was performed at the same time as *Rose et Colas* (3 November 1764), with music by Monsigny, and libretto by the socially conscious Sedaine.

17. See the prologue of the text of the play version, *Oeuvres*, I, p. 37.

18. See *Oeuvres*, I, unnumbered p. 65.

19. One of the Shepherds attacks and kills it; all the Shepherds surround their defender, raise him upon a sort of Throne of greenery and render homage to him. Gratefulness has created the first king.

20. This evaluation is abundantly confirmed in A.-J. Du Coudray, *Eloge historique de M. de Saint-Foix . . .* (London and Paris, 1776).

21. May the most glorious rank / Consecrate the courage of this conqueror; / May he be among us the image / Of the sovereign of the Gods: / Let us celebrate his victory. / May his name and his glory / Fly up to the heavens.

22. On François-Joseph Giraud (died 1790), see the article by Mary Cyr in *The New Grove Dictionary of Music and Musicians*, VII, pp. 406A–B; on Pierre-Montan Berton (1727–80), see *The New Grove*, II, pp. 641B–642A (article by P. Petrobelli).

23. The stage shows the aftermath of the Deluge which has not yet ceased: one hears the vague, muffled sounds of waves, wind, and thunder: trees and various ruins are seen as they are swept away, engulfed in the torrent: the bright cloud where Venus appears with the three Graces sheds enough light for one to perceive these sorry objects through the darkness.

24. The musical quotation corresponds to p. 7 of the printed libretto.

25. *Divertissements* had come, ever since the time of Lully, to absorb more than half of the music. See the statistics of Fajon, *L'Opéra à Paris . . .*, pp. 220ff.

26. Text in Rousseau, O.C., II, pp. 1225–31. This work was composed in 1762. First performed in 1770, it was printed in January of the following year. See O.C., II, pp. 1926–7.

10 The rustic operas of Diderot's *Neveu de Rameau*

1. In the Fabre edition, pp. 13–14.

2. One might wish that de Voltaire had the gentleness of Duclos, the ingenuousness of abbé Trublet, and the uprightness of abbé d'Olivet, but since that is impossible, let us consider the truly interesting thing about it [. . .]

3. Let us forget for the moment the point we occupy in time and space; let us cast our eyes over the centuries to come, the most distant lands and nations yet to be born. Let us think of the good of our race [. . .]   (*ibid.*)

4. Fabre, edn, note 53.

5. Jean Jacquart, *Un Témoin de la vie littéraire et mondaine au XVIIIᵉ siècle: L'abbé Trublet . . .* (Paris: Picard, 1926), esp. pp. 356–7; 376–81. The author cites (p. 372) another good example of "antiphrase" featuring Trublet, from Voltaire's *Le Russe à Paris* (1760). One suspects that Voltaire's satire is a "source" of the *Vision de Palissot* of the same year, quoted below:

Le Parisien
Nous avons parmi nous les Pères de l'Eglise.
Le Russe
Nommez-moi donc ces Saints que le ciel favorise.
Le Parisien
Maître Abraham Chaumeix, Hayer le Récollet,
Et Berthier le Jésuite et le diacre Trublet,
Et le doux Caveyrac, et Nonotte, et tant d'autres.
Ils sont tous parmi nous ce qu'étaient les Apôtres
Avant qu'un feu divin fut descendu sur eux [. . .]

6. *Préface de la comédie des Philosophes, ou La Vision de Charles Pâlissot* (Paris, 1760), pp. 3–4.

7.   And the first day of the month of January in the year of grace 1760, I was in a room in lower rue du Rempart, and I had no money.

    And Madame de ** no longer paid me, because I was no longer of any service to her, and I couldn't sell *** any more, because I had already sold him several times.

    And I said to myself: if only someone would give me *the eloquence of Chaumeix, the lightness of Berthier, and the profundity of Fréron*, I would write a good satire against one of my Benefactors, sell it for 400 francs, and buy myself a new suit of clothes at Easter.

8.   They supposed they could weep or laugh at scenes from tragedy or comedy set to music, that the tones of madness, hatred, jealousy, the genuine pathos of love, the ironies and jokes of the Italian or French stage could be presented to their ears and that nevertheless they could still admire *Ragonde* and *Platée*. You can bet your boots it didn't work.   (*ibid.*, p. 100)

9. There is an excellent study of the music to *Les Amours de Ragonde ou La Soirée du village* in Renée Viollier, *Jean-Joseph Mouret, le musicien des grâces* (Paris, 1950), pp. 101–4. On the libretto there are the deprecating remarks of Jean Hankiss, *Philippe Néricault-Destouches . . .* (Debreczen, 1920), pp. 252–4.

10. The text of this version is in *Suite des Divertissemens de Sceaux . . .* (Paris, 1725), pp. 254–89, also in Néricault-Destouches, *Oeuvres dramatiques*, 4 vols. (Paris, 1757), III, pp. 701–26.

11. Adolphe Julien, *La Comédie à la Cour . . .* (Paris, 1885), pp. 83–4; p. 182. According to Viollier, *Jean-Joseph Mouret*, p. 104, there was also a court performance in 1745. La Harpe, while dismissing the opera as "une mauvaise farce du vieux Destouches," also attested to its popularity (*Lycée*, XIV, p. 119).

12.   The Actors and Actresses, with the Dancers, are seated around a table. The women are working. Some are spinning at the distaff, others at the wheel; still others are knitting stockings.
Traditional wintertime *veillées* in country villages were indeed just as depicted in this opera. See Natalie Zemon Davis, *Society and Culture*, pp. 201ff.

13.   Yes, my darling; yes, dear heart / Three months of being a widow are enough, don't you think? / I can no longer bear these troubles. / The time has come when nights are long. / And if I don't pledge myself soon / In the end my honor may be wrecked. / A legitimate pleasure is all that I desire [. . .]

14. See David Kunzle, "World upside down . . .," in Barbara A. Babcock, ed., *The Reversible World*, p. 50.

15.   A young shepherd of twenty / Loved a shepherdess / But her mother was
        very taken with him / And she wanted to test him in spite of her teeth. /
        This old woman was a witch. / To punish the shepherd who was indifferent
        to her ardor / She made him into a tomcat who worked himself into a rage /
        And threw himself down from a roof gutter.

16.   An old woman had four teeth / Which she hardly used; / She designed to be
        a mother again / By forcibly marrying a shepherd of twenty. / He scorned
        this shrew. / She intended to punish the disdainful shepherd / But, in order
        to spoil her dangerous schemes, / He sent her to sigh at the bottom of the
        river.

17.   See Davis, *Society and Culture*, p. 107.

18.   *Les Amours de Ragonde* (Paris, 1742), p. 20.
        Blissful shepherds, / Follow the love that gives you light, / Here the
        laughter, the games, / Everything serves our wishes: / The sweet spring-
        time / Begins and ends all of our years: / Love leaves his mother / To visit
        our fields. / Let us sing a thousand times, / Let us praise the God who
        guides our choices; / He is not so much at Cythera / As he is in our woods.

19.   Viollier, *Jean-Joseph Mouret*, p. 103. The rusticity of the original version, and the
        vulgarity of the plot of the old hag running after the young swain, probably
        reflect the influence of the distinctly rustic comedies of Dancourt; see particular-
        ly the character of Mme Loricart in *Le Charivari* (1697), in *Oeuvres* (Paris, 1742),
        IV, pp. 205ff.

20.   My definition is based on that of Paul-Marie Masson, "Le 'Ballet héroïque,'"
        Revue musicale, 9:8 (1928), 133. On the "ballet héroïque" in general, see James R.
        Anthony, *French Baroque Music . . .*, 2nd edn (London, 1978). It is impossible to
        translate these librettos into modern English in a manner that would be useful
        for the present discussion. Hence no translations will be provided.

21.   Of course *Le Neveu de Rameau* is the outstanding case in point. See Donal
        O'Gorman, *Diderot the Satirist* (Toronto and Buffalo, 1971), pp. 88–9. Camille
        Desmoulins interpreted the "Saturnales" as a sort of precursor of the Revolu-
        tion: "C'était une fête commémorative, instituée pour rappeler l'égalité orig-
        inelle; c'était une espèce de déclaration chômée des droits de l'homme [...]"
        (*Discours de la lanterne aux Parisiens* [1792], in *Oeuvres*, ed. Jules Claretic, 2 vols.
        [Paris, 1874], p. 195).

22.   *A Shepherdess* / Flee the Shades / Of our Groves / You who only know the
        brilliance of the Court /

        Flee the Shades / Of our Groves / In our Woods we offer incense only to
        Love.

23.   Among the better-known examples was Vadé's *Jérome et Fanchonette ou Anacréon à
        la Grenouillère, pastorale poissarde*, 1755 (cf. Mondonville's *Daphnis et Alcimadure*).
        On opera parody in general, see Grannis, *Dramatic Parody*, pp. 111ff.

24.   The printed version termed it a "Comédie-Ballet." It was produced at Versail-
        les in 1745 and in Paris in 1749. In the Versailles cast were the two singing stars
        of the Opéra, Jelyotte and Mlle Fel, and the two most celebrated dancers, Mlles
        Camargo and Sallé. See the "Commentaire bibliographique" by Charles
        Malherbe at the head of the Saint-Saëns edition of Rameau, *Oeuvres complètes*,
        XII, pp. vii–lvi.

25.   It was with this production that the impresario Jean de Monnet opened his

theatre at the Foire St Laurent. Rameau conducted the orchestra, and among the players (though not on opening night) was Préville, later to play Beaumarchais' Figaro. The costumes and decors were designed under the direction of Boucher. Noverre did the dances. Favart claimed that the success was so great that the Comédie Française and the Italiens vowed, in their jealousy, to ruin the enterprise, and indeed they succeeded in getting the theatre closed in 1744. See Monnet's *Mémoires* (Paris, n.d.), p. 36, and cf. Isherwood, *Farce and Fantasy*, p. 95.

26. I bow to her and tip my hat; and my courteous greeting makes her blush. With one hand she toys with a corner of her apron, and with the other she hides her eyes, but she looks at me through her fingers, and I notice from her scarf that her little breast is no more tranquil than mine.

27. I pledge myself to you forever / Stay true to me. / I am not tempted / By any of their possessions and attractions; / You will compensate me for those, / Without vines or orchards / My soul will be content. / My treasures and my happiness / Are deep within your heart.

28. Text in Rousseau, O.C., II, pp. 1093–114. On the influence of Charles-Simon Favart on *Le Devin du Village*, see Daniel Heartz, "The beginnings of the operatic romance: Rousseau, Sedaine, and Monsigny," *Eighteenth-Century Studies*, 15 (1982), 149–78, esp. p. 158.

29. Heartz, "The beginnings of the operatic romance," p. 158.

30. La Harpe reproached Rousseau for making his rustics use a speech he termed "trop élégamment pastoral" (*Lycée*, XIV, p. 167). His views on this Romance, however, are quite different from my own.

31. I have lost my Servant / I have lost all my happiness / Colin has forsaken me.

32. Love scarcely knows / What it allows and what it forbids; / It is a child, it is a child.
    (The line probably looks back to Ovid's "Et puer est et nudus Amor" from the *Amores*, I, x.)

33. Reference given above, note 25.

34. Printed in Paris, 1763. (Music for the ariettes by Blaise.) Her husband had some hand in the composition of this work.

35. Three volumes (Paris, 1765), II, pp. 201–20.

36. La Harpe reproached Mme Favart "de faire entrer dans cette espèce d'églogue dramatique, des traits d'une philosophie déplacée et fausse." He particularly objected to the references to Annette's pregnancy, a liberty he associated with Diderot (*Lycée*, XIV, p. 186).

37. I am happy right here / With Annette / My cottage / Is a little palace / Where I'll always find / The days too short.

38. The Great are not happy unless they are copying us, / To them, the richest tapestry / Appears an amusing sight / Only if it faithfully depicts our fields, our verdure; / Our dances under the elm tree, our labors, our recreations, / That is what they call a landscape, I believe. *Annette*: Yes, Lubin, we must really love our pleasures / Since so much money is needed to have the image of them. *Lubin*: Silly people! / Their greatness should not tempt us. / They paint our pleasures instead of tasting them.
    Cf. Diderot, *Salons*, III (1767), edn, p. 139.

39. That is the image of true happiness. / They enjoy all the blessings while

living simply: / Artless love and pure feeling reign / Beneath the humble village roofs.

40. The only scholar who has identified the existence of this inversion and stressed its importance is Marian Hobson in *The Object of Art* (see above, chapter 4, note 2), p. 152. The first eighteenth-century example of this kind of reversal, in a musical work at least, may have occurred in one of the only Biblical operas ever performed at the Royal Academy, *Jephté* (1732), the words being by abbé Pellegrin, the music by Montclair. In the prologue, the stage is set to resemble a theater ("un Lieu destiné pour des spectacles"). Apollon, Polhymnie, Terpsicore and a chorus of twenty-seven are singing of the delights and pleasures of "la douce erreur," which apparently designates both classical mythology and the false charms of theatrical illusion. Venus calls for laughter, youth, folly, and surrender to pleasure, a theme that is taken up by the chorus. Suddenly the stage darkens, while brightly lit Truth ("la Vérité") descends from the ceiling in a *gloire*. Sternly she rebukes these "fantômes séduisants, enfants de l'imposture," and declares it is time for Truth to make lies vanish. She sends all the pagan divinities scurrying off to hell (they sink down, grumbling in their rage). Error having been banished, the stage is now ready for the Truth of Jephté, while illusion and reality are supposed to have changed places.

41. The best short introduction to the life and work of Mercier is currently that of Raymond Trousson in his edition of Mercier, *L'An deux mille quatre cent quarante, Rêve s'il en fut jamais* (Bordeaux: Ducrox, 1971). One notes, however, that Mercier's political position in this visionary novel is decidedly more conservative than the one implied in the two theatrical works we will be considering. Such contradictions are quite characteristic of Mercier.

42. "Préface" to *Jenneval ou le Barnevelt français, Drame en cinq actes en Prose* (Paris, 1769), pp. 3–15. This "Préface," in which one sees many of Mercier's most daring theatrical ideas taking form, has generally been ignored by scholars, and by Mercier himself, who apparently came to feel that his "Préface" had been superceded by his longer treatise "Du Théâtre" (reference in note 45).

43. For the Greeks the aim of tragedy was intangible. It was intended to nourish the republican seed and render monarchy odious. I understand Corneille very well; but it must be admitted that for us he has become almost a foreign Author; we have lost the right even to admire him [. . .] Corneille in fact should have been born in England.

Mercier's interpretation of Greek tragedy is curiously close to that of the arch-conservative abbé d'Aubignac. See his *La Pratique du théâtre*, ed. P. Martino (Algiers and Paris, 1927), pp. 72–3.

44. It is strange, then, that of the many authors whose taste inclined them to search for characters to portray, nearly all of them scorned commerce with inhabitants of the countryside, or only saw in them their apparent coarseness. For a moral Poet, what a treasure is nature in its simplicity! So many things to paint, to reveal to a Prince's ear! If I am not mistaken, given our progress in Philosophy, it is time for the Monarch to be brought down to the level of the audience, and for the Shepherd to go up on the stage. The inverse of the Theater would perhaps become the most auspicious form, and the most instructive as well. The Danube peasant appears for a moment in the midst of the Roman Senate, and becomes the most eloquent of Orators.

These texts by Mercier have recently been discussed in Anne Boës, *La Lanterne magique de l'histoire: Essai sur le théâtre historique en France de 1750 à 1789*, *SVEC*, 213 (1982), 80–2.

45. *Du Théâtre ou Nouvel essai sur l'art dramatique* (Amsterdam, 1773), p. vi, p. 8.
46. Adolphe Julien, *La Comédie à la Cour*, pp. 274–304.
47. See Mona Ozouf, *La Fête révolutionnaire, 1789–1799*, pp. 44–77.
48. Twelve volumes in five (Amsterdam, 1783).
49. Six vols. (Paris, n.d.). This work has been discussed in Norman Hampson, *Will and Circumstance: Montesquieu, Rousseau and the French Revolution* (University of Oklahoma Press, 1983), pp. 263–70.
50. For example, II, pp. 240–54; III, pp. 3–25; IV, pp. 101–9.
51. There is no sensitive heart that does not fondly recall that lovely autumn evening when the inhabitants of Ermenonville carried to Paris the coffin containing the author of *Emile*, beneath a cradle of greenery and flowers. The air was calm, the sky pure: a long veil of purple on the horizon screened the rays of the setting sun. A fresh wind gently stirred the last leaves.
52. The funeral ceremonies ended with the air "Dans ma cabane obscure"; and every person went away still singing it sweetly.

11 The demise of classical tragedy in France

1. In the Garnier edition, ed. P. Vernière (Paris, 1968), pp. 77–175.
2. On the concept of distance in the age of Classicism, see Jean-Marie Apostolides, *Le Prince sacrifié: Théâtre et société au XVIIe siècle* (Paris, 1982), chapter 1. A history of "aesthetic distance" and a copious bibliography will be found in John T. Ogden, "From spatial to aesthetic distance in the eighteenth century," *Journal of the History of Ideas*, 35 (1974), 63–78.
3. Striking examples are to be found in Couperin's *Leçons de ténèbres*. The observation would apply also to the sacred motets of Lully. The standard study of this topic remains Leo Spitzer's essay on the "récit de Théramène," in *Linguistics and Literary History* (Princeton, N.J., 1948), pp. 87–125. To be sure I do not accept the implications of his basic term "klassische Dämpfung."
4. The *Meditationes* are the classic exposition of this epistemology, of course.
5. *Discours préliminaire* in the *Encyclopédie*, 1st edn, I (1751), pp. vii–viii.
6. All the great writers of the eighteenth century had their say about this celebrated text. Marmontel suggested that the description of the monster was inappropriately detailed for Théramène's state of mind: "Si le sentiment dont Théramène est saisi, étoit la frayeur, il seroit naturel qu'il en eût l'objet présent, et qu'il le décrivît comme il l'auroit vu, mais peu importe à sa douleur et à celle de Thésée que le front du dragon fût armé de cornes, et que son corps fût couvert d'écailles. Si Racine eût dans ce moment interrogé la nature, lui qui la connaissoit si bien, j'ose croire qu'après ces deux vers,

> *L'onde approche, se brise, et vomit à nos yeux,*
> *Parmi des flots d'écume un monstre furieux*

il eût passé rapidement à ceux-ci,

> *Tout fuit, et sans s'armer d'un courage inutile,*
> *Dans le temple voisin chacun cherche un asyle,*
> *Hypolyte, lui seul*, etc.   (*Supplément à l'Encyclopédie*, IV, p. 17b)

In the present century Thierry Maulnier, also, wished – although for different reasons – that Racine had not been so precise. Again it was the *écailles* and the *cornes* that gave offense: "La peur grandit et se nourrit d'autant mieux qu'elle ne peut se fixer sur aucune figure précise, et que les puissances de la nuit ne trouvent pas dans un hybride de taureau et de reptile, dans je ne sais quel gros poisson cornu, une vaine et futile définition" (*Lecture de Phèdre*, new edn [Paris 1967], p. 114). See also Emilie P. Kostoroski, *The Eagle and the Dove: Corneille and Racine in the Literary Criticism of Eighteenth-Century France*, *SVEC*, 15 (1972).

7. Martin Turnell, *Jean Racine, Dramatist* (London, 1972), pp. 271–3; pp. 350–1.
8. On the functioning of Racine's language as it releases and controls eros and violence, see the perceptive discussion of Norman Bryson, *Word and Image*, pp. 92ff.
9. John Lough, *An Introduction to Eighteenth-Century France* (London, 1964), pp. 277–90. See also Auerbach, *Mimesis*, p. 344, who refers in this connection to Taine's essay on Racine in the *Nouveaux Essais de critique et d'histoire*.
10. There are hints of this scattered in all of Diderot's major writings on the theater, most especially in the letter to Mme Riccoboni, 27 November 1758, in *Correspondence*, ed. Roth and Varloot, II, pp. 89–102.
11. See R. S. Ridgway, *Voltaire and Sensibility* (Montreal and London, 1975), pp. 177–8; pp. 197–221.
12. Arthur Wilson, *Diderot* (New York, 1972), p. 326.
13. *Lettre de M. de Voltaire à l'Académie française, lue dans cette Académie, à la solennité de la Saint-Louis, le 25 Auguste 1776*, in Voltaire, *Oeuvres complètes*, ed. Moland, XXX, pp. 249–70.

   Since Voltaire had attacked Shakespeare on many previous occasions, none of the arguments he puts forth in this address is particularly new. See David Williams, ed., *Commentaires sur Corneille*, in *The Complete Works of Voltaire* (Banbury: The Voltaire Foundation), LIII (1974), pp. 276–301, and André Michel Rousseau, *L'Angleterre et Voltaire*, 3 vols., in *SVEC*, 145–7 (1976), II, pp. 479–90.

14. I would say to you that this soldier's gibe, "I have not heard a mouse scampering [trotting]" is lacking [poetic] harmony and contains no interesting truth. Whether or not this soldier had seen any mice going by is a fact that is quite useless for the tragedy of *Hamlet*: it's simply a clown's speech, a low proverb, which makes no [telling] effect.
15. Indeed, Sir, a soldier can answer thus in the guard house, but not on the stage, before the first persons of the nation, who express themselves nobly, and before whom one has a duty to do likewise.
16. All the elements of this theory are already present by implication in the preface to *Jenneval ou le Barnevelt français* (1769), which was studied in the previous chapter. However, in the work presently under consideration, *Du Théâtre ou Nouvel essai sur l'art dramatique* (Amsterdam, 1773), these elements have been more fully realized.
17. L'histoire d'où émane la pompeuse tragédie est pour la multitude un effet sans cause; elle ne voit pas les rapports. Et qu'est-ce qu'un ouvrage moral dont le but ne sçauroit être saisi et qui ne peut persuader. Eh! parlez à la multitude de ses moeurs, de sa fortune, de sa position actuelle; elle vous entendra. Les calamités d'une vie privée les frapperont plus que ces grands événemens et qui lui sont certainement étrangers. (p. 42, note a)

L'histoire est l'égoût des forfaits du genre humain, elle exhale une odeur cadavéreuse, et la masse des calamités passées [...] semble nécessiter [...] jusqu'aux calamités futures. (p. 47)

18. Homme dédaigneux, approche, que je te juge à ton tour. Qui est-tu? qui te donne le droit d'être hautain? Je vois ton habit, tes laquais, tes chevaux, ton équipage; mais toi, que fais-tu?... Tu souris, je t'entends; tu es homme de cour, tu consumes tes jours dans une inaction frivole, dans des intrigues puériles, dans des fatigues ambitieuses et risibles [...] Il ne te faut plus qu'un parchemin, pour faire gémir une province entière et lui ôter ses moeurs. Vil esclave, qui rampes par cupidité, [...] verge avilie du despotisme, un tisserand, son bonnet sur la tête, me paroît plus estimable et plus utile que toi. Si je te mets sur la scène, ce sera pour la honte. Mais ces ouvriers, ces artisans peuvent y paroître avec noblesse [...] Et toi, né pour l'opprobre du genre humain, plût à Dieu que tu fusses mort à l'instant de ta naissance! (pp. 136–9)

19. Je sçais que chez les grands les vices sont bien plus difficiles à appercevoir [...] Leurs ridicules prennent aussi un air de dignité et de noblesse qui en impose. Je sais qu'on peut les peindre, mais [...] on flatte leur vanité, on encense leurs grands airs. Il faudroit, au contraire, les mettre nuds sur la scène, et les battre de verges jusqu'à ce que le véritable cri de leur ame orgueilleuse échappe avec l'aveu de la vérité; c'est une espèce de question morale qu'il faudroit leur donner. (pp. 79–80, note b)

20. I want to see the emperor alone, unable to escape the frightening memories that his crimes retrace before him. His grief and pain bespeak his impiety; his repentance is that of a coward, his fright, womanish. He would take up the blade with a trembling hand; twenty times he would try to kill himself without having the courage to do so; he would weep; his wild eyes seeking on all sides for help, he would beg the vilest slave to do the deed for him. His infamous blood would flow. Then, I should like to see him struggling against death, falling to earth, scratching it with his hands, screaming as he approached the end which makes all equal. I should like to see the convulsions in the muscles of that face which used to be so unmoved by the torments of his peers, his arms growing stiff, his chest swelling, all his nerves distending as he fights against the terrible end which is at hand. His destruction would seem to address his terror-stricken soul, saying, "Come, Monster, come fall into the dark abyss where death will reign over you, where the justice you belittled will seize hold of you and render to you all the tortures you inflicted on your countrymen."

21. Mercier chose never to acknowledge this implication, a curious example of blindness that rather parallels that of Suzanne in *La Religieuse*. Firmly convinced that he had always been a political moderate, after the Revolution, Mercier attacked David, the painter, for doing in his pictures just what Mercier himself had done in his theatrical criticism: "[...] Ses extravagances n'en furent pas moins homicides, et j'avoue que le nom de David marié à la peinture, me fait voir dans celle-ci ce règne de terreur qu'on diroit qu'elle s'est plue à consacrer dans tous ces tableaux où l'on ne voit que martyres, décolations, chevalets, fournaises ardentes, en face de ces anciens décemvirs que David n'a que trop imités dans ces jours de crimes. O Mânes des Trudaines!" (*Le Nouveau Paris*, II, chapter 14, p. 97).

12 *The Marriage of Figaro*

1. See introduction to *Le Mariage de Figaro*, ed. Annie Ubersfeld (Paris: Editions Sociales, 1957).
2. Jean Fabre, "Beaumarchais," in *Histoire des littératures*, ed. Raymond Queneau, III (Paris: Encyclopédie de la Pléiade, 1958), p. 784.
3. See T. E. Lawrenson's edn of Lesage, *Crispin rival de son maître*, pp. 26–33, and E. J. Arnould's edn of *Le Mariage de Figaro* (Oxford: Basil Blackwell, 1952), pp. xxxvi–xxxvii.
4. *La Dramaturgie de Beaumarchais* (Paris: Nizet, 1954).
5. These and other sources are reviewed in René Pomeau, *Beaumarchais* (Paris: Hatier, 1967), pp. 168–77. A useful bibliography of this question and other problems connected with *Figaro* will be found in John Hampton, "Research on *Le Mariage de Figaro*," *French Studies*, 16 (1962), 24–31.
6. "The theme of the 'droit du seigneur' in eighteenth-century theatre," *French Studies*, 15 (1961), 228–39.
7. See Pomeau, *Beaumarchais*, pp. 169–70.
8. Pomeau, *Beaumarchais*, p. 171.
9. I intend no disagreement here with the informed and subtle discussion in Robert Niklaus' *Beaumarchais: Le Barbier de Séville* (London: Edward Arnold, 1968), pp. 21–4; it is rather that I am approaching the question from a different direction.
10. Most critics, from Sainte-Beuve and Francisque Sarcey to Arnould (edn, p. xxxiii), have found the structure defective from the standpoint of unity.
11. I am not aware of any other commentator who has used the present approach in analyzing the play. However, Philippe Van Tieghem has made some pertinent remarks about the game spirit in Beaumarchais (especially *jeux d'escrime* and *jeux d'esprit*) in *Beaumarchais par lui-même* (Paris: Editions du Seuil, 1960), pp. 32–7.
12. Marivaux is to some degree an exception; however, games in Marivaux' plays almost never exist in the pure state they do in *Figaro*.
13. *Tartuffe*, I, iv. Cf. Gaston Hall, *Molière: Tartuffe* (London: Edward Arnold, 1960), p. 20.
14. For such observations I am indebted to Iona and Peter Opie, *Children's Games in Street and Playground* (New York: Oxford University Press, 1969).
15. E.g., Pomeau, *Beaumarchais*, p. 180.
16. See his words at the conclusion of the scene of Chérubin's *brevet* (II, xxi): "(*A part*) C'est ce Figaro qui les mène, et je ne m'en vengerais pas? (*Il veut sortir de dépit.*)"
17. *Homo Ludens: A Study of Play-Element in Culture* (Boston: Beacon Press, 1955), chapter 4, "Play and Law," pp. 76–88. Cf. Arnould, edn, p. xxxiv.
18. I. and P. Opie, *Children's Games*, pp. 18–25. Children instinctively shun the role.
19. Cf. Scherer, pp. 161–3.
20. See the concluding remarks of the chapter on Beaumarchais by Robert Niklaus, *The Eighteenth Century (1715–1789)*, in vol. III of *A Literary History of France*, gen. ed. P. E. Chavet (London: Benn, and New York: Barnes and Noble, 1967). Some of the most interesting research on Beaumarchais currently being done is by the art historian, Thomas E. Crow. See, for example, his *Painters and Public Life in Eighteenth-Century Paris*, pp. 223ff. One hopes this author will do a full-length study, for undoubtedly Beaumarchais' politics in particular have been badly

misinterpreted; it is time for a whole new evaluation. On the other hand, I do not accept the implications of his statement (p. 223) about the politics of *Le Mariage de Figaro*, for in fact the revolutionary message is built into the structure of the play (not only Napoleon, but apparently Louis XVI saw it quite clearly). Professor Crow, exceptionally, fails to keep track of the chronology on this issue. His statement that "Beaumarchais was far from being a symbol of political dissent in the 1780's, . . . he stood instead in the public mind for the forces of reaction and despotism" creates a false impression because it does not take into account the shifts in public opinion during this volatile period. Beaumarchais was anything but a symbol of reaction and despotism at the time of the creation of *Le Mariage de Figaro*. He may have become so, in the eyes of many, shortly thereafter.

21. A convenient résumé of this tradition will be found in the introduction to T. E. Lawrenson's edition of *Crispin*, referred to above.

22. Text of the Comédie Française manuscript reproduced in J. B. Ratermanis' critical edition, *SVEC*, 63 (1968), 439A–441A.

23. Text found in three early pirated editions (Amsterdam, 1785; Paris, 1785; Lausanne, 1785), act v, scene 3, based on a hasty transcription taken down during actual performances of the play. However, the manuscript tradition referred to above makes it seem likely that in this instance the scribe correctly noted the stage action.

13 Deucalion's last eighteenth-century appearance

1. Rf 7, 494.

2. Athenais-Bernard-Louis-Claude, Vicomte de Tryon-Montalembert, born in 1768, would only have been about thirty at the time of this poem's publication, and his romantic, monogamous and royalist disposition shown in his published work *Table des matériaux biographiques, Concernant les femmes qui, dans la révolution se sont illustrées par leur dévouement, leur courage, leurs services, leurs souffrances, & plusieurs par leur glorieuse mort, pour leur Dieu et leur Roi* (Brussels, 1824) does not conform at all to the personality of the present narrator.

3. A "Pays de Lanternois" was also described by Rabelais in *Le Cinquiesme Livre*, chapters XXXII–XXXIIbis, and a "Pays de Lanternes" appeared in *La Bibliothèque bleue*. See François Moureau, *Dufresny, auteur dramatique (1757–1724)* (Paris: Klincksieck, 1979), p. 205, note 40.

4. I laughed 'til the tears came as she told me of the adventure of the lamps which the foolish virgins had allowed to go out, when they didn't take the precaution of providing themselves with oil as they went to meet the Bridegroom, and fell asleep waiting for him; she heartily praised the wisdom of the five other lamps, her nieces, who refused to lend them their oil (Matthew, Gospel, chap. 25). She chattered so much that for quite a while I took her for a nun's parlor lamp; she disabused me, declaring she had been in turn a monk's lamp, and a canon's lamp. Since the oracles had ceased, she had nothing to do, and amused herself by chatting with all the stangers who came to Lamptown. She had seen so many of them, she knew so much about those she had shed light on, from mother to daughter; she talked about them at such length, that I fell asleep, and she went out. Since this conversation, I always retell some of her stories every time I write.

5. Sabatier de Castres, *Journal politique-national des Etats-Généraux et de la Révolution de 1789* [. . .], 3 vols. (n.p., 1790), I, pp. 153–4: "A propos de lanterne et de réverbère un mauvais plaisant a dit que les démagogues, qui prétendent qu'on ne peut trop éclairer le peuple, devraient se dégoûter de cette maxime, en voyant l'usage que le peuple fait des lumières." Cf. Camille Desmoulins, *Discours de la lanterne aux Parisiens*, in *Oeuvres*, ed. Jules Claretic, 2 vols. (Paris, 1874), I, pp. 162–95.

6. Man, on the contrary, brought upon earth / A thirst for blood, discord and war. / He took on the hardness of these pebbles; / Insensitivity in his false heart; / He has masked himself with deceitful imposture, / Made himself tyrant even over nature; / He tramples underfoot the ties of blood and friendship; / He assassinates, while speaking of pity; / The word *virtue* is ever on his lips, / Crime dwells in his ferocious heart, / Traitor to honor, to love, to faith. / My good friends, you knew better than I, / Whether, by drowning you, one could make you over.

7. By the corner of the fire I hear the winds whistle, / The rain fall, and passers-by cursing [the weather]. / There, on the ill-tuned strings of my lyre / I strum out a few rhymes no one listens to.

8. I read, I write, I drink, I laugh, I sing, / And if, fair sex, reaching seventy, / I am no longer making love; do not take it amiss; / I'm much more vexed for me than for you.

246

Index

Index

Index

Index

Index